**American
Red Cross**

Lifeguarding

The following organizations provided review of the materials and support for **American Red Cross Lifeguarding:**

BOYS & GIRLS CLUBS
OF AMERICA

BOY SCOUTS OF AMERICA

Girl Scouts ®

StayWell®

A MediMedia USA Company

A MediMedia USA Company

American Red Cross

Content reflects the *American Red Cross 2005 Guidelines for Emergency Care and Education* and the *2005 Guidelines for First Aid*.

American Red Cross certificates may be issued upon successful completion of a training program, which uses this manual as an integral part of a course. By itself, the material in this manual does not constitute comprehensive Red Cross training. In order to issue Red Cross certificates, your instructor must be authorized by the American Red Cross, and must follow prescribed policies and procedures. Make certain that you have attended a course authorized by the Red Cross. Contact your local American Red Cross chapter *(www.redcross.org)* for more information.

The emergency care procedures outlined in this manual reflect the standard of knowledge and accepted emergency practices in the United States at the time this manual was published. It is the reader's responsibility to stay informed of changes in the emergency care procedures.

The Girl Scout service mark is a registered trademark of Girl Scouts of the USA.

Printed by Banta Book Group.

StayWell
780 Township Line Rd.
Yardley, PA 19067

Library of Congress Cataloging-in-Publication Data

Lifeguarding. — 3rd ed.
    p. cm.
   Includes bibliographical references and index.
   ISBN 1-58480-320-7
   1. Lifesaving. 2. Lifeguards—Training of. I. American Red Cross.

GV838.7.L54 2007
797.2'10289—dc22

                                          2006031662

ISBN-10 1-58480-320-7
ISBN-13 978-1-58480-320-1

   09 10/ 9 8 7 6 5 4

ACKNOWLEDGMENTS

American Red Cross Lifeguarding was developed through the dedication of both employees and volunteers. Their commitment to excellence made this manual possible.

The American Red Cross team for this edition included—

Pat Bonifer
Director
Research and Product Development

Jennifer Deibert
Project Manager
Research and Product Development

Mike Espino
Project Manager, Aquatics Technical
    Development
Research and Product Development

Kelly Fischbein
Associate, Evaluation
Research and Product Development

Connie Harvey
Manager
Research and Product Development

John Hendrickson
Senior Associate
Chapter Business Development and
    Sales Support

Tom Heneghan
Senior Associate
Program Administration and Support

Steve Lynch
Senior Associate
Business Planning

Marc Madden
Senior Associate
Research and Product Development

Barbara Muth
Manager, Evaluation
Research and Product Development

Lindsay Oaksmith, CHES
Senior Associate, Aquatics Technical
    Development
Research and Product Development

Greta Petrilla
Manager
Communication and Marketing

Mary Kate Martelon
Volunteer Intern
Research and Product Development

Betty J. Butler
Administrative Assistant
Research and Product Development

Rhadames Avila
Administrative Assistant
Research and Product Development

Guidance and support was provided by the following individuals—

Scott Conner
Vice President
Preparedness and Health and Safety
    Services

Don Vardell
National Chair
Preparedness and Health and Safety
    Services

The StayWell team for this edition included—

Nancy Monahan
Senior Vice President

Bill Winneberger
Senior Director of Manufacturing

Paula Batt
Executive Director
Sales and Business Development

Reed Klanderud
Executive Director
Marketing and New Product
    Development

Shannon Bates
Managing Editor

Lorraine P. Coffey
Senior Developmental Editor

Bryan Elrod
Senior Developmental Editor

Kate Plourde
Marketing Manager

Stephanie Weidel
Senior Production Editor

The following members of the American Red Cross Advisory Council on First Aid and Safety (ACFAS) also provided guidance and review:

David Markenson, MD, FAAP, EMT-P
Chair, American Red Cross Advisory
    Council on First Aid and Safety
    (ACFAS)
Chief, Pediatric Emergency Medicine
Maria Fareri Children's Hospital
Westchester Medical Center
Valhalla, New York

Roy R. Fielding
Member, American Red Cross
    Lifeguarding Advisory Group
University of North Carolina—
    Charlotte, Dept. of Kinesiology
Director of Aquatics
Charlotte, North Carolina

Francesco A. Pia, PhD
Member, American Red Cross
    Lifeguarding Advisory Group
Water Safety Films, Inc.
President, Pia Consulting Services
Larchmont, New York

M. Kathryn Scott
Director, Physical Education
University of California
Berkeley, California

The Lifeguarding Advisory Group for this edition included—

Joyce A. Bathke
American Red Cross
St. Louis Area Chapter
Director, Health and Safety
St. Louis, Missouri

David W. Bell, PhD
National Aquatic Committee
National Health and Safety
    Committee
Boy Scouts of America
Ponca City, Oklahoma

Tina M. Dittmar
City of Laguna Niguel, Parks &
    Recreation Aquatics
Aquatics Supervisor
Laguna Niguel, California

Dan L. Jones
City of Newport News—Aquatics and
    Beach Safety
Director, Aquatics and Beach Safety
Newport News, Virginia

John A. Kaufmann
United States Navy
Supervisor Training Specialist
Pensacola, Florida

Bryan J. Nadeau
Busch Entertainment Corporation
Admission Systems Manager
St. Louis, Missouri

Jorge L. Olaves, EdS
Florida A&M University—Aquatic
    Center
Aquatic Director/Coordinator
Tallahassee, Florida

The following organizations provided external review:

American Camp Association—Education
Catherine M. Scheder
Director, Educational Partnerships
Martinsville City, Indiana

Boy Scouts of America—National Council
Bill Steele
Director
Leadership Support Service
Irving, Texas

Boys & Girls Clubs of America
Rachel C. Falgout
Director, Teen Services
Atlanta, Georgia

Girl Scouts of the U.S.A.
Kathleen M. Cullinan
Program Consultant, Safety-Wise
    Lead
New York, New York

Jewish Community Centers Association
JoyAnn Brand
Associate Director of Professional
    Development
New York, New York

National Recreation & Park Association
Sharon L. Mannion
Aquatic Manager
Ashburn, Virginia

US Navy—CNIC—MWR—Mission Essential Branch
John K. Powell
Head, Mission Essential Branch
Millington, Tennessee

USA Swimming
Sue Pitt Anderson
Resource Development
Colorado Springs, Colorado

The following individuals provided external review:

Gerald DeMers, PhD
Chair, Kinesiology Department
California Polytechnic State
    University
San Luis Obispo, California

Jennifer Espino-Smith
Supervisory Recreation Specialist
30th Services Division
Vandenberg AFB, California

Jim O'Connor
Aquatics Coordinator
Miami-Dade Park and Recreation
Miami, Florida

The following individuals provided external review for American Red Cross and StayWell:

Susan T. Dempf, PhD
Associate Professor, The Sage Colleges
Troy, New York

Terri Eudy, MA
Health and Safety Course
    Instructor/Trainer
Department of Campus Recreation
Oakland University
Rochester, Michigan

Bonnie Griswold
Aquatics Supervisor
City of Madison
Madison, Wisconsin

The American Red Cross and Stay-Well thank Casey Berg, Rick Brady, Vincent Knaus, Jessica Silver and Lynn Whittemore for their contributions to the development of this manual.

Photo Locations

A.D. Barnes Pool
Metro-Dade Parks and Recreation
Miami, Florida

Anacostia Pool
District of Columbia
Department of Parks and Recreation
Washington, DC

Army Navy Country Club
Arlington, Virginia

Camp Oneka
Wayne, Pennsylvania

Camp Saffran
Broad Creek Memorial Scout
    Reservation
Baltimore Area Council, Boy Scouts
    of America
Whiteford, Maryland

Carpinteria Community Pool
City of Carpinteria
Parks and Recreation
Carpinteria, California

Crown Valley Community Pool
City of Laguna Niguel
Parks & Recreation
Laguna Niguel, California

Cypress Lakes
Lee County Parks and Recreation
Fort Myers, Florida

Gunpowder Falls State Park
Hammerman Area
Chase, Maryland

Huntington Park Beach
City of Newport News
Department of Parks, Recreation &
    Tourism
Newport News, Virginia

Larry and Penny Thompson Park
Metro-Dade Parks and Recreation
Miami, Florida

Los Baños Pool
City of Santa Barbara
Parks & Recreation
Santa Barbara, California

Magruder Swimming Pool
City of Newport News
Department of Parks, Recreation &
    Tourism
Newport News, Virginia

Matheson Hammock Park
Metro-Dade Parks and Recreation
Miami, Florida

Midtown Aquatic Center
City of Newport News
Department of Parks, Recreation &
    Tourism
Newport News, Virginia

North Shore Pool
Reston Association
Reston, Virginia

Paul Nelson Aquatic Center
City of Santa Maria
Recreation & Parks Department
Santa Maria, California

Turkey Thicket Pool
District of Columbia
Department of Parks and Recreation
Washington, DC

University of Maryland
Campus Recreation Center
    Natatorium
College Park, Maryland

**Vandenberg AFB Family Aquatic
Center**
30th Services Division
Vandenberg AFB, California

Ventura Aquatic Center
City of Ventura
Community Recreation Division
Ventura, California

Walt Disney World
Orlando, Florida

Wet 'n Wild
Orlando, Florida

Wild Rivers Waterpark
Irvine, California

William Woollett Jr. Aquatics Center
City of Irvine
Community Services
Irvine, California

PREFACE

This manual is for lifeguards, whom the American Red Cross profoundly thanks for their commitment to safeguarding the lives of children and adults who enjoy aquatic facilities. As the number of community pools and waterparks grows nationwide, participation in aquatic activities is also growing. With this growth comes the need for even more lifeguards.

To protect this growing number of participants, lifeguards must receive proper and effective training. Lifeguards also need to maintain their skills to ensure their ability to work effectively with others as a part of a lifeguard team. Participation in frequent and ongoing training is essential.

Lifeguards must be able to recognize hazardous situations to prevent injury. They must be able to supervise swimmers, minimize dangers, educate facility users about safety, enforce rules and regulations, provide assistance and perform rescues.

Being a lifeguard carries a significant professional responsibility, but lifeguarding also offers opportunities for personal growth. Experience as a lifeguard can help one develop professional and leadership skills that will last a lifetime—through college, career and family.

There are a half million American Red Cross-trained lifeguards working at swimming pools, waterparks and waterfronts across our country. Every day on the job, these lifeguards are part of a critical force for good—ensuring the safety of patrons and protecting lives.

BRIEF TABLE OF CONTENTS

TABLE OF CONTENTS

Chapter 1

Chapter 2

Chapter 3

Chapter 4

Chapter 5

Chapter 6

Chapter 7

Chapter 8

Chapter 9

Chapter 10

Chapter 11

The Professional Lifeguard

LIFEGUARDING CAN BE A REWARDING JOB. BEING A LIFEGUARD IS—

- **Dynamic.** Each day on the job may present new situations.
- **Challenging.** Doing the job well requires quick judgments.
- **Important.** Responding to an emergency at any moment may be required.
- **Inspiring.** The knowledge, skills and attitude learned when becoming a lifeguard can save a life.

This chapter describes the characteristics and responsibilities of a lifeguard, the rewards of being a professional lifeguard and the importance of maintaining lifeguarding knowledge and skills.

CHARACTERISTICS OF A PROFESSIONAL LIFEGUARD

Lifeguard professionalism begins with training and certification. Professional lifeguards are mentally, physically and emotionally prepared at all times to do their job **(Fig 1-1)**. Professional lifeguards must be—

- **Knowledgeable and have appropriate skills.** Participate in training, including annual or preseason orientation and training, and regular and frequent in-service training to always be able to prevent and respond to emergencies.
- **Reliable.** Arrive to work on time, accept assignments willingly, be committed to the work and respond to all incidents quickly and effectively.
- **Mature.** Be a leader, act responsibly, obey all facility rules and lead others by example.
- **Courteous and consistent.** Be polite and enforce the rules firmly and equally for everyone.
- **Positive.** Show a positive attitude in all job activities.
- **Professional.** Look and be prepared to respond appropriately to any situation:
  - Wear the lifeguard uniform only when on duty.
  - Be well groomed.
  - Keep rescue equipment positioned for immediate use when on duty.
  - Keep essential personal gear, such as sunglasses, on or nearby at all times.
  - Sit or stand upright at the lifeguarding station.
  - Keep eyes focused on the assigned area of responsibility at all times.
  - Keep interactions with others brief and do not let them interrupt patron surveillance.
  - Transfer and handle equipment carefully.
  - Observe all facility rules, regulations and policies.
  - Eat and use mobile phones only when on break or off surveillance duty.

Fig. 1-2

- **Healthy and fit.** To stay healthy and fit—
  - **Exercise.** An exercise program should include swimming and water exercises that focus on building endurance and developing strength **(Fig 1-2)**. Regular exercise helps lifeguards—
    - Stay healthy.
    - Perform strenuous rescues.
    - Stay alert.
    - Cope with stress and fatigue.
  - **Eat and hydrate properly.** Good nutrition and a balanced diet help provide the energy needed to stay alert and active. Drink plenty of water to prevent dehydration.
  - **Rest adequately.** Proper rest and sleep during off-duty hours are essential for staying alert while on duty.
  - **Use sun protection.** Overexposure to the sun can cause many problems, such as—
    - Sunburn.
    - Skin cancer.
    - Dehydration.
    - Heat exhaustion.
    - Heat stroke.

  These problems can be prevented by using a sunscreen with a sun protection factor (SPF) of at least 15, reapplying as needed, and by wearing light-colored, light-weight clothing, like a shirt and a hat that covers the head and shades the face, neck and ears. Using an umbrella provides shade. Wearing wrap-around polarized sunglasses with UVA/UVB protects eyes and reduces glare. Drinking plenty of water and taking breaks in cool or shaded areas throughout the day also helps prevent overexposure.

Fig. 1-1

Dehydration and the Lifeguard

Lifeguards have the job of looking out for patrons, but sometimes forget about themselves. This sometimes is the case with dehydration. Dehydration is a condition that occurs when a person loses more fluids than he or she consumes. Knowing the signs of dehydration and understanding how it affects an individual's ability to remain alert can be helpful to a lifeguard. Some of the mild-to-moderate signs of dehydration include—

- Excessive thirst.
- Sleepiness or tiredness.
- Dry mouth.
- Decreased urine output—8 hours or more without urination for teenagers.
- Few or no tears when crying.
- Muscle weakness.
- Headache.
- Dizziness or light-headedness.

Some severe signs of dehydration include—

- Extreme thirst.
- Irritability and confusion in adults.
- Very dry mouth, skin and mucous membranes.
- Lack of sweating.

- Little or no urination—any urine that is produced will be dark yellow or amber.
- Sunken eyes.
- Shriveled and dry skin that lacks elasticity and does not bounce back when pinched into a fold.
- Low blood pressure.
- Rapid heart beat.
- Fever.
- In the most serious cases, delirium or unconsciousness.

Dehydration can be prevented by—
- Keeping properly hydrated by drinking water regularly and whenever becoming thirsty before, during and after a shift. A plastic water bottle filled with water should be kept at the lifeguard station.
- Eating well-balanced meals before a shift and during breaks.
- Taking breaks in cool or shaded areas.
- Avoiding beverages containing caffeine and/or sugar.
- Avoiding alcohol.

■ **Do not use alcohol and other drugs.** On- or off-duty use of alcohol and other drugs can negatively affect job performance and can jeopardize the safety of patrons, co-workers and oneself.

RESPONSIBILITIES OF A PROFESSIONAL LIFEGUARD

The **primary responsibility** of a lifeguard is to ensure patron safety and protect lives—including his or her own. This can be done in several ways, such as—
- Preventing injuries by minimizing or eliminating hazardous situations or behaviors.

- Enforcing facility rules and regulations and educating patrons about them.
- Recognizing and responding quickly and effectively to all emergencies.
- Administering first aid and cardiopulmonary resuscitation (CPR) or using an automated external defibrillator (AED) in an emergency and, if trained, administering oxygen when needed.
- Informing other lifeguards, facility staff and management when more help or equipment is needed.

Other tasks for which a lifeguard is responsible are called **secondary responsibilities**. Secondary responsibilities must never prevent the lifeguard from meeting his or her

So, You Want to be a Lifeguard

Now that you have decided to accept the challenge of becoming a professional lifeguard, the American Red Cross can help. Red Cross Lifeguarding provides lifeguard candidates with the knowledge and skills they need to prevent and respond to aquatic emergencies.

The Red Cross Lifeguarding program offers four customized courses to choose from:

- **Lifeguarding** prepares lifeguard candidates to work at traditional pools and multi-attraction facilities.
- **Waterfront Lifeguarding** teaches lifeguard candidates surveillance and rescue skills specific to nonsurf, open-water environments, such as lakes and rivers.
- **Waterpark Lifeguarding** teaches lifeguard candidates surveillance and rescue skills specific to waterpark environments.
- **Shallow Water Attendant** trains candidates to work at water attractions up to 4 feet deep, such as zero-depth pools, catch basins at the foot of slides, winding rivers and kiddie pools.

For more information on Red Cross Lifeguarding courses, including course prerequisites and certification requirements, go to *www.redcross.org*.

Although the Red Cross does not offer training for the surf environment, our lifeguarding courses provide an excellent base for any type of lifeguarding. For information on becoming a lifeguard in the surf environment, visit the United States Lifesaving Association's Web site at: *www.usla.org*.

primary responsibility. Secondary responsibilities can include—

- Filling out required records and reports on schedule and submitting them to the proper person or office.
- Performing maintenance or other tasks assigned by his or her supervisor. (Some duties, such as monitoring pool water chemistry, require additional training beyond American Red Cross lifeguarding courses.)
- Inspecting the facility daily and reporting any unsafe conditions or equipment to a supervisor.

LIFEGUARDING TIP: Never perform secondary responsibilities when performing patron surveillance.

LIFEGUARD WORK SETTINGS

There are many opportunities in different environments in which to be a lifeguard. Lifeguarding is a challenging and rewarding experience. These environments include—

- **Swimming pools.** Swimming pools are enclosed bodies of treated water used for recreational or competitive swimming or other aquatic activities. Swimming pools can be rectangular in shape or free-form (**Fig 1-3**).

Fig. 1-3

Job Description for a Lifeguard

Job Title: Lifeguard (entry-level)
Job Description: Responsible for ensuring the safety of facility patrons by preventing and responding to emergencies.

Minimum Qualifications:
- Current certification in the following:
  - Lifeguarding:
    - American Red Cross Lifeguarding and First Aid
    - American Red Cross Shallow Water Attendant and First Aid (up to 4 feet)
    - American Red Cross Waterfront Lifeguarding and First Aid for nonsurf open-water positions
    - American Red Cross Waterpark Lifeguarding and First Aid for waterpark and multi-attraction facility positions
  - American Red Cross CPR/AED for the Professional Rescuer
  - Other certifications required by local or state laws
- Preemployment testing of lifeguarding knowledge and skills

Knowledge and Skills:
- Thorough knowledge and application of lifeguarding surveillance and rescue techniques
- An understanding of facility characteristics, rules, policies and procedures
- Leadership and public relations skills
- Decision-making skills

Responsibilities:
- Recognize and respond quickly and effectively in emergencies.
- Enforce all aquatic facility policies, rules and regulations.
- Inspect the facility on a daily schedule and report any unsafe conditions or equipment to the supervisor.
- Complete records and reports.
- Participate in regular in-service training sessions.
- Maintain fitness level (swimming skills, strength and endurance).
- Complete additional duties as assigned by supervisor.

Responsible to:
- Head lifeguard, lifeguard supervisor, pool manager or aquatics director/supervisor.

- **Multi-attraction aquatic facilities.** Multi-attraction aquatic facilities can include swimming pools, but also include play structures, inflatable play equipment, water slides and activity pools (**Fig 1-4**).
- **Waterfronts.** Waterfronts are open-water areas, such as lakes, rivers, ponds and oceans. This manual covers nonsurf, waterfront swimming areas, such as those at national and state parks, summer camps and campgrounds. Every waterfront is unique. They vary in water quality, clarity, currents and beach conditions (**Fig 1-5**).
- **Waterparks.** Waterparks are aquatic theme parks with attractions, such as wave pools, speed slides and winding rivers. Each waterpark is different and has its own unique attractions (**Fig 1-6**).

Fig. 1-4

Fig. 1-5

Fig. 1-6

Lifeguards learn the specific characteristics of their facility through orientation and in-service trainings. This manual does not discuss lifeguarding at surf environments where strong waves or strong currents are present. Surf lifeguarding requires other specialized skills and equipment.

DECISION MAKING

Decision making is an important component to lifeguarding. Lifeguards make many kinds of decisions, including—

- When and how to make a rescue.
- When and how to perform first aid or CPR and give other emergency care.
- How to work with their lifeguard team and the facility's management.

- How to interact with patrons and deal with them in a variety of settings and circumstances.

Decision making can be difficult, especially in an emergency. The **FIND** decision-making model can be a useful tool to make informed decisions. This can help lifeguards to clearly understand what is involved in a decision. **FIND** means—

- **F** = Figure out the problem.
- **I** = Identify possible solutions.
- **N** = Name the pros and cons for each solution.
- **D** = Decide which solution is best.

The **FIND** decision-making model applied to lifeguarding decisions can help lifeguards find the best action to take in most situations.

LEGAL CONSIDERATIONS

To avoid liability, it is important to understand the legal principles involved in being a professional lifeguard.
- **Duty to act.** While on the job, a lifeguard has a legal responsibility to act in an emergency.
- **Standard of care.** Lifeguards are expected to meet a minimum standard of care, which may be established in part by their training program and in part by state or local authorities. This standard requires lifeguards to—
  - Communicate proper information and warnings to help prevent injuries.
  - Recognize a victim in need of care.
  - Attempt to rescue a victim needing assistance.
  - Provide emergency care according to their level of training.
- **Negligence.** If a lifeguard fails to follow the standard of care or fails to act, which results in someone being injured or causes further harm to the victim, the lifeguard may be considered negligent. Negligence includes—
  - Failing to provide care.
  - Providing care beyond the scope of practice or level of training.
  - Providing inappropriate care.
  - Failing to control or stop any behaviors that could result in further harm or injury.
- **Good Samaritan laws.** The vast majority of states and the District of Columbia have Good Samaritan laws to protect people who willingly provide emergency care without accepting anything in return. These laws differ somewhat from state to state, but generally help protect people who act in good faith, within the scope of

Multi-Attraction Aquatic Facilities and Spray Parks

Multi-attraction aquatic facilities and spray parks continue to grow and increase in popularity. These provide a greater variety of activities for patrons.

Multi-Attraction Facilities

Many park and recreation departments, communities and private pool owners are adding play structures, inflatable play equipment, water slides and activity pools—sometimes replacing other equipment, such as diving boards. The idea is to turn a pool into a miniature waterpark. As new facilities are built, attractions are often part of the facility's design. Facility owners realize that people want to get the most entertainment for their money, so they provide more options for their customers.

Because of the variety of attractions in multi-attraction facilities, lifeguards need additional training on the use and care of this equipment and for the differences in surveillance that are needed to keep patrons safe.

Spray Parks

Spray parks are playgrounds, but with water. These parks create a unique interactive play experience for children who want to get wet without ever getting in a pool. They are becoming popular due to the fact that admission typically is free, and they provide children exciting play opportunities while at the same time providing a low-cost alternative to building a pool. Some communities do not have the budget to build pools, so spray parks are an attractive alternative since they do not have standing water and are computer controlled.

Some of the attractions that can be found in a spray park include spray cannons, ground sprays and above-ground features, such as forts, waterfalls, rain showers, animals that spray water and structures that simulate a car wash.

---

their training and are not negligent. Some Good Samaritan laws, however, do not provide coverage for individuals who have a duty to respond. For this reason, it is important that lifeguards consult a lawyer or the facility's legal counsel to determine the degree to which their state's Good Samaritan laws will help protect them.

- **Consent.** An injured or ill victim must give permission before responders can provide first aid and emergency care. To obtain consent—
  - State your name.
  - Tell the victim you are trained and what level of training you have.
  - Ask the victim if you may help.
  - Explain to the victim that you would like to assess him or her to find out what you think may be wrong.
  - Explain what you plan to do.

With this information, the victim can grant his or her informed consent for care. Someone who is unconscious, confused or seriously injured or ill (such as in a nonfatal submersion) may not be able to grant consent. In these cases, the law assumes the victim would give consent if he or she were able to do so. This is called *implied consent.* Implied consent also applies to a minor who needs emergency medical assistance and whose parent or guardian is not present.

- **Refusal of care.** Some injured or ill victims, even those who desperately need care, may refuse care. Parents may also refuse care for children. Even though the victim may be seriously injured, his or her wishes must be honored. However, a lifeguard should explain to the victim why he or she needs care and request the victim to at least allow someone more highly trained, such as emergency medical services

(EMS) personnel, to evaluate the situation. It must be made clear that care is neither being denied nor withheld, and the victim is not being abandoned. Someone else, such as another lifeguard, must witness the victim's refusal and document it. Any refusal of care must be documented.

- **Abandonment**. Once care is initiated, it must be continued until EMS personnel or someone with equal or greater training arrives and takes over. Responders can be held legally responsible for abandoning a person who requires ongoing care if they leave the scene or stop providing care.
- **Confidentiality**. While making a rescue or providing care, a lifeguard may learn something about the injured or ill victim, such as information about medical conditions, physical problems and medications taken. The victim's right to privacy is protected by keeping information learned about the victim confidential. Reporters, insurance investigators or attorneys may ask questions. This information must never be shared with anyone except EMS personnel directly associated with the victim's care, facility management or the facility's legal counsel. The Health Insurance Portability and Accountability Act (HIPAA) of 1996 was created by the federal government to protect a victim's privacy. Sharing personal information with individuals not directly associated with a victim's medical care may constitute a breach in the victim's privacy. Further information on HIPAA is available at *www.hhs.gov/ocr/hipaa.*
- **Documentation**. Documenting injuries and incidents is very important. If a legal action occurs later, a record can provide legal documentation of what was seen, heard and done at the scene. Required forms should be completed as soon as possible after the incident occurs. As time passes, critical details may be forgotten. Reports should state facts of the incident, not opinion. Responders should sign, date and keep a copy of the report, even if care was provided when not on duty.

THE LIFEGUARD TEAM

A *lifeguard team* is formed when 2 or more lifeguards are on duty. Team members may be trained and evaluated together. Team members practice working together as a unit. Everyone who works at the facility needs to know and understand his or her role in an emergency and how and when to call for more help. To be a good team, all staff must practice the facility's emergency action plans (EAPs) together until everyone knows his or her responsi-

bilities and can perform them correctly. EAPs are the written procedures that guide the actions of lifeguards and other staff in emergencies.

Team members will work together better when they understand the expectations of management as well as what they can expect from each other. Management should put its expectations in an employee handbook or other written guidelines. To learn what team members should expect from one another, it is important that team members communicate and practice together. On-the-job or in-service training is ideal for reviewing and practicing EAPs and talking with teammates.

The lifeguard team is also part of a larger team—the aquatic safety team. The *aquatic safety team* is a network of people who prevent, prepare for, respond to and assist in an emergency at an aquatic facility. This team is comprised of other facility staff and local emergency service personnel. Chapter 4 discusses the responsibilities of the aquatic safety team.

HOW FACILITY MANAGEMENT PROMOTES LIFEGUARD PROFESSIONALISM

Facility management supports and helps lifeguards develop professionally by providing—
- A policies and procedures manual.
- Annual or preseason orientation and training and regular and frequent in-service training.
- Opportunities for recognition and career development.

If the facility does not have professional development opportunities, lifeguards should talk to their supervisors, who may be able to develop these opportunities or help find other options.

Policies and Procedures Manual

Management should be certain that all lifeguards have the information they need to work safely and to perform their duties effectively. A policies and procedures manual can provide this information. This manual usually includes—
- A mission statement.
- Administrative policies and procedures.
- Rules and regulations.
- EAPs.
- Opening and closing procedures.
- Sample record and report forms.
- Guidelines for daily pool activities and supervision needed for each (e.g., swim lessons, fitness classes and diving).

- Guidelines for special pool activities and supervision needed for each (e.g., large groups, day camps, parties and movies).
- Instructions for administering swim tests.
- Guidelines for personnel (including preemployment requirements, hiring policies, conditions of employment and standards of performance and conduct).
- An organizational chart (with a chain of command and job descriptions).
- A floor plan of the facility that shows emergency evacuation routes and where emergency equipment is located.
- Instructions for equipment use.
- Diagrams of areas of responsibility for patron surveillance.
- Rotations and assigned stations.

Orientation

An orientation session about facility operations and the lifeguards' responsibilities helps both new and returning lifeguards understand the facility, their responsibilities and management's expectations. Lifeguards should ask their employer questions about, and become completely familiar with, their facility's operations.

In-Service Training

In-service training helps lifeguards maintain their knowledge and skills at the appropriate level. The facility manager, lifeguard supervisor, a head lifeguard or an individual who is an expert in a particular subject matter, such as a public health official, risk manager or human resources representative, may conduct sessions **(Fig 1-7)**. In-service training sessions might address issues such as—

- Potential hazards at the facility.
- Facility rules and regulations.

Fig. 1-7

- EAPs.
- Surveillance and water rescue skills.
- First aid; CPR; AED; caring for head, neck or back injuries; and, when appropriate, bloodborne pathogens and administering emergency oxygen training.
- Personal protection equipment.
- Physical conditioning.
- Decision making.
- Internal staff issues, such as communication, teamwork and morale.
- Facility operations.
- Records and reports (proper documentation).
- Customer service.

LIFEGUARDING TIP: Professional lifeguards need to regularly participate in in-service training sessions.

Recognition and Career Development

Recognition for a job well done may come in the form of an award, a promotion or a written letter expressing appreciation for a lifeguard's efforts. Some facilities offer career opportunities through in-service training, special events like lifeguard competitions, additional training or course work or attendance at conferences or workshops. The Red Cross offers basic- and instructor-level courses to enhance careers in lifeguarding, such as Waterpark Lifeguarding, Waterfront Lifeguarding, Emergency Response, Administering Emergency Oxygen, Bloodborne Pathogens Training and Lifeguard Management.

MAINTAINING LIFEGUARDING KNOWLEDGE AND SKILLS

Earning a lifeguarding certification means a candidate has successfully completed course material and passed written and skill tests on a given date. *It does not mean that the candidate has learned everything there is to know about lifeguarding.* It is important that lifeguards maintain their professionalism by retaining their knowledge and skills at an appropriate level. Lifeguards should have annual certification training. This is especially important for seasonal lifeguards, who can lose knowledge and skills during the off-season. Annual certification training can include CPR and AED review courses, lifeguarding review courses and review of lifeguarding knowledge and skills. One of the best ways a lifeguard can keep his or her knowledge and skills current and stay in peak physical form is by participating in in-service training sessions.

PUTTING IT ALL TOGETHER

Being a professional lifeguard means being fully prepared for this challenging and important work. Looking
and acting professional indicates readiness to do the
job. Staying professional requires practice and commitment. No one is a natural born lifeguard; it takes hard
work. A lifeguard can meet the challenges and gain the
rewards of being a professional through practice and
dedication.

Chapter 2

Injury Prevention and Facility Safety

Lifeguards are essential for keeping aquatic facilities safe. Unlike most other professional rescuers, lifeguards are present to prevent emergencies from occurring. Lifeguards focus most of their time on injury prevention, which means preventing situations in which patrons can be harmed. Therefore, an understanding of how injuries occur and how they can be prevented is essential.

PREVENTING INJURIES: PATRON SAFETY

Aquatic injury prevention is a part of the facility's risk management program. *Risk management* involves identifying dangerous conditions or behaviors that can cause injuries and then taking steps to minimize or eliminate them. Even though lifeguarding requires performing emergency rescues, far more time will be spent on preventive lifeguarding—trying to make sure emergencies do not happen in the first place.

Although not all emergencies can be prevented, knowing what causes life-threatening injuries helps lifeguards prevent them. Injuries are either life threatening or nonlife-threatening. Examples of life-threatening injuries include—

- Submersion (nonfatal submersion or drowning).
- Injuries to the head, neck or back (spinal injuries).
- Unconsciousness.
- Breathing emergencies.
- Cardiac emergencies.
- Severe bleeding.

The two most serious aquatic emergencies to prevent are drowning and head, neck or back injuries. *Drowning* happens when a person suffocates in the water. Drowning may result when a nonswimmer enters water that is over his or her head, when a poor swimmer becomes exhausted or when a patron is incapacitated in the water due to a medical emergency, such as a seizure or cardiac emergency. Most head, neck or back injuries result from head-first entries into shallow water. If a victim's head strikes the bottom or the side of the pool, the spinal cord can be damaged and cause paralysis or death.

Nonlife-threatening injuries also occur in aquatic facilities. Examples of nonlife-threatening injuries include—

- Suspected fractures or dislocations.
- Abrasions (scrapes).
- Superficial burns (sunburns).
- Muscle cramps (caused by overexertion).
- Sprains and strains.

Understanding how injuries occur helps lifeguards know how to prevent them by—

- Increasing their awareness of risks and hazards.
- Helping patrons avoid risky behavior.
- Developing a safety-conscious attitude at their facility.

Lifeguards use the following three injury-prevention strategies:

- Communication with patrons
- Facility safety checks
- Patron surveillance (covered in Chapter 3)

COMMUNICATION WITH PATRONS

Communication as an injury-prevention strategy requires lifeguards to—

- Inform patrons about the potential for injury.
- Educate patrons about inappropriate behavior.
- Enforce rules and regulations.

Inform Patrons About the Potential for Injury

Patrons need to know about risks that could cause injury. Signs give them warnings, tell them how to use equipment and list rules and regulations to help prevent behaviors that can lead to injury. Lifeguards also help inform patrons about the potential for injuries. Therefore, lifeguards need to understand the rules and regulations of the facility where they work.

Common Rules and Regulations

Every facility should have rules and regulations posted **(Fig. 2-1)**. The lifeguard's job is to understand these rules and help patrons understand and comply with them. Lifeguards should use a positive approach to promote acceptable behavior. For example, if a patron is running on the deck, the lifeguard should tell the patron to "Please walk."

Pool Rules

- Swimming is permitted only when a University Lifeguard is on duty.
- Bathing suit required. Cut-off shorts are not permitted.
- Children under 16 years of age must be supervised by a parent/guardian/teacher/coach on the deck.
- Soap showers must be taken prior to entering pool.
- Water in closed, resealable plastic containers is allowed. All other drinks, food and glass are prohibited.
- When more than 2 swimmers are in a lane, laps must be "circle swum" counter clockwise.
- Individuals having skin lesions; mouth, nose or ear discharges; or any communicable disease may not use the pool without written permission from a medical professional.
- One person permitted on diving board at a time. A maximum of one bounce is permitted.

PROHIBITED:

- Street shoes on pool deck
- Running or rough play
- Hanging on lane ropes
- Swimming under bulkheads
- Diving into shallow water or areas marked "NO DIVING"
- Back dives or flips from the edge of pool
- Swimming in Diving Area while springboards are in use

Fig. 2-1

Rules do not keep patrons from having fun. They exist for everyone's health and safety, including facility staff. Posted rules help patrons enjoy their experience without endangering themselves or others. Rules should be posted in plain view for all patrons and staff to see. Facilities that attract large numbers of international guests or facilities that are located in multi-cultural communities may also post rules in other languages or use international signs or symbols. Rules posted at aquatic facilities may include—

- Swim only when a lifeguard is on duty.
- Obey lifeguard instructions at all times.
- No running, pushing or horseplay.
- Shower with soap and water before entering the water.
- Dive only in designated areas.
- Proper swimwear required.
- No glass containers in the pool area and locker rooms.
- No alcoholic beverages or other drug use allowed.
- No smoking.

The facility may also have other rules, such as—

- Only members and their guests allowed.
- Nonswimmers and children under a set age or height must be supervised by an adult.
- Children using flotation devices must be supervised by a parent or guardian within arm's reach.
- No personal flotation devices (PFDs) allowed except for U.S. Coast Guard-approved life jackets.
- Patrons may have to demonstrate their swimming ability before entering deep water.
- Extended breath-holding exercises prohibited.
- No weapons allowed.
- No pets allowed in the facility.

Additional rules for waterfront facilities may include—

- No playing or swimming under piers, rafts, platforms or play structures.
- No boats, sailboards, surfboards or personal water craft in swimming areas.
- Dive only in designated areas.
- No running or diving head-first into shallow water.
- No fishing near swimming areas.
- Stay off lifeguard stands (stands are for lifeguards only).
- Keep a clear path between the lifeguard stand and the water.
- No umbrellas at the waterline (umbrellas present a surveillance obstruction).
- No swimming in unauthorized areas.
- Rescue craft and rescue boards are for lifeguard use only.

At waterparks, rules and regulations may also be played as recorded messages. Rules may vary based on

Fig. 2-2

the type of facility and attractions available. Additional rule considerations at waterparks include—

- The minimum or maximum number of people allowed on an attraction or on a tube at a time.
- Patron height or weight restrictions to use an attraction **(Fig. 2-2)**. For example, on waterslides, typically, patrons must be at least 6 inches taller than the depth of a shallow catch pool. A *catch pool* is a small pool at the end of a slide where patrons enter water deep enough to cushion their landing.
- Child height or age restrictions in some areas designated for small children for safety reasons.
- Warning signs that state the water depth in a catch pool. Some catch pools are shallow and patrons can stand up, but others are very deep. Patrons may expect a shallow catch pool and be surprised in a deep catch pool.
- Common rules for winding rivers, such as—
  - Enter and exit the winding river only at designated places.
  - No jumping or diving into the water.
  - No people on shoulders.
  - Stay in tubes at all times.
  - No walking or swimming in the winding river if tubes are used.
  - Only one properly fitted life jacket per patron.
  - No stacking of tubes or life jackets.
  - No forming chains of tubes or life jackets.
  - Only one patron allowed per tube, except for an adult holding a small child. The child must be wearing a U.S. Coast Guard-approved life jacket in case the adult tips over.
- Common rules for waterslides include—
  - No running, stopping, standing, kneeling, rotating or tumbling on the slides.
  - No swimsuits or shorts with metal rivets, buttons or fasteners.

Life Jackets

Anyone who cannot swim well should wear a life jacket if they are going to be in or around the water at an aquatic facility. Facilities may have policies addressing the use of life jackets in a pool, waterfront or attraction—whether or not they can be worn. In some cases, life jackets may be available at a facility for rent or free of charge.

There are several types and many styles of life jackets, and they are rated for their buoyancy and purposes. Swimming ability, activity and water conditions help determine which type to use. For any type, it should be U.S. Coast Guard-approved and in good condition. The U.S. Coast Guard has categorized personal flotation devices (PFDs) into five types:

- Type I—Offshore life jacket

- Type II—Near shore buoyant vest

- Type III—Flotation aid

- Type IV—Throwable device

- Type V—Special use device

The common types of life jackets that are seen at aquatic facilities are the Type II and Type III life jackets. If the facility allows, rents or loans life jackets, the life jacket should be checked to ensure that it is in good condition (no broken buckles, missing straps or torn fabric) and is the right size for the intended user. Size is determined by the weight of the user. Patrons should observe fitting requirements, such as wearing the proper size life jacket and buckling all buckles, facing forward.

Inflatables, such as water wings, swim rings and other flotation devices, are **not** designed to be used as substitutes for U.S. Coast Guard-approved life jackets or adult supervision. Swimmers may go beyond their ability and fall off an inflatable, which may lead to a drowning situation. Inflatable materials deteriorate from sun and rough surfaces, leading to deflation and leaks.

- No eyeglasses, sunglasses or goggles.
- No life jackets allowed.
- No aqua socks or aqua shoes.

Facility Equipment and Structures

There are other rules for specific equipment and structures. These rules depend on the facility and may include the following:

- One person at a time on a ladder.
- Do not sit or hang on lifelines or lane lines.
- Do not climb on lifeguard stands or towers.
- Lap swimmers may use kickboards, hand paddles, pull buoys, masks, fins and snorkels only for swimming in assigned lanes.
- Starting blocks may be used only by swim team members in scheduled practices, competitions and instruction when supervised by a coach or instructor (**Fig. 2-3**).

Diving Areas

Rules for diving boards and towers should be posted in the diving area (**Fig. 2-4**). The rules may include the following:

- Only one person on the diving board at a time.
- Use the ladder to climb onto the diving board.

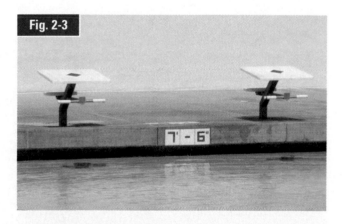

Fig. 2-3

Fig. 2-4   **DIVING BOARD RULES**
- One bounce on board.
- Jump straight off diving board, then swim to ladder.
- One person on the diving board at a time.
- Make sure area is clear under diving board before jumping.
- No back dives off edge.
- No swimming in the diving well.

REGLAS DEL TRAMPOLÍN
- Solamente un rebote en el trampolín.
- Brinque hacia enfrente del trampolín, luego nade hacia las escaleras.
- Solamente una persona a la vez en el trampolín.
- Asegurarse que no este nadie debajo del trampolín antes de brincar.
- No se permiten clavados hacia atrás.
- No nade en area   clavados

- Only one person on the ladder at a time.
- Look before diving or jumping to make sure the diving area is clear.
- Only one bounce allowed on the diving board.
- Dive or jump forward straight out from the diving board.
- Swim immediately to the closest ladder or wall.
- Dive only when supervised by a lifeguard, swimming instructor or coach.

Spas, Hot Tubs and Therapy Pools

Spas, hot tubs and therapy pools are popular, but their hazards include drowning, hyperthermia (high body temperature) and disease transmission. State and local laws may regulate their operation. Ask a supervisor about regulations governing the facility's spas, hot tubs and therapy pools. Rules common to these areas include—

- Use only when a lifeguard is present.
- Shower with soap and water before using.
- Enter and exit slowly and cautiously.
- People with heart disease, diabetes, high or low blood pressure, seizures, epilepsy or other medical conditions are not allowed to use the spa or hot tub.
- Pregnant women and young children should seek their doctor's approval before using a spa or hot tub.
- No unsupervised use by children.
- Do not use the spa or hot tub while under the influence of alcohol or other drugs.
- No diving, jumping or horseplay in the spa or hot tub.
- Limit time in the spa to 10 minutes. Patrons may then shower, cool down and return again briefly. Prolonged use may result in nausea, dizziness, fainting or hyperthermia.
- No body lotions, oils or sunscreen in the spa or hot tub.
- No food or drink in the spa area or hot tub.
- No exercising in the spa or hot tub.
- Report any safety issues to the lifeguard.
- Remove swim caps before entering the spa or hot tub.

Play Structures

Play structures are common at many facilities and come in many shapes and sizes. Permanent play structures include tube and drop slides, rope swings, sprays, fountains and moving water (**Fig. 2-5**). Removable play structures include floating toys, large inflatables and water games. Follow manufacturer's guidelines for safe operation. Common rules for play structures include—

- Do not let a play structure become overcrowded.
- Only clean, soft toys are allowed in the water.
- No climbing on inflatable play structures on dry land.
- No swimming beneath structures.

Fig. 2-5

rules. It is important to let them know what could happen because of an unsafe act. Explaining rules in a positive way encourages patrons to behave safely. The following steps can prevent a patron from engaging in risky behavior:

- Get the patron's attention, for example by blowing a whistle, and say, "Excuse me, but what you are doing is dangerous."
- Explain the hazard or danger, for example, "Diving into shallow water can cause you to hit your head on the bottom and be injured," or "You may slip and hurt yourself if you run." Simply telling them not to do something often does not work. People usually understand and cooperate when they know why something is dangerous.

If the facility has play structures, extra precautions are needed. Careful observation helps patrons stay safe and keeps the play structures in good condition. Be alert for—

- Some nonswimmers or weak swimmers becoming careless over the excitement of using play structures. They might try things they would not otherwise do, or they might unexpectedly enter deep water.
- Swimmers may be surprised by the fall from a drop slide or rope swing, especially if they did not realize they are over deep water. Watch that they come up to the surface and swim to the side.
- Excited children, who may run, fall and be injured around sprays and fountains in shallow water. A very young child who falls may not be able to get back up without assistance.
- Moving water may cause patrons to lose their balance and fall over.
- Patrons who may jump into the water from floating toys and inflatables without noticing what is around them and land on other swimmers.

Guidelines for permanent slides include—
- Follow manufacturer's guidelines for all slides.
- Enforce age, height and weight guidelines.
- Only one rider allowed on the slide at a time.
- Enter, ride and exit the slide feet-first.
- Keep hands inside the slide.
- No standing or stopping.
- Keep slide entry and exit points clear.
- No metal objects, locker keys, jewelry, metal snaps/zippers, eyewear or watches.
- Station lifeguards at the top and bottom of slides.

Educate Patrons About Inappropriate Behavior
Patrons may be unfamiliar with a facility's features or get so excited that they do not read signs or pay attention to the

Using a Whistle Wisely

A whistle is an important communication tool a lifeguard uses for activating emergency action plans and signaling other lifeguards and staff for backup. A whistle is often used to attract the attention of a patron involved in unsafe activity or a rule infraction. A lifeguard should never hesitate to use a whistle as necessary to intervene to prevent or respond to an emergency. However, sometimes a verbal or visual signal will suffice without the accompaniment of a loud blast. Sometimes young children will look at the lifeguard immediately before or after breaking a rule. A lifeguard can frequently correct minor infractions by simply making eye contact, nodding the head or giving an appropriate hand signal. If whistles are used too frequently, patrons may become conditioned to ignore them.

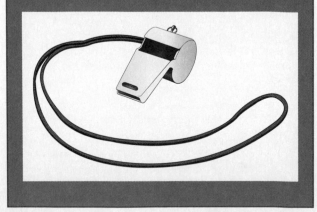

Interacting Positively with the Public When Not Conducting Patron Surveillance

Any time a lifeguard interacts with the public, his or her actions should promote an atmosphere of trust and goodwill. The following general guidelines help develop a positive relationship with patrons:

- Treat people as one would like to be treated. Make every patron feel welcome, important and respected.
- Be professional at all times. Be courteous, mature and responsible. Never insult or argue with a patron.
- Speak clearly and calmly, at a reasonable pace and volume.
- Use appropriate language, but do not patronize or speak down to anyone, including children.
- When interacting with patrons, make frequent and direct eye contact. Remove sunglasses, if necessary.
- Keep interactions brief, direct and firm but pleasant in tone and manner.
- Take all suggestions and complaints seriously, and follow up as necessary. Avoid blaming anyone. Direct complaints to facility management if they cannot be resolved, and follow the facility's procedures.
- It is helpful to repeat the concern expressed by the patron back to him or her. This helps to ensure an understanding of the concern.
- Do not make promises that cannot be kept.
- Enforce rules fairly and consistently. Be positive and non-judgmental. Reinforce correct behavior.
- Take a sincere interest in all patrons.

Nonverbal Communication

Spoken words make up a surprisingly small part of the overall communication. A listener automatically tends to make judgments about the speaker's attitude based on voice volume, pace, tone and pitch. A listener reacts positively or negatively to visual cues or body language. A lifeguard can gauge a person's attitude as cooperative or confrontational by these cues. A lifeguard should be aware that the listener will also be doing the same.

To convey a positive message, even when correcting someone, a lifeguard should—

- Act professional.
- Make frequent eye contact. If possible, remove sunglasses to do so.
- Point to features, such as signs, as they are referred to.
- When speaking to small children, kneel down to be at eye level with them.

A lifeguard should not—

- Pace back and forth.
- Glare at the person.
- Frown, sneer or scowl.
- Point, jab or wag a finger at the person.
- Stand over the person with arms crossed.
- Stand too close to the person.

- Explain a safe alternative behavior or activity. For example, tell them, "If you want to dive, please go to the deep end of the pool, where it is safe." Or say, "Excuse me, diving into shallow water is dangerous and can cause a head injury. Please use the deep end." Or say, "Please walk."

This type of explanation—

- Gets the patron's attention.
- Clarifies the danger.
- Emphasizes the consequences of the risky behavior.
- Offers safe alternatives, if available and appropriate.

Dealing with Uncooperative Patrons and Violence

No matter how fairly lifeguards enforce the rules, they may encounter an uncooperative patron. Before assuming a patron is uncooperative, lifeguards should make sure that he or she hears and understands them.

Uncooperative behavior may occur for different reasons:

- Some patrons let their fun get out of hand.
- Some patrons do not understand instructions because of language barriers.
- Some patrons may be under the influence of alcohol and other drugs.
- Conflicts between some patrons keep them from paying attention to the rules.
- Some patrons do not like to be corrected and get angry and embarrassed.

If a patron breaks the rules and is uncooperative, a lifeguard should take action right away because breaking the rules is a danger to the uncooperative patron and others. Most facilities have procedures for handling uncooperative patrons. If the facility does not have established procedures, the lifeguard supervisor or facility manager should be called for help as soon as possible.

A patron may threaten or commit a violent act with a weapon, such as a knife or a gun, a bottle or another type of implement or even a fist or foot. Lifeguards must be realistic about what can be done in a violent situation. If violence is likely to erupt, the supervisor or facility manager should be called immediately. If violence does erupt, a lifeguard should not try to stop it. A lifeguard should never confront a violent patron physically or verbally nor approach a patron who has a weapon. In such a situation, retreating and following the facility's EAP for violence is the best approach. Safety is still the main goal: safety for patrons and facility staff.

ENFORCE RULES AND REGULATIONS

Enforcing rules helps prevent injuries and encourages safe patron behavior. When enforcing rules, lifeguards must always be consistent and fair. Sometimes the patron may not know the rules at the facility or just does not understand the rules. Enforcement methods that are age appropriate and are approved by the facility's policies should be used.

For example, if there are children who repeatedly break the rules, have them sit out of the water for a set time. Another lifeguard who is not engaged in patron surveillance or a supervisor can read and explain the rules to the children. If the parent or guardian seems uncooperative, the rules should be clearly explained to them as well. If a parent or guardian continues to be uncooperative, a lifeguard should not get into an argument, but rather ask a supervisor or facility manager for help.

Since most people want to be treated with respect, just explaining the rules is usually enough. If someone keeps breaking the rules, however, the patron may need to be asked to leave the facility for the safety of all patrons. This should be done as a last resort. If a patron repeatedly breaks the rules, a supervisor or facility manager may even have to call the police or security personnel. The pool may be temporarily cleared until the situation is over. Every facility needs a procedure for removing someone from the facility. This procedure should have specific steps and guidelines to follow. Any such action should be recorded in the facility's daily log or on the appropriate form or report.

SAFETY CHECKS

Safety checks are the primary method of facility surveillance. These checks may be performed by lifeguards, by others, such as those who are trained to handle facility operations and maintenance, or a combination of both **(Fig. 2-6)**. A lifeguard supervisor or facility manager will instruct lifeguards about the procedures for a facility.

Safety checks are conducted before opening the facility, during daily operations and at closing. Several facility safety checks are done each day. These checks may also include a test ride of all attractions before opening the facility. If an unsafe condition is found, it should be corrected, if possible, before the facility opens. If the problem cannot be corrected, a supervisor should be informed immediately. If the condition is serious, the supervisor or facility manager may close or delay the opening of the facility, attraction or area until the condition is corrected. Signs, ropes or cones can keep patrons away from an area of the facility not open to the

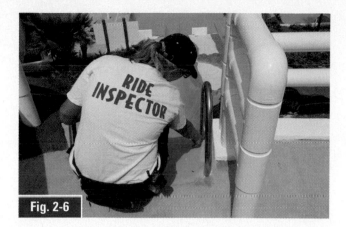

Fig. 2-6

4 FT 0 IN

Fig. 2-7

- Communication equipment and safety equipment.
- Pool decks or waterfront shorelines.
- Pools, waterfront swimming areas or waterpark attractions.
- Locker rooms (dressing areas, shower areas and restrooms).
- Recreational equipment and play structures.

Hazards at Waterfront Facilities

It is important to know the potential hazards at waterfront facilities, such as—
- Underwater hazards.
- Pier formations.
- Changing water conditions.

Dangerous conditions may change with the wind, tides and weather. On some days, the water may be totally calm and flat. Other days, there may be large waves. Potentially hazardous conditions specific to a facility should be covered during orientation. If not, lifeguards should ask facility management to cover any situations for which the lifeguards feel ill-at-ease or not adequately prepared.

Underwater Hazards

Common underwater hazards include—
- Holes in the swimming area.
- Sudden drop-offs.
- Submerged objects, such as rocks, tree stumps and underwater plants (Fig. 2-8).
- Bottom conditions (sand, rock, silt, weeds and mud).
- Slope of the bottom and water depth.
- Shells and barnacles.
- Broken glass or other sharp objects.
- Marine life.

If possible, underwater hazards should be removed. If hazards cannot be removed, swimming areas should be positioned away from them. Floating buoys may mark underwater hazards to warn patrons of their danger.

public (Fig. 2-7). Other lifeguards should be informed about the hazard so that they can direct patrons away from the area. All such incidents should be recorded in the daily log or on the appropriate form or report.

LIFEGUARDING TIP: Lifeguards should never perform safety checks while also performing patron surveillance. If problems with equipment are observed during surveillance, notify the lifeguard supervisor or another lifeguard not performing patron surveillance immediately so that the problem can be corrected.

Specific Areas to Inspect for Safety

The facility's safety checklist form is the guide for performing a safety check. The general areas and equipment to inspect include—

Fig. 2-8

Typical Items Found on a Safety Checklist

All Environments
- Walkways are free of slipping or tripping hazards.
- Sharp objects or objects sticking out are eliminated or isolated.
- Handrails or guardrails are tight and stable.
- Fire exits are clear and accessible.
- Walkways or paths are clear and accessible.
- Doors to nonpublic areas are locked.
- Equipment or chemicals are stored in locked areas.
- All first aid supplies are present.
- First aid station is clean.
- Restroom and public facilities are clean.
- Signs are in good condition and properly displayed.
- Play structures are in good condition.
  - Nonmoving parts on play structures are secured.
  - Removable play structures are tethered properly.
  - Water flows properly on slides.
- Communication equipment, such as whistles, telephones and two-way radios, are in good working order.
- Safety equipment is in proper operating condition and location, including—
  - Rescue tubes.
  - Resuscitation masks.
  - First aid kit.
  - AEDs.
  - Emergency oxygen delivery system.
  - Backboards (including head immobilizers and straps).
  - Life jackets.
  - Lifeguard stands.

Pools, Multi-Attraction Facilities and Waterparks
- Ladders are secured properly.
- Drain covers are secured properly and are undamaged.

- Water clarity is satisfactory. The bottom of the pool, attraction or the main drains can be clearly seen.
- Water temperature is satisfactory.
- Pool is free of debris and algae.
- Water quality is satisfactory.
- Water level is satisfactory.

Waterpark Attractions
For each attraction, visually check or test that—
- Rafts, tubes or sleds are properly inflated and handles are secure.
- Communication equipment, such as light signals, public address systems, telephones and two-way radios, is in good working order.
- Water quality is satisfactory.
- Water flow is satisfactory.
- Water level is satisfactory.
- Water temperature is satisfactory.
- Emergency shut-off systems (E-stops) are working properly.

Waterfronts
- Bottom is free of hazards.
- Shoreline is free of sharp objects, broken glass, rocks and litter.
- Sand in front of and around lifeguard stands is clear of objects that could injure lifeguards when they jump off the stand to make a rescue.
- Piers are stable—no protruding nails, rotting wood and weak or frayed anchor lines.
- Rescue craft, such as rescue boards, rowboats and kayaks, are in proper operating condition.
- Air horns and megaphones are in good working order.

Fig. 2-9

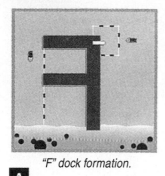

"F" dock formation.

A

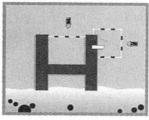

"H" dock formation.

B

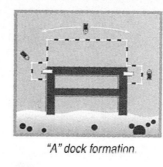

"A" dock formation.

C

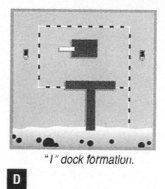

"I" dock formation.

D

Pier Formations

Piers in the water are often used for different activities **(Fig. 2-9, A-D)**. The following precautions should be taken with piers:

- Ensure that floating piers and rafts are anchored securely.
- Be aware of *blind spots* (obstructed views) caused by piers.
- Ensure that patrons dive from piers only in designated areas. Check the water depth daily. Be aware of bottom and tidal changes before allowing head-first entries.
- Prohibit swimming in fishing areas around piers.

Changing Water Conditions

There are many factors that can influence water conditions, which can also affect patron safety, such as—

- Water depth and currents. Examples include—
  - When a dam releases water, the water depth above the dam drops and the river depth below the dam rises.
  - Heavy rainfall that makes a lake or river rise, or a long, dry period that makes it too shallow for diving.
  - Tidal changes.
- Debris in the water or cloudiness.
- Water temperature, which is usually colder early in the summer and after rain. Although surface water may be warm and comfortable, water at a depth of several feet can be much colder. This condition, called a *thermocline*, can cause *hypothermia* (low body temperature).

When dealing with changing water conditions, lifeguards should—

- Warn patrons of hazards by using signs, buoys and safety announcements.
- Check for objects that may have washed into the area.
- Check for changes in bottom conditions and water depth.
- Alert patrons to cold water, and watch for signs of hypothermia.
- Check and document scheduled high and low tides in the daily log each morning before opening, and plan for depth changes.

WEATHER CONDITIONS

Weather affects the safety of swimmers both outdoors and indoors. Lifeguards should be aware of the weather conditions in their area and know how to act when severe weather occurs. The NOAA Weather Radio All Hazards is a nationwide radio network that provides detailed weather information 24 hours a day to most areas. A special radio receiver is needed to receive the signal and can be set to sound an alarm when a warning is issued for a specific area. These radios have battery back-up in case of power failure. Local up-to-date forecasts and weather warnings are also available from the National Weather Service at *www.nws.noaa.gov*. In addition, local radio stations, television channels and cable services also provide forecasts and emergency weather warnings. The facility's emergency action plan (EAP) for severe weather conditions should be followed. EAPs are discussed in detail in Chapter 4.

Lightning and Thunderstorms

Lightning and thunderstorms happen more often in the summer. The facility's procedures for clearing patrons from the water should be followed before an impending storm. Patron safety should never be at risk. If a storm or other bad weather is predicted, stay alert for signs of the coming storm, such as thunder and lightning or high winds.

In the event of thunder or lightning, lifeguards should—

- Clear everyone from the water at the first sound of thunder or first sight of lightning. Lifeguards in an elevated station should get down immediately. Move everyone to a safe area. For outdoor facilities, move everyone inside. Large buildings are safer than smaller or open structures, such as picnic shelters or gazebos.
- Keep patrons and staff out of showers and locker rooms during a thunderstorm. Water and metal can conduct electricity.
- Refrain from using a telephone connected to a landline except in an emergency.
- Keep everyone away from windows and metal objects (e.g., doorframes, lockers).
- Keep watching for more storms and monitor weather reports on a broadcast radio or weather radio.

Lightning

What Is Lightning?

Lightning is the result of the build-up and discharge of electrical energy. The air in a lightning strike is heated to 50,000° F. It is this rapid heating of the air that produces the shock wave that results in thunder.

A cloud-to-ground lightning strike begins as an invisible channel of negatively charged particles moving from the cloud toward the ground. When one channel nears a positively charged object on the ground, a powerful surge of electricity from the ground moves upward to the clouds and produces the visible lightning strike.

- Lightning can heat its path five times hotter than the surface of the sun.
- One ground lightning strike can generate between 100 million and 1 billion volts of electricity.
- Lightning often strikes as far as 10 miles away from any rainfall. Even when the sky looks blue and clear, be cautious.
- Lightning injuries can lead to permanent disabilities or death. On average, 20 percent of strike victims die; 70 percent of survivors suffer serious, long-term effects.

Lightning Facts

- 25 million cloud-to-ground lightning strikes occur in the United States each year.

Source and excerpts taken from the National Weather Service Web site: *www.lightningsafety.noaa.gov/index.htm.*

The National Lightning Safety Institute recommends waiting 30 minutes after the sound of thunder is heard before resuming activities.

If caught outside in a thunderstorm and there is not enough time to reach a safe building, lifeguards should take the following steps:

- Keep everyone away from structures in open areas, such as picnic shelters.
- Keep away from tall trees standing alone and any tall structures.
- Keep away from water and metal objects, such as metal fences, tanks, rails and pipes.
- Keep as low to the ground as possible: squat or crouch with the knees drawn up, both feet together and hands off the ground.
- Do not lie flat on the ground; minimize ground contact.

Heavy Rain and Hail

Heavy rain and hail can be dangerous. Rain can make it difficult to see the bottom of the pool or beneath the surface. In addition, hail can cause serious physical injury. Patrons should be cleared from the water and directed to shelter.

Tornadoes

If the aquatic facility's area is prone to tornadoes, lifeguards or facility staff should monitor weather forecasts. A *tornado watch* means that tornadoes are possible. A *tornado warning* means that a tornado has been sighted and that everyone should take shelter immediately.

In the event of a tornado, lifeguards should—

- Clear the water and surrounding area.
- Move everyone to the location specified in the facility's EAP, such as a basement or an inside area on the lowest level of a building.
- Keep everyone away from windows, doors and outside walls.
- Have everyone lie flat in a ditch or on a low section of ground, if adequate shelter is unavailable at or near the facility.
- Keep patrons in the safe location until the all-clear signal is sounded, if a tornado siren warning is heard.

High Wind

High wind may cause waves or turbulence that make it hard to see patrons in the water. Wind also increases the risk of hypothermia, especially for small children and the elderly.

Safety guidelines for high wind include—

- Clearing the pool or waterfront if visibility is impaired by waves or increased turbidity.
- Moving all patrons and staff indoors.
- Securing all facility equipment that could be blown and become dangerous, but only if it is possible and safe to do so.

Fog

In some areas, fog can occur at any time of the day or night with changing weather conditions. If the fog limits visibility, the facility may need to be closed.

Weather Conditions and Indoor Facilities

Indoor facilities are safe from most weather problems but still may be affected. Severe weather can cause a power failure; therefore, the facility should have some type of portable or emergency lighting. In cases of power failure, clear the pool and deck immediately. The facility's EAP for severe weather conditions should be followed.

MANAGEMENT AND SAFETY

Just as lifeguards have a responsibility to protect patrons, management has an obligation to protect lifeguards, as well as the patrons they are guarding. Management is responsible for—

- Creating, reviewing and revising a facility's policies and procedures, rules and regulations and EAPs as needed.
- Warning patrons and staff about actual and potential dangers.
- Addressing unsafe or dangerous conditions.
- Complying with local, state and federal regulations for facility operations and employment.
- Maintaining records on the facility and its employees.
- Assisting after an emergency.

Warning Patrons and Staff

Management can help prevent injuries by posting signs, markings and warnings to inform patrons about dangers **(Fig 2-10)**. Management must also protect staff members from dangers at the facility by giving specific written and spoken information, as well as protective equipment.

Fig. 2-10

CAUTION SHALLOW WATER NO DIVING ALLOWED

Addressing Unsafe Conditions

Lifeguards work with management to address unsafe conditions at a facility. Management tells the lifeguards what to check during safety checks. Management relies on the lifeguards to find and report dangers. When an unsafe condition is found and reported, management is responsible for correcting it.

Complying with Regulations

Government regulations protect people. The facility and staff must comply with all regulations. The following sections describe some federal regulations that affect lifeguards.

Age Limitations

Federal and state departments of labor set conditions on the number of hours and the types of tasks that employees under the age of 18 are allowed to perform. The requirements are typically more stringent for 15 year olds than for those 16 and 17 years of age. A facility's policy and procedures manual should cover how these regulations affect a lifeguard's duties relative to those of other lifeguards at the facility.

Hazard Communication Standard

Federal regulations protect people from chemical hazards in and around a facility. For example, the Hazard Communication Standard has rules regarding hazardous chemicals to prevent injury and illness caused by an exposure. Management is required to provide lifeguards and other employees with information and training about the chemicals stored and used at their workplace if their jobs involve handling such items. Each chemical has an information sheet called a Material Safety Data Sheet (MSDS). The MSDS for each hazardous chemical must be easy to find and use. Be sure to know where MSDSs are kept and how to find the information **(Fig. 2-11)**. Employees have a right to know—

- Which hazardous chemicals are in the facility.
- Where those chemicals are stored in the facility.
- The specific dangers of those chemicals.
- How to identify chemical hazards in their facility.
- How to protect themselves and others from being exposed to hazardous chemicals.
- What to do if they or others are exposed to such hazards.

Hazardous chemicals must be handled and stored properly, as specified in the Hazard Communication Standard. Keep unauthorized personnel away from chemical storage areas. Consider all chemical products as dangerous and treat them carefully.

Fig. 2-11

Bloodborne Pathogens Standard

The federal Occupational Safety and Health Administration (OSHA) developed the Bloodborne Pathogens Standard to reduce the risk of disease spreading from one person to another. This standard helps protect employees from contact with body fluids that may contain bacteria and viruses called *bloodborne pathogens*. The facility's management should help protect employees from being exposed to bacteria and viruses that can cause disease and let employees know what to do if an exposure occurs. Chapter 6 provides detailed information on bloodborne pathogens and prevention of disease transmission.

Local and State Regulations

Many local and state regulations also affect the operation of aquatic facilities, such as—

- Lifeguard certification requirements.
- Facility design and safety features.
- Pool capacities.
- Staff training requirements.
- Ratio of lifeguards to patrons.
- Water sanitation procedures.
- First aid equipment and supplies.
- Lifeguarding equipment.
- Diving depths.

Local and state regulations are specific to individual areas. Lifeguards need to learn about those that affect

Recreational Water Illness

When people use pools, waterparks, spas, hot tubs, lakes, rivers and the ocean, they share the same water. If someone is ill, he or she can contaminate the water for everyone who is in it. Contaminated recreational water can cause a variety of illnesses, such as diarrhea or skin, ear, eye and upper respiratory infections. Young children who wear diapers are just learning to control their bowels and are more prone to contaminate the water. These children are more likely to have fecal accidents and, if they are ill with diarrhea, the germs in their stool can contaminate the pool. Once the pool is contaminated, patrons may accidentally swallow the fecally contaminated water, which could make them ill. In addition, some germs, such as *cryptosporidium*, may take days to be killed by chlorine, increasing the risk of spreading illness.

Pool and Attraction Closures

When a fecal accident happens, lifeguards should follow their facility's procedures on how to handle and document such an accident. The facility's procedures should have been developed based on state and local health regulations or the Centers for Disease Control and Prevention's recommendations.

Fecal accidents are a concern and an inconvenience to lifeguards, pool operators and patrons. Carefully explain to swimmers the need to close the pool or attraction in response to a fecal accident for their own health and safety. Understanding that pool or attraction closure is necessary for proper disinfection and protection of the health of swimmers is likely to promote public support rather than frustration. Pool closures allow chlorine to inactivate harmful pathogens and protect swimmers from recreational water illnesses.

Excerpts taken from the Centers for Disease Control and Prevention's *Healthy Swimming.* Available at *www.cdc.gov/healthyswimming*

their facilities. Facility management should provide this information during orientation or in-service training.

Maintaining Records and Reports

Facility management uses a variety of records and reports. They are important for the facility's daily operation. Records and reports at a facility may include—
- Employee schedules.
- Lifeguard rotations.
- A safety checklist.
- Health, sanitation and maintenance records.
- Daily attendance or facility use logs.
- Training records (orientation, preseason and in-service training).
- Water conditions (pool temperature, clarity, chlorine and pH levels).
- Incident and injury reports.
- Time sheets.

Management will help the lifeguards complete the records and reports and will give instructions for how and when to complete them, as well as show examples. It is important that lifeguards fill out the forms on time, accurately and thoroughly. Management then maintains the records and reports, which are used to—
- Give information about equipment, personnel, procedures and improvements.
- Give information about the cause and prevention of injuries.
- Comply with federal, state and local laws requiring information about facility sanitation and maintenance.
- Document incidents.
- Protect the facility and its employees from possible legal actions.

Lifeguards must know what records and reports need to be completed. This will be covered during orientation or in-service trainings, or they will be located in the facility's policies and procedures manual.

Assisting After an Emergency

Management also has responsibilities after an emergency at a facility. Chapter 4 describes these responsibilities and the support management can provide to lifeguards involved in the incident. After an emergency, management is generally responsible for—

- Closing and reopening the pool.
- Interacting with the media.
- Reporting procedures.
- Helping lifeguards with problems related to the incident.
- Reviewing the incident and addressing any needed changes in operations or in the facility's EAP.

Lifeguards should be comfortable knowing that management is there to support them on the job whenever an emergency occurs.

PUTTING IT ALL TOGETHER

The more a lifeguard understands how injuries occur, the more he or she is able to prevent them. Good communication with patrons is important to help prevent injuries. Patrons should be informed about the potential for injury and educated about the consequences of risky behavior. Rules and regulations should be for safety. These actions will help patrons have an enjoyable experience. To prevent injuries, as many hazards as possible should be eliminated or reduced. Frequent safety checks help to control hazards. Facility surveillance, injury prevention, communication and patron surveillance add up to a good overall approach for safety at a facility.

Chapter 3

Patron Surveillance

A lifeguard's primary responsibility is to ensure patron safety and protect lives. A primary tool to accomplish this function is patron surveillance—keeping a close watch over the people in the facility. Lifeguards will spend most of their time on patron surveillance. To do this effectively, they must be alert and attentive at all times, supervising patrons continuously.

EFFECTIVE SURVEILLANCE

With effective surveillance, lifeguards can recognize behaviors or situations that might lead to life-threatening emergencies, such as drownings or injuries to the head, neck or back, and then act to modify the behavior or control the situation. Effective surveillance has several elements:

- Victim recognition
- Effective scanning
- Lifeguard stations
- Area of responsibility

The previous chapter focused on eliminating hazardous situations. This chapter concentrates on recognizing patrons who either need, or might soon need, assistance.

Victim Recognition

When conducting surveillance, lifeguards should look for behavior that indicates a patron needs immediate assistance. Lifeguards are better able to identify these behaviors because they are universal responses that indicate a patron is in trouble in the water. Deciding that a patron is in trouble must be based on his or her behavior, not on physical characteristics or appearance, such as age or ethnic or racial background.

It is important to understand the behaviors that a victim shows when in distress or drowning. **Table 3-1** compares the behaviors of a swimmer with those of a distressed swimmer, an active drowning victim and a passive drowning victim. Notice differences in—

- Breathing.
- Arm and leg action.
- Body position.
- Body propulsion or locomotion (movement) through the water.

Understanding these behaviors enables a lifeguard to recognize quickly when someone needs help. Quick action can mean the difference between life and death for a distressed or drowning victim.

Swimmer

Depending on his or her proficiency with the stroke, a swimmer's arms and legs work in a coordinated and effective way. The body position is nearly horizontal, and there is some breath control. The person is able to make recognizable progress through the water (**Fig. 3-1**). Note that a person with a physical disability (such as the loss of a leg) might have to modify a stroke, but that person's unique swimming style can soon be recognized.

Distressed Swimmer

For a variety of reasons, such as exhaustion, cramp or sudden illness, a swimmer can become distressed. A distressed swimmer makes little or no forward progress and may be unable to reach safety without a lifeguard's assistance.

Distressed swimmers can be recognized by the way they try to support themselves in the water. They might float or use swimming skills, such as sculling or treading water. If a safety line or other floating object is nearby, a distressed swimmer may grab and cling to it for support. Depending on the method used for support, the distressed swimmer's body might be horizontal, vertical or diagonal (**Fig. 3-2**).

The distressed swimmer usually has enough control of the arms and legs to keep his or her face out of the water to continue breathing and call for help. In most cases, a distressed swimmer is also able to wave for help. He or she can use the legs and one arm for support, while raising the other arm to wave for assistance. The distressed swimmer generally has the ability to reach for a rescue device.

As conditions such as fatigue, cold or sudden illness continue to affect the distressed swimmer, he or she is less and less able to support him or herself in the water. As this occurs, the victim's mouth moves closer to the surface of the water, and anxiety increases. If a distressed swimmer is not rescued, he or she may become an active drowning victim.

Active Drowning Victim

Active drowning victims have distinctive arm and body positions. They try to keep their mouths above the surface of the water (**Fig. 3-3**). This universal behavior is called the *instinctive drowning response* (Pia, 1974). This means that all active drowning victims have the same behaviors. An active drowning victim—

- Struggles to keep the face above water in an effort to breathe. If unable to do this, he or she begins to suffocate.
- Has arms extended to the side, pressing down for support.
- Has a vertical body position in the water with no supporting kick.
- Might continue to struggle underwater.
- Might eventually lose consciousness and stop moving.

An active drowning victim is struggling to breathe. His or her mouth repeatedly sinks below the surface and reappears. While the mouth is below the surface, the drowning victim keeps it closed to avoid swallowing water. When the mouth is above the surface, the drowning victim quickly exhales and then tries to inhale before the

TABLE 3-1 BEHAVIORS OF DISTRESSED SWIMMERS AND DROWNING VICTIMS COMPARED TO SWIMMERS

	Fig. 3-1 Swimmer	Fig. 3-2 Distressed Swimmer	Fig. 3-3 Active Drowning Victim	Fig. 3-4 Passive Drowing Victim
Breathing	Rhythmic breathing	Can continue breathing and might call for help	Struggles to breathe; cannot call out for help	Not breathing
Arm and Leg Action	Relatively coordinated	Floating, sculling or treading water; might wave for help	Arms to sides alternately moving up and pressing down; no supporting kick	None
Body Position	Horizontal	Horizontal, vertical or diagonal, depending on means of support	Vertical	Horizontal or vertical; face-down, face-up or submerged
Locomotion	Recognizable	Little or no forward progress; less and less able to support self	None; has only 20 to 60 seconds before submerging	None

mouth goes below the surface again. While the victim is gasping for air, he or she also might take water into the mouth. Although some people believe active drowning victims can call out for help, this is not the case. They can barely take in enough air to breathe, so there is no air left over to call out for help.

Active drowning victims do not make any forward progress in the water. All of the person's energy is devoted to keeping the mouth above the surface of the water, and the person is unable to reach for a rescue device. The active drowning victim usually stays at the surface for only 20 to 60 seconds. The victim may continue to struggle underwater but eventually loses consciousness and stops moving.

Passive Drowning Victim

A victim might progress from active to passive drowning or suddenly slip under water without a struggle. Passive drowning victims might float face-down at or near the surface or might sink to the bottom **(Fig. 3-4)**. A passive drowning can result from a variety of conditions that can lead to a loss of consciousness, including—

- A heart attack or stroke.
- A seizure.
- A head injury.
- A heat-related illness.
- Hypothermia.
- Hyperventilation.
- Use of alcohol and other drugs.

Once a victim submerges and loses consciousness, water can enter the trachea (windpipe). This may cause a spasm of the vocal cords (*laryngospasm*), which blocks the airway to keep fluid or food out of the airway. Water might get into the lungs after submersion or loss of consciousness. Anyone who is submerged or floating facedown and motionless for 30 seconds should be considered a passive drowning victim. Lifeguards should check the victim's condition immediately. If the victim is conscious and was just holding his or her breath, the patron needs to be directed to stop doing so.

Heart Attack, Stroke, Seizure and Head Injury. A person who has suffered a heart attack, stroke, seizure or head injury might feel dizzy or faint or be temporarily paralyzed. These conditions cause great difficulty in swimming or even walking in the water. The person might also suddenly stop swimming and become a passive drowning victim. **Table 3-2** lists the signs and symptoms for these conditions.

Heat-related Illness. A *heat-related illness* occurs when a person's inner core temperature rises above its normal temperature of 98.6° F (37° C) to 102.6° F (39° C) or higher. The victim becomes weak and dizzy, and might become confused or lose consciousness. See Chapter 9 for the signs and symptoms and care for heat-related emergencies.

For facilities with a spa, exposure to hot water can make it difficult for a person to get out. It is important for lifeguards to monitor patrons as they use spas and hot tubs and to advise them not to stay in the water too long. Also, advise pregnant women, adults with cardiac or circulatory problems and parents or guardians of young children about the risk hot water can pose to their health. Since many health clubs and recreation departments with

TABLE 3-2	SIGNS AND SYMPTOMS OF A HEART ATTACK, STROKE, SEIZURE AND HEAD INJURY			
	Heart Attack	**Stroke**	**Seizure**	**Head Injury**

Signs and Symptoms	• Persistent chest pain or pressure (a primary signal of a heart attack) that lasts longer than 3 to 5 minutes, or goes away and comes back
	• Chest pain spreading to the shoulders, neck, jaw or arms
	• Shortness of breath or trouble breathing
	• Nausea or vomiting
	• Dizziness, lightheadedness or fainting
	• Pale, ashen (grayish) or bluish skin
	• Sweating
	• Denial of signals
		• Sudden weakness or numbness to the face, arm or leg; usually to one side
		• Difficulty with speech or vision
		• Severe headache
		• Confusion, dizziness or disorientation
			• Confusion, dizziness or disorientation
			• Difficulty breathing
			• Body might stiffen
			• Convulsions followed by—
			  ▪ Relaxed state
			  ▪ Fatigue and confusion
			  ▪ Headache
				• Swollen or bruised areas
				• Unconsciousness
				• Confusion or loss of memory
				• Severe pain or pressure in the head
				• Profuse or external bleeding of the head

swimming pools now include spas, it is important to be aware of the risks associated from the effects of hot water.

Hypothermia. *Hypothermia* develops when the body can no longer generate sufficient heat to maintain normal body temperature. In hypothermia, body temperature drops below 95° F (35° C). As the body cools, an abnormal heart rhythm might develop and the heart eventually stops. A person can develop hypothermia even if environmental temperatures are not extreme. See Chapter 9 for the signs and symptoms and care for hypothermia.

Hyperventilation. Hyperventilating is a dangerous technique some swimmers use to try to swim long distances underwater or to hold their breath for an extended period while submerged in one place. They mistakenly think that by taking a series of deep breaths in rapid succession and forcefully exhaling that they can increase the amount of oxygen they breathe, allowing them to hold their breath longer underwater. This is not true. Instead, it lowers the carbon dioxide level in the body.

The practice is risky because the level of carbon dioxide in the blood is what signals a person to breathe. As the level of carbon dioxide increases, a person normally takes a breath. When a person hyperventilates and then swims underwater, the oxygen level in the blood can drop to a point where the swimmer passes out before the body knows it is time to breathe. Then, when the person finally does take a breath instinctively, water rushes in and the drowning process begins.

Alcohol. The following are some ways alcohol can affect a person in the water and lead to drowning or head, neck or back injuries.

- **Alcohol affects balance.** Some people with alcohol in their body have drowned in shallow water when they lost their balance and were unable to stand up. "Ordinary" actions on steps, ladders, diving boards or play structures become hazardous for an intoxicated person.
- **Alcohol affects judgment.** A person might take risks, such as diving into shallow water, which he or she would not normally take.
- **Alcohol slows body movements.** It can greatly reduce swimming skills, even those of an excellent swimmer.

One of the biggest myths about alcohol is that an intoxicated person can sober up by going swimming. Splashing water on a person's face or immersing a person in water **will not** reduce the amount of alcohol in the bloodstream, nor reduce the effects of alcohol.

EFFECTIVE SCANNING

Knowing how to recognize a victim in trouble in the water is the first step, but lifeguards also need to know how to scan effectively. *Scanning* is a visual technique for

Fig. 3-5

watching patrons in the water (**Fig. 3-5**). It is an active process. When scanning, a lifeguard should not just passively watch patrons in the water. The lifeguard should actively observe the swimmers' behaviors and look for signals that someone in the water needs help. The lifeguard's head needs to move while scanning to look directly at each area rather than staring in a fixed direction. Movement may be noticed with peripheral (side) vision, but recognition requires looking directly at the person.

Guidelines lifeguards should follow for effective scanning include:

- Scan the patrons in the assigned area of responsibility.
- Scan above and below the surface of the water, and include the bottom of the pool in the scan.
- Scan thoroughly and repeatedly. Do not neglect any part of the assigned area of responsibility, including any deck or beach areas and those areas under, around and directly in front of the lifeguard station.
- Scan from point to point, rapidly watching all movements of the patrons in the area.
- Do not focus on a scanning pattern itself, but stay focused on effective patron surveillance.
- Scan for potential problems. Arm and leg action, body position and movement through the water are good indicators of weak swimmers and those in trouble in the water.
- If a weak swimmer is slowly moving toward safety, check him or her more frequently while scanning the whole area of responsibility.
- Spend less time and attention on patrons who are good swimmers or who are safely enjoying the water, but still include them while scanning.
- Scan crowded areas carefully. Partially hidden arm movements might indicate that a victim is actively drowning.

- While scanning, do not be distracted by people or activities. Keep focused on the assigned area of responsibility.
- Do not interrupt scanning an area except during an emergency or to stop someone from breaking a rule. The facility's emergency action plan (EAP) should address back-up coverage if a lifeguard must make a rescue or provide emergency care, such as first aid or CPR. If only one lifeguard is performing patron surveillance and must stop someone from breaking a safety rule, the lifeguard should do this quickly. Get the person's attention, explain the danger and how he or she can become injured, and, if necessary, how to avoid the injury. This should take only a few seconds, and it can be done while still scanning. If the patron needs a detailed explanation, the lifeguard should call for assistance or tell the patron that his or her questions can be discussed further during a break.
- Do not interrupt scanning an area if a patron asks a question or has a suggestion or concern. A lifeguard should acknowledge the patron and quickly explain that he or she cannot look at him or her while talking, but he or she is still listening to the patron. Politely but briefly answer the patron's question, suggestion or concern, or refer him or her to the head lifeguard, facility manager or another staff member.
- Do not wait for patrons or other lifeguards to indicate that someone is drowning. A drowning victim is often surrounded by others who are unaware the drowning is happening right next to them. New lifeguards sometimes feel unsure of themselves and mistakenly wait for patrons or more experienced lifeguards to tell them that someone is in trouble.
- Be aware of areas that cannot be seen or that are difficult to see. Areas might be blocked when patrons cluster together or from water movement, such as fountains or bubbles that block the view underwater. The lifeguard should adjust body position to see into blind spots.
- Be aware of conditions that affect visibility, such as glare from the sun or overhead lights, cloudy water or shadows on the water at different times of the day. The lifeguard should adjust his or her position or move to a point with clear visibility.
- Various factors can affect a lifeguard's scanning technique. Make adjustments for—
  - Area of responsibility.
  - The type and location of the lifeguard station.
  - The variety of patron activities in the area being scanned.
  - The number of patrons in the area of responsibility.
  - Fatigue.

Fatigue

There are many things that can cause fatigue when performing patron surveillance. These include—
- Dehydration.
- Heat exhaustion.
- Overexposure to the sun.
- Lack of sleep.
- Poor nutrition and lack of regular meals.

The following guidelines will help lifeguards prevent fatigue:
- Always drink plenty of water. Keep a plastic bottle of water around at all times.
- Use adequate sun protection, such as hats, polarized wrap-around sunglasses with UVA/UVB protection and umbrellas.
- Come to work well-rested and well-nourished.
- Rotate stations and take breaks.

Lifeguard Stations

Patron surveillance might be performed in an elevated lifeguard chair or by standing on the deck, beach, pier or in the water. The goal is to provide optimum coverage for the whole facility. A lifeguard must be in a position to recognize and respond to an emergency at all times.

The location of the lifeguard station must allow lifeguards to see their entire area of responsibility. The lifeguard stand may need to be moved or the position adjusted during the day to adapt to the changing sun, glare, wind or water conditions. Having a clear view of the whole area so that everyone can be seen in it is critical. Additional coverage at waterfront areas can be provided by foot patrols, boat patrols and four-wheel drive vehicles.

Elevated Stations

Elevated lifeguard stations usually provide the most effective position for patron surveillance because they offer an excellent place for scanning the area of responsibility **(Fig. 3-6)**. This is particularly important at a facility where a single lifeguard is doing patron surveillance. An elevated stand provides a much better view of patron activities than the view from a ground-level lifeguard station.

Fig. 3-6

While walking, lifeguards need to face the patrons in the area of responsibility. The primary purpose of ground-level stations is to be close to patrons. Here a lifeguard can easily make assists and enforce safety rules for patrons in the water and on the deck. While maintaining surveillance, a lifeguard can also educate patrons about the reasons behind the rules, but he or she should never become distracted from surveillance duties by talking socially with patrons.

The area under, around and directly in front of the stand should be included in the scan. Lifeguards on opposite sides of a pool can solve this problem by scanning below each other's stands. Movable stands should be positioned close to the edge of the water with enough room to climb up and down from the stand.

The area surrounding an elevated stand must be kept clear of patrons or objects that might interfere with the lifeguard's ability to respond. A safety zone should be established that allows access to the water in case of an emergency. At a waterfront, this area should be thoroughly inspected with rakes and shovels before opening each day. This helps prevent injuries to lifeguards during emergency exits from the lifeguard stand.

Ground-Level Stations

Lifeguards might be assigned to a walking patrol, a fixed location on the deck or a position in the water near a play structure (**Fig. 3-7**). In these positions, the view of the entire swimming area is limited, and patrons might be hidden from view by play structures or other patrons.

Fig. 3-7

Rescue Water Craft

In many waterfront facilities, lifeguards watch swimmers from water craft. Rescue water craft typically patrol the outer edge of a swimming area. Often, someone in trouble in the water can be reached more quickly from water craft.

Fig. 3-8

In a small, calm area, a rescue board or a flat-bottom rowboat might be used (**Fig. 3-8**). In rough water, a v-hull or tri-hull rowboat might be used. Power-boats, inflatable boats, kayaks and personal water craft also can be used as rescue water craft (**Fig. 3-9, 3-10**). Facility management normally provides on-the-job training in the use of water craft at a facility.

Fig. 3-9

It is important that water craft are properly equipped. Inspect equipment at the start of each shift, and inform the lifeguard supervisor or facility manager about any damaged or missing equipment. Water craft should have at least the following equipment:

Fig. 3-10

- Extra oars or paddles
- Several life jackets in various sizes
- Rescue tube(s)
- Throwable personal floatation devices
- Extra anchor and line
- First aid kit
- Fire extinguisher

- Bailing device
- Communication equipment (radio, whistle, flag, flares and air horn)
- Basic tool kit

If stationed on water craft in water with a current, a lifeguard might have to row or paddle to stay in position. In rough water or a strong wind, a lifeguard needs to be in good physical condition for constant rowing or paddling. Some water craft use a special anchor line with a quick release for making a rescue. In some larger water craft, one lifeguard maintains the craft's position while a second watches the swimming area.

Lifeguards should make sure they are well trained in operating the facility's water craft before using it for surveillance or to make a rescue. They should be even more cautious with water craft with a motor, and take care to avoid injuring swimmers or damaging lifelines when crossing into the swimming area to make a rescue.

Lifeguard Rotations

Periodic rotations from one station to another, along with breaks, help lifeguards stay alert and decrease fatigue. Rotating from station to station also helps lifeguards learn conditions and hazards in the entire facility, instead of in just one location. Lifeguards must maintain patron surveillance when rotating from one station to another.

Each lifeguard may carry a separate rescue tube during the rotation. If not, then the rescue tube is passed from the lifeguard on duty to the new guard during the rotation. Patron surveillance must always be maintained while the rescue tube is removed and passed on to the next lifeguard.

At a ground-level station, the relieving lifeguard should—

1. Walk to the side of the lifeguard being relieved and begin scanning (**Fig. 3-11, A**).
2. Ask the lifeguard being relieved whether any patrons in the area of responsibility need closer than normal supervision (**Fig. 3-11, B**).
3. Once scanning has started, signal or tell the outgoing lifeguard that he or she can leave (**Fig. 3-11, C**).

At an elevated station, the relieving lifeguard should—

1. Take a position next to the stand and begin scanning the area of responsibility. After a few moments of scanning, signal the lifeguard in the stand to climb down (**Fig. 3-12, A**).
2. Once on the deck, this lifeguard takes a position next to the stand and resumes his or her surveillance of the area. Climb up in the stand and begin scanning (**Fig. 3-12, B**).

Fig. 3-11

A

B

C

3. Ask the lifeguard being relieved whether any patrons in the area of responsibility need closer than normal supervision.
4. Signal or tell the outgoing lifeguard that he or she can leave (**Fig. 3-12, C**).

Lifeguards should take a break at least once an hour. In one system of surveillance, a lifeguard might spend 20 or 30 minutes at one station, rotate to another station for 20 or 30 minutes, and then take a 20- or 30-minute break. In another system, a lifeguard might spend 45 minutes at

Fig. 3-12

Lifeguard Rotations at Waterparks. Lifeguards typically move from one station to another during a shift. They might rotate through different attractions or different positions at the same attraction. Usually they rotate positions every 30 to 45 minutes to help them stay alert.

Lifeguard rotations are usually based on—
- Locations of stations.
- Type of station (sitting or standing).
- The need to be in the water at some stations.
- The number of patrons using the attraction.

Area of Responsibility

The lifeguard supervisor or the facility manager establishes each lifeguard's area of responsibility for patron surveillance. This might be total coverage (the whole pool, attraction or waterfront area) or zone coverage (only part of a pool, attraction or waterfront area). Another type of coverage is back-up coverage, in which a lifeguard takes over part or all of an area for another lifeguard who is making a rescue.

The area of responsibility assigned to a lifeguard in a waterfront environment may be larger than that assigned to a lifeguard working at a pool or waterpark. In addition, lifeguards who work at a waterfront may also contend with more swimmers in their area and a wide variety of activities. For example, lifeguards are primarily responsible for watching swimmers but might also have to warn people on boats, fishing, operating personal watercraft or using water skis to stay away from the swimming area.

Total Coverage

Total coverage is used at facilities where a single lifeguard is conducting patron surveillance at a time or when only one lifeguard is needed for a small number of patrons present. If there is only one lifeguard conducting patron surveillance, that lifeguard has to scan the entire area, rescue distressed swimmers or drowning persons, control the activities of patrons in and out of the water and recognize and respond to other emergencies **(Fig. 3-13)**. If the lifeguard cannot provide adequate coverage for all patrons, he or she needs to inform a supervisor that help is needed.

Zone Coverage

In zone coverage, the swimming area is divided into separate areas of responsibility for each lifeguard station **(Fig 3-14, A-B)**. Areas can be marked by ladders, lane lines, lifelines, visual markers or the shape of the pool. Zone coverage is effective for high-risk areas, avoiding blind spots and reducing the number of patrons watched by each lifeguard.

one stand, take a break for 15 minutes and then go to another stand.

Lifeguards should not make changes or substitutions in the schedule of rotations and breaks or leave the facility during a break without permission from the lifeguard supervisor or facility manager. If only one lifeguard is performing patron surveillance, then he or she should clear the water during breaks. Never leave patrons in charge while on a break. Another lifeguard or staff member should monitor the pool while the lifeguard is on a break to prevent patrons from entering the water.

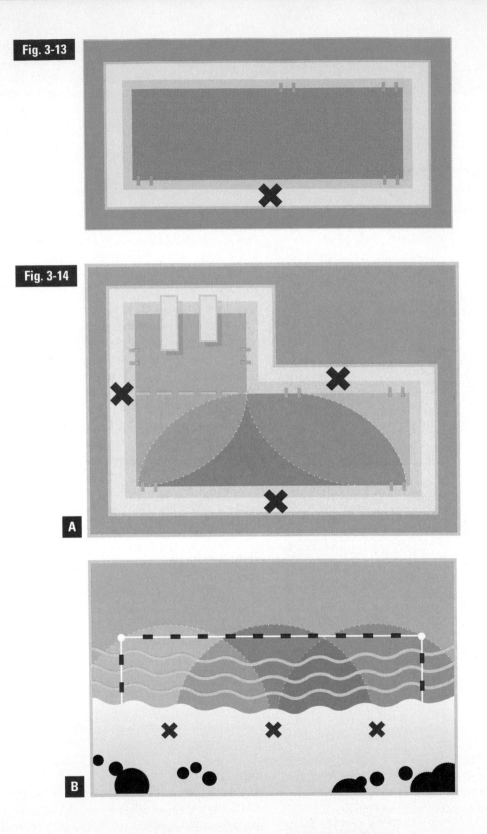

Fig. 3-13

Fig. 3-14

A

B

At a minimum, zones should overlap by several feet so that the boundaries between them have double coverage. This prevents any area from not being scanned. It is important for lifeguards to know the zone for each guarding position.

Back-Up Coverage

In emergency situations when there are two or more life-guards on duty and one lifeguard must enter the water, lifeguards who remain out of the water must now supervise a larger area. They might need to move to better

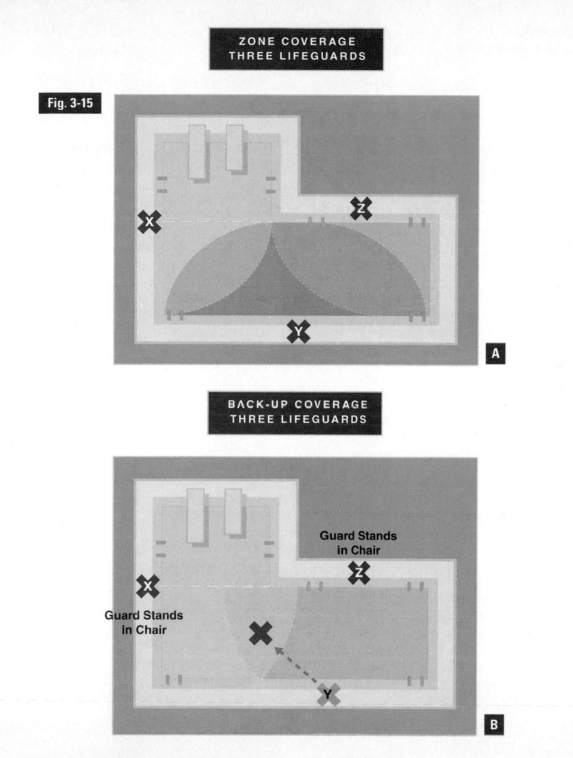

ZONE COVERAGE THREE LIFEGUARDS

Fig. 3-15

A

BACK-UP COVERAGE THREE LIFEGUARDS

Guard Stands in Chair

Guard Stands in Chair

B

vantage points, depending on the facility's design. **Figure 3-15, A**, illustrates zone coverage when three lifeguards are on surveillance duty. **Figure 3-15, B**, shows an example of back-up coverage for the same three-lifeguard facility. In Figure 3-15, B, lifeguard Y is the primary rescuer. He or she signals and enters the water (indicated by a dotted line). The other two lifeguards (lifeguards X and Z) each stand in the lifeguard chairs and divide the responsibility for scanning the pool.

The "RID Factor"

Most drownings at supervised swim areas happen when neither lifeguards nor other patrons notice that a victim has slipped below the surface. Except for passive drownings, drownings in areas where lifeguards were on duty resulted from one or more of three causes, summarized as the RID factor (Pia, 1984)—**R**ecognition, **I**ntrusion and **D**istraction:

- The failure of the lifeguard to **recognize** the instinctive drowning response

- The **intrusion** of secondary duties on the lifeguard's primary responsibility of patron surveillance
- **Distraction** from surveillance duties

Recognition

Knowing how to recognize that a swimmer is in distress or a person is drowning is one of the most important lifeguarding skills. Lifeguards must be able to distinguish such behavior from that of others who are swimming or playing safely in the water. Lifeguards must recognize when someone needs to be rescued. A lifeguard cannot expect the victim or others to call for help in an emergency.

Even when a victim slips underwater without a struggle, with good surveillance and scanning techniques, a lifeguard can recognize someone lying motionless within seconds in clear water.

Intrusion

Intrusion happens when secondary duties, such as maintenance tasks, intrude on a lifeguard's primary responsibility of patron surveillance. Lifeguards often have to sweep the deck, empty trash cans, pick up towels, check locker rooms and perform other maintenance duties. While these duties might be part of the job, they must not be performed while conducting patron surveillance. Another lifeguard must first take over surveillance for the assigned area of responsibility.

A lifeguard cannot perform adequate surveillance duties while also coaching a swim team or teaching a swimming lesson. There should be a separate lifeguard, coach or instructor for these additional activities, even if no other patrons are in the water.

Distraction

Distractions also will affect patron surveillance, for example, a lifeguard talking with other lifeguards or friends. A brief conversation might seem innocent, but during that time a 20- to 60-second struggle of a young child could be missed. The child could die because a lifeguard was distracted! Social conversations should not be held while on duty.

SPECIAL CONSIDERATIONS FOR PATRON SURVEILLANCE

Facilities with Play Structures

Some facilities may have play structures that are either permanent or removable. Permanent structures include items such as regular or drop-off slides, sprays and fountains. Removable structures include items such as large floating toys, inflatable play structures and water basketball and volleyball nets. Some play structures require their own lifeguards, while others are watched by life-

guards surveying a larger area. The surveillance of patrons at play structures depends on—

- Location of the feature.
- Number of patrons in the facility.
- Number of patrons using the structures.
- Age and skill of patrons using the structures.
- Activity and excitement level.
- The lifeguard's ability to see around and under tethered structures.

The following techniques should be used when performing patron surveillance at play structures **(Fig. 3-16)**:

- Pay close attention to nonswimmers or weak swimmers. The added excitement of play structures may lead nonswimmers or weak swimmers to become careless. They might try things they would not otherwise do, or they might accidentally enter deep water.
- Do not let a play structure become overcrowded. Be prepared to restrict the number of patrons using it at one time.
- Watch that patrons return to the surface after dropping into the water from a drop-off slide. Swimmers can be surprised by the fall from a drop-off slide, especially if they do not realize the slide is over deep water. Be certain that they return to the surface after dropping into the water.
- Pay close attention to children playing in sprays and fountains. These attractions are usually in shallow water. Excited children may run and fall and be injured. A very young child who falls might not be able to get back up.
- Pay close attention to patrons in moving water. Moving water can surprise people. They might lose their balance and be unable to stand up again.
- Keep play safe and orderly.
  - Patrons may climb onto floating toys and jump back into the water. They may not notice what is around them and jump onto other swimmers.
  - Patrons may throw balls and other toys and hit unsuspecting swimmers, resulting in injury.

Fig. 3-16

Fig. 3-17

Fig. 3-18

Waterparks

Lifeguards perform patron surveillance in a waterpark similar to that at pools, but they need to adapt their techniques for the specific attractions. Lifeguards should follow these general principles:

- Watch patrons as they enter and exit an attraction **(Fig. 3-17)**.
  - Dispatch patrons safely on a ride at set intervals. Dispatching is the method of informing patrons when it is safe for them to proceed on a ride.
- Keep patrons in view as long as possible.
  - On some attractions, this is a problem. Lifeguards might be able to see only the beginning or end of a long water slide. Caves, enclosed tubes, bridges, buildings and other structures might keep a lifeguard from seeing patrons at all times. When a patron goes out of sight behind something, watch to make sure he or she emerges safely on the other side.
- Be aware of any special risks on the play equipment.
  - Structures that patrons sit, climb on or swim over or under pose hazards. Lifeguards should supervise patrons carefully. A patron who falls off a mat, raft or tube might be injured or pose a hazard to someone else.

Winding Rivers

In a winding river, water flows in a long circular or twisting path through a waterpark. Depending on the winding river, patrons float along slowly with or without inner tubes or walk or swim. Lifeguards might be stationed at the entrance and exit and at other positions with overlapping zones **(Fig. 3-18)**.

Water Slides

Water slides are long, winding slides usually made of fiberglass or concrete. Water is pumped down the slide from the top to the catch pool. Some slides are in enclosed tubes and others are open **(Fig. 3-19)**.

On some slides, patrons ride on an inner tube, raft or mat. On other slides, they do not use riding equipment. Do not let patrons stop, slow down or form a chain of riders. On most slides, only one person is allowed on an inner tube or a raft. On some slides, two or more people can go together on a special tube or raft. On an inner tube or raft, the rider goes feet-first in a sitting position. If no equipment is used, the rider goes face-up and feet-first.

Fig. 3-19

Fig. 3-20

Fig. 3-21

The lifeguard at the top of a slide should perform the following duties:
- Instruct riders how to ride down the slide properly.
- Help riders with the equipment.
- Check that patrons are tall enough to use the slide (**Fig. 3-20**). A measuring pole or line on a wall may be used to check their height.
- When dispatching—
  - Dispatch riders at proper intervals to keep them from colliding on the slide.
  - Be cautious of hand placement on the tube. When available, use tube handles. Avoid pushing or pulling riders by their shoulders, arms or legs.
  - Do not pair unfamiliar riders.
  - Do not allow other patrons to force a reluctant patron to ride an attraction.

The lifeguard at the bottom of a slide in the catch pool should perform the following duties:
- Supervise riders on the slide and help them out of the water.
- Watch riders exit the slide into the catch pool (**Fig. 3-21**).
- Watch and help riders who might be caught in a hydraulic (**Fig. 3-22**). (A *hydraulic* is a strong downward flow in the catch pool that can knock a person off balance or hold a small person or nonswimmer under water.)
- Make sure that riders exit from the catch pool quickly and do not cross in front of any slide when getting out of the catch pool.

At some very long slides, a lifeguard in the middle of the slide watches and helps riders.
- Riders might need help in the middle of a slide.
- Riders might stop, slow down or stand up on the slide. They could be injured doing this.
- Riders might lose their mat, tube or raft and have trouble getting down the slide.
- Riders might hit their heads on the side of the slide.

Fig. 3-22

Drop-Off Slides

A drop-off slide ends with a drop of several feet into the catch pool (**Fig. 3-23**). Patrons might not realize the depth of the catch pool and need assistance.

When supervising a drop-off slide, a lifeguard should make sure—
- Riders are aware of the depth of the water.
- Riders sit or lie in a feet-first position.
- Each rider has moved out of the catch pool before dispatching the next rider.

Fig. 3-23

Fig. 3-24

Fig. 3-25

Speed Slides

A speed slide is straight and steep and may have small hills or rises **(Fig. 3-24)**. It usually has a runout into water several inches deep to slow patrons to a stop.

If stationed at the top of a speed slide, the lifeguard should—

- Allow only one rider down the slide at a time.
- Ensure that riders are in the correct riding position (e.g., feet-first, lying on their back, with legs crossed at the ankles and arms crossed over the chest). This position is faster and reduces the risk of injury.
- Not dispatch a rider until the previous rider has left the runout or the catch pool and the lifeguard at the bottom signals for the next rider.
  - If the lifeguard at the bottom can be seen, a hand signal and a whistle might be used.
  - If the lifeguard at the bottom cannot be seen, a mechanical signal might be used.

If stationed at the bottom of a speed slide, the lifeguard should—

- Help riders, if needed, from the runout or catch pool. (Some might be disoriented or frightened from the ride.) **(Fig. 3-25)**.
- Signal the lifeguard at the top when it is clear to send the next rider.

Free-Fall Slides

A free-fall slide has a nearly vertical drop that provides a sensation of falling. It is like a speed slide with a steeper angle **(Fig. 3-26)**.

Lifeguarding responsibilities for a free-fall slide are like those for speed slides. The lifeguard at the top should give patrons specific directions, such as—

- Riders in line must stand back away from the slide.
- Riders must wait for the lifeguard's signal to start. The lifeguard should signal only when he or she is sure that the previous rider has left the runout.
- Riders should be lying flat on the back, with ankles crossed and arms crossed over the chest.
- Riders must not sit up until they come to a complete stop.

Fig. 3-26

When dispatching a rider, the lifeguard needs to confirm that the rider is ready to go.

Riders who do not follow these directions could be injured, which may result in—

- Friction burns on the legs and arms.
- Bumps and bruises if the rider sits forward and tumbles down the slide.
- Head, neck or back injuries; broken bones; or sprains if the rider tumbles or twists down the slide.

Fig. 3-27

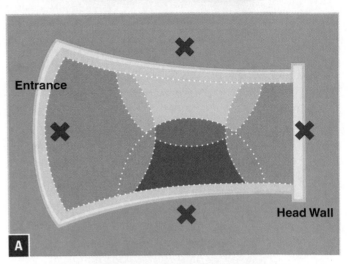

Fig. 3-29

FOUR PERSON ZONE COVERAGE

Entrance

Head Wall

A

Fig. 3-28

EIGHT PERSON ZONE COVERAGE

Entrance

Head Wall

B

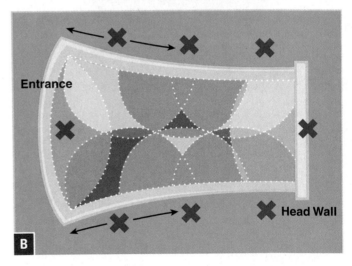

Wave Pools

Wave pools are popular attractions that produce waves of various heights, intervals and patterns.

- Wave pools vary in size, shape and depth **(Fig. 3-27)**.
- At one end is the head wall, where a mechanical system creates the waves.
- Lifeguards may be stationed on the head wall for a better view of the wave pool **(Fig. 3-28)**.
- Many pools operate on a cycle, such as 10 minutes on and 10 minutes off. Times may vary. When waves are present, lifeguards should stand up to get a better view of patrons. When the waves are off, lifeguards might be allowed to sit, but should keep scanning. Lifeguards should rotate positions when the waves are off.
- Lifeguards are often stationed at various places around or in the pool.

Wave pools have special guidelines:

- As in other pools, the number of lifeguards depends on the size and shape of the pool, how many people are in the water as well as state and local health codes **(Fig. 3-29, A-B)**.

- Lifeguard chairs often have an emergency stop button to turn the waves off in an emergency before a lifeguard performs a rescue **(Fig. 3-30)**. The facility's EAP should tell how lifeguards cover all areas of responsibility while a rescue is being performed.
- Patrons often go to where the waves break because of the excitement. Inexperienced swimmers can be knocked over by the waves or carried into deeper water by the undercurrent.
- Patrons must enter the pool only at the shallow end. Do not let patrons dive into the waves. Keep the areas around ladders and railings clear so that patrons can exit from the pool quickly.
- If the waterpark has inner tubes or inflatable rafts for the wave pool, watch for inexperienced swimmers falling off

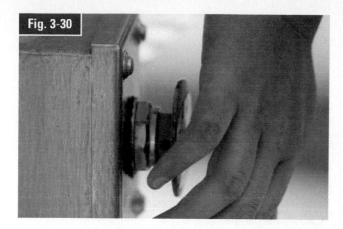

Fig. 3-30

Fig. 3-31

Fig. 3-32

their tubes in deep water. When there are many inner tubes in the water, it is difficult to see everyone and the bottom. In a very crowded pool, someone who falls off an inner tube or raft might have trouble coming up for air if the surface is blocked by tubes or rafts. In addition, someone who is hit by an inflatable raft might be knocked down, hit the bottom and get into trouble.

- Lifeguards should change their scanning technique or move to a different position to eliminate any blind spots, and watch carefully in high-risk situations.
- Some wave pools have special activities like surfing at certain times. During these activities, other patrons should stay out of the pool because the surfboards or boogie boards in the wave pool present a hazard.

Kiddie Areas

Many waterparks have shallow pools for small children. Often, these areas have play equipment like slides, fountains, inflatable play equipment and climbing structures (**Fig. 3-31**). Lifeguards should provide effective patron surveillance at kiddie areas, even though the water may be shallow. Lifeguards need to enforce the rules, such as height and age requirements, fairly and consistently. Note that—

- Older children might be too large for some structures, or their play might be too rough for small children.
- Children often get lost. Ask adults to supervise their children at all times.
- Watch out for small children using the pool as a toilet. The facility should have a procedure for handling this situation, following local health department guidelines.
- Children usually do not consider overexposure to the sun or hypothermia. If a child is becoming sunburned or overly cold, tell the child's parent or guardian immediately.

Special Attractions

Some deep-water pools have activities like specialty slides, diving platforms, cable swings or hand-over-hand structures like ropes, nets and rings (**Fig. 3-32**). These attractions might make surveillance difficult. Orientation and in-service training will include these attractions. Lifeguards must—

- Carefully watch both the water below and activities overhead.
- Allow only one person to swing at a time on a rope or cable swing over a deep-water pool. Do not allow horseplay on platforms. Patrons might not know the depth of the water, and nonswimmers could get in trouble in deep water.
- Not allow diving in water less than 9 feet deep.
- Watch for overcrowding and horseplay on "lily pads"—flat, floating structures tethered to the bottom of the pool that allow patrons to walk from one lily pad to another, holding on an overhead rope (**Fig. 3-33**).
- Carefully watch patrons using inner tubes or rafts on a rapids ride, which is a rough-water attraction that is like white-water

Fig. 3-33

rafting. Lifeguarding responsibilities are similar to those for water slides and winding rivers. Patrons should be in the same body position as on water slides. Lifeguards should be positioned at the top, the bottom and in between to watch all parts of the ride **(Fig. 3-34)**.

- Enforce the height requirement on slides in which the rider sits on a plastic sled. Lifeguarding responsibilities are similar to those at other slides, such as free-fall slides. The lifeguard at the top of the slide starts sledders with a mechanical control. The lifeguard at the bottom watches for a sled flipping over. A signaling system is used to start riders.

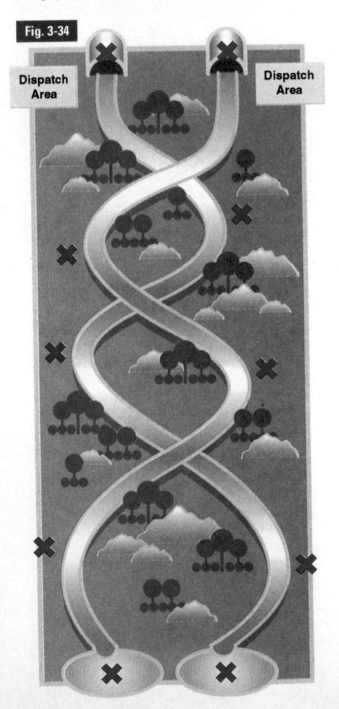

Fig. 3-34

Dispatch Area

Dispatch Area

Youth Camps

Waterfront and swimming pool facilities operated by youth camps implement additional prevention strategies. Prevention strategies may include—

- **Safety orientation.** All campers are familiarized with water safety rules and regulations prior to in-water activities.
- **Smaller swimmer-to-supervisor ratios.** Lifeguard areas of responsibility and patron loads are generally smaller than at many public facilities. Although trained lifeguards are essential for proper supervision, they may be supplemented at some camps by other personnel serving as spotters or lookouts after proper orientation. These individuals do not take the place of lifeguards or reduce the number of lifeguards needed to provide effective patron surveillance. In addition, lifeguards must not reduce the size of their area of responsibility or become less attentive when scanning due to the presence of spotters or lookouts.
- **Classification of swimming abilities.** Campers are classified by swimming ability and limited to water depths and activities appropriate to their demonstrated skills.
- **Buddy pairs.** Campers always swim in buddy pairs and are assigned the task of informing a lifeguard if their buddy experiences difficulty.
- **Buddy checks.** Although buddy checks are primarily designed to remind buddies to look after one another, common procedures also allow repeated confirmation of the number of campers known to be in the water.
- **Health screening.** Most camps require every camper to present a health history or physical examination. Any chronic or temporary conditions that indicate special precautions while swimming are discreetly communicated to the appropriate aquatic staff members.

Careful patron surveillance and prompt emergency response are just as important at youth camps as they are at other aquatic facilities. Common practices at waterfront and swimming pool areas operated by camps help make supervision more effective. Some of these practices include the classification of swimmers and the use of a buddy system and buddy boards.

Classification of Swimming Abilities

At the beginning of the camping session, the swimming skills and abilities of all campers and staff who will be participating in aquatic activities, such as swimming and boating, should be tested through a demonstration of swimming skills and abilities. The screening results, which should be conducted prior to any other aquatic programming, will determine which aquatic activities are appropriate for each person. Appropriate safety measures must be in place during the screening process. For example, a lifeguard provides surveillance while swimming instructors or

Swim Tests

Swim tests are used to determine if a person has the minimum level of swimming ability required to participate safely in activities, such as swimming in deep water, riding a slide that empties into deep water or jumping off a diving board into deep water. There is no single set of swim test criteria that best meets the needs of all facilities or organizations. Each facility or organization establishes swim test requirements based on the facility's design and features, the activities offered and common practice.

Procedures for conducting swim tests should be provided to lifeguards by facility management in the facility's policies and procedures manual. Swim testing should occur at established times during a facility's normal operating hours and be administered by lifeguards when not on surveillance duty.

aquatic staff cross-trained as both swimming instructors and lifeguards administer the tests. A lifeguard cannot administer a test while performing patron surveillance.

The swim test allows camp participants to be classified by swimming ability. Some camps may use a system to classify swimmers and nonswimmers, while some camps may use a three-tier system, such as shallow, intermediate and deep. At the swimming area, camp participants are grouped based on their classification. In some camps, campers are assigned a color-coded tag that is used to check into swimming and boating areas.

After the initial test, additional swim tests should be conducted at intervals throughout the camping session to determine if swimming abilities have improved or for campers who arrive after the initial test has been given.

Swimming Area Sections. The swimming area is clearly marked and divided into sections for each group as defined by each of the swim classification tests. The aquatics staff should be sure that campers remain in areas where they are assigned. Nonswimmers should never be allowed in water greater than chest height. There should be some type of continuous barrier, such as buoyed lifelines, piers, decks or a beach, around the perimeter of areas set aside for nonswimmers to prevent them from accidentally straying into deep water. Areas for swimmers may be defined with individual buoys.

Buddy System

Camps use the buddy system to pair a camp participant with another camp participant of similar swimming skills and abilities and then assign them to a specific swimming area. If buddies do not have similar swimming skills and abilities, the pair should be assigned to the swimming area to which the weaker swimmer is assigned. If there are an uneven number of participants in the group, consider forming one set of three participants or pairing the extra participant with a camp counselor.

Buddies must be instructed to be responsible for one another and to stay together in their assigned swimming area. If one leaves the swimming area for any reason, the other buddy must also leave. They must be taught that they are paired to watch out for each other. They need to tell a lifeguard immediately if their buddy is in trouble or missing. *Notifying the lifeguard is the first safeguard provided by the buddy system and should prompt immediate action.* The notification focuses the lifeguard's attention on the buddy in trouble and an appropriate response is to call for an immediate buddy check.

Buddy Checks. Buddy checks are often used at camps to reinforce the concept of the buddy system, and for that reason, buddy checks are often timed. That is, the person conducting the check may count out loud to ten while inattentive buddies strive to find one another. The primary purpose of the buddy checks is to account for all swimmers and to teach buddies to continuously monitor their partner by automatically conducting their own individual buddy checks.

During instructional periods, buddies do tasks together or watch each other perform a skill one buddy at a time. Instructional techniques are geared to support the buddy concept; the class does not need to be interrupted by a group buddy check. During recreational periods, buddy checks are called as needed to maintain order and to condition buddies to stay near one another.

To initiate a buddy check, a lifeguard, lookout or supervisor gives a prearranged signal, such as a whistle blast. The buddies grasp each other's hand, raise their arms over their heads and hold still while the staff confirms that everyone has a buddy **(Fig. 3-35)**.

When buddy checks are being performed, buddies do not have to leave the water. Those in shallow water may stand in place; those in deep water may move with their buddy to the side and raise hands without leaving the water. Those already on deck should remain there. If the area needs clearing at the end of the period or for an evacuation, everyone is asked to exit the water in an orderly fashion after accounting for all buddies.

During a buddy check, lifeguards should quickly become aware of anyone without a buddy. *A person without a buddy during a buddy check is the second safe-*

Fig. 3-35

guard provided by the buddy system. A buddy check is needed only if both the buddy and the lifeguard fail to notice a problem as it occurs. If a buddy check reveals a missing person, the lifeguards should immediately suspect the buddy is submerged.

In clear water, the bottom can be quickly scanned from the surface during a buddy check to locate a submerged swimmer. In water where the bottom cannot be seen and a buddy is missing, the EAP for a submerged swimmer must be activated immediately. An in-water search must not be delayed while searching for the missing person outside of the swimming area. In the process of initiating an in-water search, the buddy check must be completed to ensure there is not an additional victim.

Counting the people in the area during a buddy check is the third safeguard provided by the buddy system. Normally, a count simply confirms that the system is working. Emergency situations should be noticed long before a miss-match between the number of people known to be in the area and the actual number of swimmers indicates a problem.

Two methods are commonly used to confirm the count of swimmers after everyone has located their buddy and grasped hands. Both use a buddy board or other tracking system to note everyone who enters and leaves the area. That task is assigned to a lifeguard or other staff member.

- Method 1: Lifeguards may count the swimmers in each area and relay those numbers to the monitor.
- Method 2: Each pair of buddies is given a number. The monitor calls off the numbers in order and buddies respond when their number is called.

If everything matches, the buddy check is over. If there is an inconsistency, the EAP for a missing person should be activated.

The buddy check is especially helpful during busy times when lifeguards want to account for swimmers who are present. The buddy check gives lifeguards the opportunity to check periodically the bottom of the pool and also gives swimmers a brief rest.

Although the buddy system provides useful safeguards, buddy checks are not conducted frequently enough to substitute for normal surveillance. Lifeguards should never depend on the buddy system as the only method of supervision. They must constantly watch their areas of responsibility, looking for the behaviors of swimmers in trouble.

Buddy Boards

Some type of buddy board is needed to keep track of campers in the swimming area **(Fig 3-36)**. They are typically large permanent structures located at the swimming area.

Based on the initial swim test, every camper should get a colored tag with his or her full name and group designation, for example, a cabin or campsite number. Tags should be color-coded or labeled by swimming ability, such as "swimmer" or "nonswimmer." Numbered tags should only be used in place of individual name tags if a complete list of campers and their numbers is available at the swimming area to identify quickly any missing or injured person. The camper's name is needed to access medical files and emergency contact information on file at the camp office or first aid station.

If using a permanent board, it should be mounted within the confines of the swimming area and divided into sections matching how the swimming areas are divided. Tags are placed on hooks in the appropriate section

Fig. 3-36

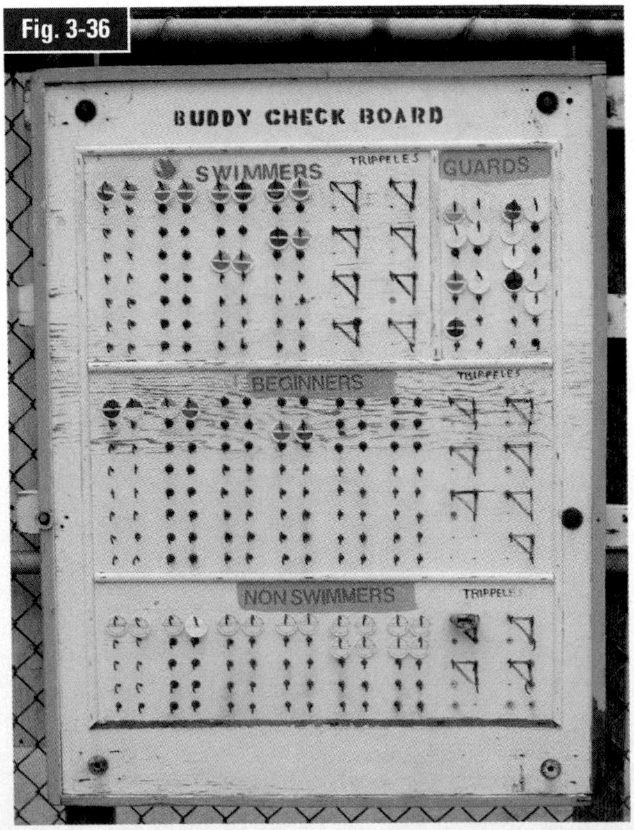

when campers are within the area and removed when the campers leave. Tags not in use may be kept on a separate "out" board outside the swimming area, kept by the camper or collected by a counselor. Out boards are normally sectioned by campsite or cabin groups for easy retrieval. Removing the tags from the swimming area facilitates their use for boating activities as well. A single board may include both "in" and "out" sections for swimming-only tags provided the sections are clearly distinguished. Different camps have different arrangements to prevent tag loss and unauthorized use.

Before buddies enter the water, they should hang their tags on the section of the board that indicates the swimming area in which they will be swimming. If buddies decide to move from one section to another, such as from the deep section to the shallow area, they must first notify the person at the board and move their tags. Each buddy's tag should be next to each other to indicate that they are a pair. Tags should be placed on separate hooks to facilitate a reliable count. A lifeguard or other staff member should be stationed at the buddy board to make sure the tags are placed correctly and that no one enters or leaves the swimming area without moving their tags appropriately. When swimmers leave the swimming area, they return their tags to the "out" section.

Color Caps. Another system for keeping track of campers in the swimming area is to use colored bathing caps, headbands or wristbands to distinguish swimming abilities. For example, nonswimmers wear red, swimmers wear blue or green and activity leaders or lifeguards wear white. This system can be used in addition to the buddy system or the buddy board. The advantage of using colored bathing caps is that the lifeguard can easily spot a cap in a swimming area, particularly if it is in the wrong section **(Fig. 3-37)**.

Competitive Events

Participants in competitive events like swimming or diving meets, water polo games, synchronized swimming and life-

Fig. 3-38

guarding competitions usually have good swimming skills, but they still need effective surveillance **(Fig. 3-38)**. Lifeguards need to adapt their scanning techniques to their specific needs.

- Consistently enforce facility rules during competitive events as would be done during everyday operations.
- Know and understand the rules and regulations for events and the safety policies for the competitive program.
- Plan how to perform a rescue if needed. For example, a victim should not be towed across lane lines. Check the facility's EAP for how to remove a victim from the water when lane lines are in place. Know how to remove lane lines (and where the tool is kept) in case this is needed during a rescue. The same is true for boundary lines in water polo.
- Have swimmers follow the rules set for the lanes. For example, accidents can occur when swimmers attempt to enter already crowded lanes. Enforce feet-first entries into the pool; racing starts are allowed only in designated, supervised lanes.
- If a pool has bulkheads, take a position where the water on both sides can be seen, or make sure there are enough lifeguards to scan both sides of the bulkhead **(Fig. 3-39)**. Do not allow swimmers under the bulkhead.

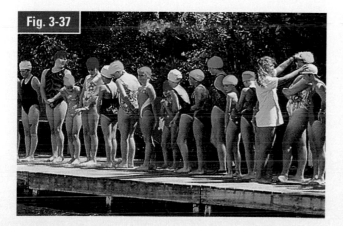

Fig. 3-37

Fig. 3-39

- During swim practices, scan the bottom frequently since practices can be crowded. Be aware of and watch for the possibility of swimmers colliding with the pool wall during turns and finishes and with other swimmers.
- In diving practices and competitions, watch for each diver to return to the surface. Take a position with a good view of the bottom.

Instructional or Therapeutic Activities

It is recommended that a lifeguard, in addition to the instructor, be present during instructional activities, such as swimming and diving lessons, water exercise and water therapy classes. Lifeguards should follow these guidelines:

- Different precautions might be needed, depending on the ages and abilities of participants. Note how tall participants are and the water depth where they are practicing. Make sure nonswimmers do not enter water more than chest deep without their instructor.
- Be sure infants and young children are with a parent or other responsible adult while in the water.
- Watch for signs of any participant becoming fatigued or chilled.
- In therapy programs for people with medical conditions, be familiar with the conditions of the participants.

PUTTING IT ALL TOGETHER

A lapse in coverage—even for just a few seconds—might result in injury or death. A lifeguard must be able to recognize a distressed swimmer and an active or passive drowning victim. Effective scanning techniques and lifeguard stations are needed to locate people in trouble.

Chapter 4

Emergency Preparation

A serious incident can happen even when everyone works to prevent injuries. In an emergency, follow the facility's emergency action plan(s). Be prepared to respond to emergencies, such as the following:

- A young child, playing with friends in the water, starts to drown.
- A person has a seizure, heart attack or stroke and slips underwater.

- A young person dives into shallow water, strikes his or her head and becomes paralyzed.
- The facility's power system suddenly fails.
- A hazardous chemical spills, requiring the facility to be evacuated.
- A severe thunderstorm is approaching a facility.

RESPONDING TO EMERGENCIES

A professional lifeguard is part of a safety team **(Fig. 4-1)**. Also on the team are supervisors, swimming instructors, security guards, concession staff and emergency medical services (EMS) personnel. At waterfronts, other team members may include park rangers, game wardens or marine safety officers. At waterparks, other team members may include equipment rental personnel and admissions personnel.

Even if there is only one lifeguard performing patron surveillance, other staff members can help in an emergency. Although bystanders may not have the training required to handle emergencies, with proper guidance they also can help by controlling a crowd, relaying a message to other team members, getting equipment or supplies or summoning EMS personnel. It is important for a lifeguard to know who is on the safety team and how to respond in an emergency.

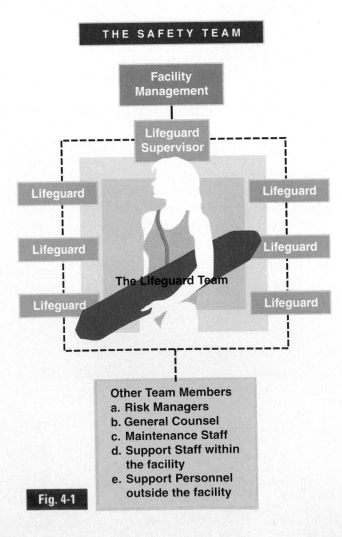

THE SAFETY TEAM

Facility Management

Lifeguard Supervisor

Lifeguard

Lifeguard

Lifeguard

The Lifeguard Team

Lifeguard

Lifeguard

Lifeguard

Other Team Members
a. Risk Managers
b. General Counsel
c. Maintenance Staff
d. Support Staff within the facility
e. Support Personnel outside the facility

Fig. 4-1

Safety Team Responsibilities

Everyone must know his or her role in an emergency action plan (EAP). Team members may have several different roles in a small facility or one main role in a large facility. When everyone on the team knows his or her responsibilities, the team works together effectively. Responsibilities of the safety team members in an EAP may include—

- Summoning EMS personnel by calling 9-1-1 or the local emergency number.
- Performing or assisting with a rescue.
- Providing back-up coverage.
- Controlling bystanders.
- Clearing the pool or facility.

Staff must know where equipment is stored, including the first aid kit, resuscitation mask, disposable gloves, automated external defibrillator (AED) and backboard. The EAP states who is responsible for retrieving equipment and getting it to the injured victim.

EMERGENCY ACTION PLANS

EAPs are detailed plans describing everyone's responsibility in an emergency. EAPs should be in the facility's policies and procedures manual. During orientation and in-service training, lifeguards should learn and practice their assigned responsibilities in the EAPs. In addition, EAPs should be practiced often to develop teamwork.

Emergency Action Plan Steps

A sample EAP for an emergency in the water or on land includes the following steps:

1. **The lifeguard recognizes that someone needs immediate help.**
   The lifeguard recognizes an emergency in the water or on land.
2. **The lifeguard activates the EAP.**
   Before leaving his or her station, the lifeguard first activates the EAP by giving a prearranged signal, such as a long whistle blast, to alert other lifeguards and staff. They provide back-up coverage, give additional help, get additional equipment and call EMS personnel if necessary.
3. **The lifeguard follows the general procedures for emergencies that occur in the water or on land.**
   See Chapter 5 for more information on emergencies that occur in the water and Chapter 6 for more information on emergencies that occur on land.

General Procedures

Water Emergencies

- Assesses the victim's condition.
- Safely enters the water, if needed.
- Performs the appropriate rescue.
- Moves the victim to safety.
- Removes the victim from the water.
- Provides emergency care, if needed.
  - Performs an initial assessment.
  - Summons EMS personnel.
  - Performs a secondary assessment.

Land Emergencies

- Sizes up the scene and approaches the victim.
- Provides emergency care, if needed.
  - Performs an initial assessment.
  - Summons EMS personnel.
  - Performs a secondary assessment.

4. Safety team members assist in the emergency.
Depending on the emergency, safety team members may assist with the rescue, provide back-up coverage, clear the facility, retrieve equipment or call EMS personnel.

5. The chain of command is notified.
The lifeguard supervisor or facility manager is notified. With a serious injury or death, the lifeguard supervisor or facility manager notifies the appropriate management administrator(s) as soon as possible. This supervisor contacts the victim's family.

6. Witnesses are interviewed.
As soon as possible, the designated safety team member individually interviews witnesses who saw the incident. Interviews are done privately and documented in writing.

7. Reports are completed.
The lifeguard who made the rescue fills out an incident report as soon as possible. Other lifeguards and other staff involved in the incident must also fill out separate incident report forms.

8. Equipment is checked.
The staff checks the equipment and supplies used in the rescue. Any damaged or missing items are reported or replaced. Any equipment exposed to blood or other potentially infectious materials is properly cleaned and disinfected. If the facility was cleared during the incident, all required equipment must be back in place before reopening the facility.

9. Corrective action taken.
Any situation that may have contributed to the incident is corrected before the facility is reopened or as soon as possible. If needed, restrict access to any unsafe area.

10. Follow-up staff discussion.
If the incident involved a serious injury or death, a professional may help facility personnel and lifeguards cope with the experience.

Emergency Preparation for Waterfronts

EAPs at waterfronts and camps may include additional steps because of the environment, the weather or the size of the waterfront and its surroundings. In rural areas, it may take longer for EMS personnel to arrive than at an urban pool setting. Therefore, the waterfront's EAP should factor in a longer response time.

Emergency Preparation for Waterparks

Factors to consider in an EAP for waterparks include—
- Stopping the waves or slide dispatch.
  - At a wave pool, pushing the emergency stop button to stop the waves (**Fig. 4-2**).
  - The lifeguard stationed at the top of an attraction not dispatching any more riders.
- Having set whistle signals, hand signals, flags or lights to communicate with other lifeguards.
- If another lifeguard is making a rescue, making sure that the lifeguard's area of responsibility is covered.
- In a deep water attraction, having all lifeguards stand in their chairs and adjust their zone coverage to cover the area of responsibility of the lifeguard making the rescue.
- In a shallow water attraction, having a nearby lifeguard move to cover both his or her area of responsibility and the rescuing lifeguard's area of responsibility.

Fig. 4-2

Missing Person Procedure

All staff should be trained in missing person procedures. Time is critical because the "missing person" may be in the water or it may be a child who wandered off and cannot be found by his or her parent. Therefore, every missing person report is serious. During all missing person search procedures, one person is in charge of the search to avoid confusion and wasted time. This may be the lifeguard supervisor or facility manager.

If the missing person is not found immediately, additional support may be needed from other EMS personnel. Continue the search until EMS personnel arrive on the scene to assist with the search. The EMS response can be canceled if the victim is found and does not need medical assistance. The facility's EAP for a missing person search may include some of the following actions:

- Use of a predetermined signal that alerts all staff that a person is missing. Lifeguards should clear the swimming areas. In clear water, all swimming areas can be quickly scanned from the surface to determine if the person is in the water. At facilities with turbid water or with limited visibility, lifeguards report to a designated area.
- All support staff should report immediately to the designated location. The individual who reported the missing person should give a detailed description of the person and wait to identify the person.
- A public address system announcement should be made describing the missing person.

Follow facility policy whether to describe a missing child. Ask everyone to stay calm, and ask for volunteers if needed. Tell the missing person to report to the main lifeguard area. Often the person does not know someone reported him or her missing.

- All other lifeguards should search the swimming area, starting where the missing person was last seen. At waterfront facilities:
  - One lifeguard acts as the lookout above the water level on a pier, raft or water craft with rescue equipment.
  - Lifeguards should look under piers, rafts and in other dangerous locations.
  - Adult volunteers can help search shallow areas, but only lifeguards should search beyond chest-deep water.
- Other facility staff should check the bathrooms, showers, locker rooms, dining areas and other locations.
- At a camp, staff should quickly check the missing person's cabin or tent and other areas.
- At a camp, all campers should be moved to a central location to do a count. Lifeguards should continue to search the entire waterfront until every person has been accounted for or until proper authorities take over.
- At parks, staff should search playgrounds, campsites and wooded areas. Park rangers, maintenance staff and volunteers can help while lifeguards search the water areas.

During an Emergency

Being prepared for an emergency is more than knowing how to rescue someone. It also means understanding the communication systems used at the facility, including any back-up systems. When first recognizing an emergency, signal other lifeguards and staff. The signal tells other lifeguards there is an emergency and that they should cover the lifeguard's area of responsibility (back-up cov-

erage). If there is only one lifeguard on patron surveillance duty, patrons should be signaled to leave the water.

All communications need to be simple and clear. The signals used depend on the nature of the facility and the number of staff. Common signals are—

- Whistles.
- Hand signals.
- Public address systems.

- Telephones.
- Two-way radios.
- Flags.
- Megaphones.

Summoning EMS Personnel

Many areas have a 9-1-1 emergency telephone system for summoning EMS personnel. In some communities, a local emergency number is used. In some facilities, an 8, 9 or other number must be dialed first for an outside line. Emergency numbers should be posted on or near all telephones, along with the information to give the dispatcher **(Fig. 4-3)**. Wasting minutes to find the emergency number could cost a life.

LIFEGUARDING TIP: Summoning EMS personnel is important in all EAPs. Everyone, including patrons, should be able to call EMS personnel immediately and give correct information to the dispatcher.

If a victim's injury is determined not to be serious enough to summon EMS personnel, provide the necessary first aid and follow facility procedures. Decide if the person should or should not go back in the water. In some cases, the person should be advised to see a health-care professional.

Some waterparks and remote youth camps may have medical equipment and staff, such as emergency medical technicians (EMTs) or nurses, on site. In this case, these members of the safety team may be contacted first. The facility's EAP will outline the procedures when medical personnel are on staff.

Controlling Bystanders

Lifeguards and/or safety team members in an emergency are responsible for controlling bystanders to prevent interference with a rescue or emergency care. Controlling bystanders might involve—

- Using a firm, but calm voice to ask bystanders to move back so that care can be given. Do not yell at patrons.
- Roping off areas or positioning chairs around the emergency site.
- Recruiting bystanders so they can assist lifeguards and facility staff in crowd control.
- Using the public address system to help control bystanders.
- Repeating commands and requests as often as necessary.
- Ensuring that EMS personnel have a clear path.
- Keeping bystanders and any children away from the water's edge if the facility is cleared.

AFTER AN EMERGENCY

After a victim has received care or has been released to EMS personnel, lifeguards and other members of the safety team still have several tasks to complete.

Completing Reports

After the emergency, lifeguards and other staff involved in the incident must fill out an incident report form (see Sample Incident Report Form on pages 54-55). Write down only factual information, not personal opinion or anything heard from someone else.

Witness statements may also be required. Getting a statement or witnesses' names, addresses and phone numbers may be the responsibility of a lifeguard, although usually a lifeguard supervisor or facility manager does this. Witnesses write their statements on separate, dated forms. They describe the incident in their own words. Lifeguards and other staff should not tell witnesses what to say in this statement. Witnesses should not be together when completing their statements as they may talk to each other and may begin to doubt what each has seen.

Checking Equipment

All equipment and first aid supplies used in the emergency must be replaced. Use the facility's safety checklist to check equipment and supplies. Equipment involved in the emergency, such as a tube, sled or mat, should be removed from rotation until cleared by the lifeguard supervisor or facility manager. If an injured victim was put on a backboard, EMS personnel will usually use that backboard while transporting the victim to a hospital. If that happens, ask EMS personnel to temporarily exchange backboards with the facility. Otherwise, the backboard must be immediately replaced or the facility closed until a backboard is available on site. Equipment exposed to blood or other potentially infectious materials

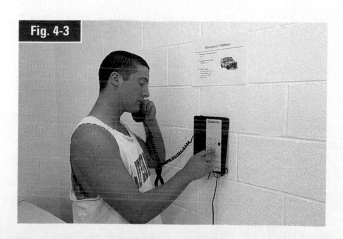

Fig. 4-3

Sample Incident Report Form

Date of Report: _____ Date of Incident: _____ Time of Incident: _____ AM ☐ PM ☐

Facility Information

Facility: _____ Phone Number: _____

Address: _____ City: _____ State: _____ Zip: _____

Information on Person Assisted (Complete a separate form for incidents involving more than one person)

Name: _____ Age: _____ Gender: Male ☐ Female ☐

Address: _____ City: _____ State: _____ Zip: _____

Phone Number(s): Home: _____ Work: _____

Family Contact (name and phone number): _____

Incident Data

Location of Incident: _____

_____

Description of Incident: _____

_____

Did an injury occur? Yes ☐ No ☐

If yes, describe the type of injury: _____

_____

Witnesses (Attach witness descriptions of incident)

1. Name: _____ Phone Number: _____

   Address: _____ City: _____ State: _____ Zip: _____

   Witness description of incident: _____

   _____

2. Name: _____ Phone Number: _____

   Address: _____ City: _____ State: _____ Zip: _____

   Witness description of incident: _____

   _____

Care Provided

Did victim refuse medical attention by staff? Yes ☐   No ☐

If yes, have victim (parent or guardian for a minor) sign here: _____   Date: _____

Signature of witness to the refusal of care: _____   Date: _____

Did facility provide care? Yes ☐   No ☐

Name of person(s) who provided care: _____

Describe in detail the care provided: _____

_____

_____

_____

Were emergency medical services (EMS) personnel called? Yes ☐   No ☐

If yes, by whom? _____

Time EMS personnel called: _____   AM ☐   PM ☐

Time EMS personnel arrived: _____   AM ☐   PM ☐

Was the victim transported to an emergency facility? Yes ☐   No ☐

If yes, where? _____ If no, person returned to activity? Yes ☐   No ☐

If the victim is a minor, were the minor's parents contacted (if not present)? Yes ☐   No ☐

Facility Data

Number of lifeguards on duty at time of incident: _____

Number of patrons in facility at time of incident: _____

Weather condition at time of incident: _____

Water condition at time of incident: _____

Deck condition at time of incident: _____

Name(s) of lifeguard(s) involved in incident: _____

Report Prepared By:

Name: _____   Position: _____

Signature: _____   Date: _____

Attachments

Note any attachments such as an EMS personnel report or follow-up conversations with victim and/or parents or guardian.

must be properly cleaned and disinfected. Report other missing or damaged items to the lifeguard supervisor or facility manager.

Reopening the Facility

During or after a significant incident, the lifeguard supervisor, facility manager or another individual as identified in the EAP decides whether to close the facility temporarily and then, when to reopen. The decision may depend on if enough lifeguards are ready to go back to surveillance, if all the required equipment is in place, if spills involving blood or other potentially infectious materials have been cleaned up or if the facility is safe to reopen. Lifeguards must inform their supervisors if they are too upset by the incident to do a good job of surveillance.

Staff Debriefing

This meeting usually is held after incident reports are completed. The entire safety team attends the meeting. The staff talks about what happened before, during and after the emergency (**Fig. 4-4**). Avoid assigning blame or criticizing anyone's actions. Goals of the debriefing are to—

- Examine what happened.
- Assess the effectiveness of the EAP.
- Consider new ways to prevent similar incidents in the future.
- Be alert for critical incident stress reactions.

Dealing with Questions

Television or newspaper reporters, insurance company representatives, attorneys and curious people may ask questions about the emergency. Do not give out any information about an injured person. Only management or a designated spokesperson should talk to the media or others about an incident. Talking about what happened can lead to legal action. The procedure for dealing with the media and others should be in the policies and procedures manual and the EAP. If people ask questions, refer them to the manager or spokesperson. Do not discuss the emergency with anyone not on the facility staff, except for counselors who are there to assist staff. If the area where the incident happened is visible from public property, individuals cannot be prevented from taking a picture from a public area. Anyone requesting to take a photo in the facility, however, needs permission from management.

Critical Incident Stress

In an emergency, the body reacts in several ways. The muscles tense, the heart rate and breathing increase and other reactions occur. The stress of the emergency can cause distress or disruption in a person's mental or emotional balance. The stress can cause sleeplessness, anxiety, depression, exhaustion, restlessness, nausea, nightmares and other problems. Some effects may happen right away, but others may appear days, weeks or even months after the incident. People react to stress in different ways, even with the same incident. Someone may not even recognize that he or she is suffering from stress or know its cause.

A critical incident may cause a strong emotional reaction and interfere with a lifeguard's ability to cope and function during and after the incident. For lifeguards, critical incidents include—

- A patron's death, especially the death of a child or a death following a prolonged rescue attempt.
- An event that endangers the rescuer's life or threatens someone important to the rescuer.
- The death of a co-worker on the job.
- Any powerful emotional event, especially one that receives media coverage.

Rescues involving severe injury or death are stressful for lifeguards. Rescues are especially stressful if the lifeguard believes he or she did something wrong or failed to do something—even after doing exactly what he or she was trained to do. This stress is called *critical incident stress*. It is a normal reaction. Someone experiencing this usually needs help to recognize it, understand it and cope with it. If this type of stress is not identified and managed, it can also disrupt a lifeguard's personal life and his or her effectiveness on the job. Facility management should help by contacting a licensed mental health professional.

PUTTING IT ALL TOGETHER

EAPs are blueprints for handling emergencies. Everyone must know his or her role in an EAP. Teamwork and practice of the EAP helps members of the safety team know how to respond in an emergency and how to manage the stress it may cause.

Fig. 4-4

Chapter 5

Rescue Skills

A lifeguard must always be prepared to enter the water to make rescues. After determining that the victim needs help, the lifeguard should assess the victim's condition and use an appropriate rescue. The skills in this chapter can be used in most aquatic environments, although they may have to be modified in some situations.

GENERAL PROCEDURES FOR A WATER EMERGENCY

In all rescue situations, the lifeguard recognizes an emergency in the water, activates the emergency action plan (EAP) **(Fig. 5-1)**, uses rescue equipment and follows these general procedures:

LIFEGUARDING TIP: A lifeguard must always provide for his or her own safety and the safety of the victim when making a rescue.

1. **Assesses the victim's condition.** Determines whether the victim is a distressed swimmer, is an active or passive drowning victim at the surface or submerged or has a possible head, neck or back injury.
2. **Safely enters the water, if needed.** Chooses the best entry based on—
   - Water depth.
   - Whether the lifeguard station is elevated or at ground level.
   - Obstacles in the water.
   - Location and condition of the victim.
   - Facility design.
3. **Performs an appropriate rescue.** Swims to the victim, if needed, and performs a rescue appropriate for the victim's condition.
4. **Moves the victim to safety.** Brings the victim to the side of the pool or pier or to the shoreline.
5. **Removes the victim from the water.** Uses the removal technique appropriate for the victim's condition and the facility's design.

6. **Provides emergency care as needed.** Depending upon the victim's condition, gives rescue breathing, cardiopulmonary resuscitation (CPR) or other care until emergency medical services (EMS) personnel arrive.

RESCUE EQUIPMENT

The use of rescue equipment makes a rescue safer for both the lifeguard and the victim. The primary piece of rescue equipment used by lifeguards is the rescue tube. However, state and local laws and regulations may require facilities to have specific rescue equipment available, such as ring buoys and reaching equipment. Specific or specialty rescue equipment may also be used by a facility due to the nature of the environment, such as in a waterfront environment.

Rescue Tube

The *rescue tube* is a 45- to 54-inch vinyl, foam-filled tube with an attached tow line and shoulder strap **(Fig. 5-2)**.

When performing patron surveillance, a lifeguard should always keep a rescue tube ready to use.

- Keep the strap of the rescue tube over the shoulder and neck.
- Hold the rescue tube across the thighs when sitting in a lifeguard chair or across the stomach when standing.
- Hold the excess line to keep it from getting caught in the chair or other equipment when starting the rescue.

Reaching Pole and Shepherd's Crook

A *reaching pole* is made of aluminum or fiberglass and is usually about 10 to 15 feet long. The *shepherd's crook* is a reaching pole with a large hook on one end **(Fig. 5-3)**. A reaching pole or shepherd's crook can be used to reach out to a distressed victim to pull him or her to safety.

Fig. 5-1

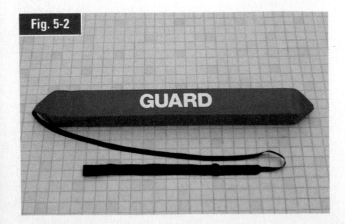

Fig. 5-2

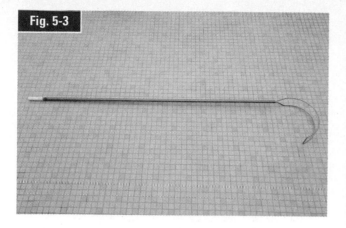

Fig. 5-3

Ring Buoy

The *ring buoy* is made of buoyant material typically ranging from 20 to 30 inches in diameter **(Fig. 5-4)**. A ring buoy with an attached line allows the lifeguard to pull the victim to safety without entering the water. The typical line length ranges from 30 to 60 feet.

Rescue Board

Some waterfronts use *rescue boards* as standard equipment. Rescue boards are made of plastic or fiberglass and are shaped similar to a surf board **(Fig. 5-5)**. The rescue board is fast, stable and easy to use. It is used by

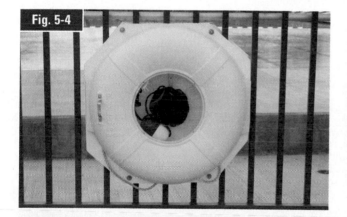

Fig. 5-4

Fig. 5-5

Rescue Buoy

Rescue buoys, also known as rescue cans or torpedo buoys, often are used as rescue equipment at waterfronts and surf beaches. Most rescue buoys are made of lightweight, hard, buoyant plastic and vary in length from 25 to 34 inches. Molded handgrips along the sides and rear of the buoy allow the victim to keep a firm hold on the buoy. Rescue buoys are buoyant enough to support multiple victims.

While approaching the victim, the lifeguard should allow the rescue buoy to trail behind. When close to the victim, the lifeguard should reach back and grasp the buoy with one hand, extend the buoy to the victim and carefully tow the victim back to safety. The buoyancy of the rescue buoy, along with reassuring talk, should comfort and calm the victim.

lifeguards to quickly paddle out long distances and can hold the lifeguard and one or more victims.

ENTRIES

There are several ways to enter the water for a rescue. The type of entry used depends on—
- The depth of the water.
- The lifeguard station—whether it is elevated or at ground level.

Fig. 5-6

Fig. 5-7

A

B

- Obstacles in the water, such as people, lane lines and safety lines.
- The location and condition of the victim.
- The design of the facility.

Slide-In Entry

The slide-in entry is slower than other entries, but it is the safest entry to use in most conditions (**Fig. 5-6**). It is especially useful in shallow water, crowded pools or when a victim with a head, neck or back injury is close to the side of the pool or pier. To perform a slide-in entry, the lifeguard should—

1. Sit down on the edge of the pool deck or pier, facing the water. Place the rescue tube on the surface of the pool deck or pier or in the water.
2. Gently slide into the water.
3. Retrieve the rescue tube.
4. Place the rescue tube across the chest with the tube under the armpits and begin the approach.

C

Stride Jump

A lifeguard should use the stride jump with a rescue tube only if the water is at least 5 feet deep and he or she is no more than 3 feet above the water. To perform a stride jump, the lifeguard should—

1. Squeeze the rescue tube high against the chest with the tube under the armpits (**Fig. 5-7, A**).
2. Hold the excess line to keep it from getting caught in the lifeguard chair or other equipment when jumping into the water.
3. Leap into the water with one leg forward and the other leg back (**Fig. 5-7, B**).
4. Lean slightly forward, with the chest ahead of the hips, and focus on the victim when entering the water.
5. Squeeze or scissor the legs together for upward thrust (**Fig. 5-7, C**).
6. Focus on the victim and begin the approach (**Fig. 5-7, D**).

D

Compact Jump

A lifeguard should use the compact jump when more than 3 feet above the water, such as on a lifeguard stand or pier, but only if the water is at least 5 feet deep. The compact jump can also be done from a pool deck into the water. To perform a compact jump, the lifeguard should—

1. Squeeze the rescue tube high against the chest with the tube under the armpits.
2. Hold the excess line to keep it from getting caught in the lifeguard chair or other equipment when jumping into the water (Fig. 5-8, A).

Fig. 5-8

3. Jump out and away from the lifeguard chair, pool deck or pier (Fig. 5-8, B). In a wave pool, time the jump to land on the crest (top) of a wave (Fig. 5-8, C).
4. Bend the knees and keep the feet together and flat to absorb the shock if hitting the bottom. Do not point the toes or keep the legs straight or stiff.
5. Let the buoyancy of the rescue tube bring the lifeguard back to the surface.
6. Focus on the victim when surfacing, and begin the approach.

Run-and-Swim Entry

To enter the water from a gradual slope, such as a shoreline or wave pool, the lifeguard should use the run-and-swim entry. To perform a run-and-swim entry, the lifeguard should—

1. Hold the rescue tube and the excess line and run into the water, lifting the knees high to avoid falling (Fig. 5-9, A).
2. When the lifeguard can no longer run, he or she should either put the rescue tube across the chest and lean forward or drop the tube to the side and start swimming, letting the rescue tube trail behind (Fig. 5-9, B). Do not dive or plunge head-first into the water; this could result in a serious head, neck or back injury.

Fig. 5-9

RESCUE APPROACHES

The best way to swim to the victim is with a modified front crawl or breaststroke **(Fig. 5-10, A-B)**. The lifeguard should keep the rescue tube under the armpits or torso, and swim toward the victim with the head up. The lifeguard should keep the rescue tube in control at all times. For longer distances, or if the rescue tube slips out from under the arms or torso while swimming to the victim, the lifeguard can let the tube trail behind **(Fig. 5-11)**. Slow down and reposition the tube before contacting the victim.

Fig. 5-10

A

B

Fig. 5-11

In shallow water it may be quicker or easier to walk to the victim. Hold the rescue tube at the side and walk quickly toward the victim. Slow down and reposition the tube before contacting the victim.

ASSISTS

Assists are the most common help given to patrons, especially at waterparks. Assists include—
- Helping patrons enter and exit an attraction.
- Helping patrons in or out of inner tubes or rafts.
- Helping tired swimmers reach shallow water or a ladder.
- Helping a patron who is stuck in a slide or becomes frightened. In this instance, the lifeguard should—
  - Climb up a slide to reach a patron, or catch a patron coming down.
  - Talk to the patron to help calm him or her.
  - If a rescue is needed instead of an assist, activate the EAP.

Simple Assist
In shallow water, a simple assist may be as easy as helping a person to stand. This can be done in two ways:
- The lifeguard keeps the rescue tube between him or herself and the person who needs help, reaches across the tube and grasps the person at the armpit to help the person maintain his or her balance **(Fig. 5-12)**.
- If the person is underwater, the lifeguard should grasp under the person's armpits with both hands and help him or her stand up.

Extension Assist from the Deck
The safest way to help is to stay on the pool deck or pier and extend a rescue tube to a distressed swimmer who is close to the side of the pool or a pier. To

Fig. 5-12

Fig. 5-13

Fig. 5-14

A

B

perform an extension assist from the deck, the lifeguard should—
1. Remove the shoulder strap.
2. Hold the shoulder strap in one hand, and extend the rescue tube to the distressed swimmer with the other hand (Fig. 5-13). The lifeguard should be sure to keep his or her body weight on the back foot and crouch to avoid being pulled into the water.
3. Tell the victim to grab the rescue tube.
4. Slowly pull the victim to safety.

Reaching Assist with Equipment
If the victim is close enough to the deck, pier or shoreline, use a reaching assist to pull him or her to safety. To perform a reaching assist with equipment, the lifeguard should—
1. Brace him or herself on a pool deck, pier surface or shoreline.
2. Extend a reaching pole or shepherd's crook to the victim (Fig. 5-14, A).
3. When the victim grabs the pole or the crook, slowly and carefully pull the victim to safety. Keep the body low and lean back to avoid being pulled into the water (Fig. 5-14, B).

LIFEGUARDING TIP: Be careful not to strike other patrons when extending the reaching pole or shepherd's crook to the victim during the assist.

Throwing Assist
Throwing assists work well for distressed swimmers who are beyond the range of a reaching device. To perform a throwing assist with a ring buoy, the lifeguard should—
1. Hold the coil of line in the open palm of the nonthrowing hand and grasp the side of the ring buoy with the throwing hand (Fig. 5-15, A). If the line has a wrist loop,

place the hand that will hold the line through it. If there is not a wrist loop, step on the nonthrowing end of the line.
2. Hold the buoy vertically, step back with the leg on the throwing side, swing the ring buoy backwards and then forward for an underhand toss (Fig. 5-15, B-C).
3. Aim the throw so that the ring buoy lands just beyond the victim with the line lying on the victim's shoulder (Fig. 5-15, D-E). Tell the victim to grab the ring buoy. If there is a crosswind or current, throw upwind or up current of the victim.
4. After the victim has a firm grasp on the ring buoy or line, drop the remaining coil, if any, and pull the victim to safety. Keep the body low and lean back to avoid being pulled into the water (Fig. 5-15, F). Reassure the victim.
5. Slowly pull the victim to safety by reaching out with one hand and grasping the line with the thumb inward. Pull the line in to the side with that hand while reaching out with the other (Fig. 5-15, G). Continue the alternate pulling and reaching action until the victim is at the side or is able to stand in shallow water.

A successful throwing assist for an active drowning victim requires the ring buoy to land within the grasp of

Fig. 5-15

A

B

C

D

E

F

G

the person's arm movements. Victims will not be able to reach for or move even a short distance toward either the line or the buoy.

RESCUES AT OR NEAR THE SURFACE

Use the following skills to rescue a distressed swimmer or an active drowning victim at or near the surface of the water.

Fig. 5-16

A

B

Fig. 5-17

A

B

C

D

Swimming Extension Rescue

The swimming extension rescue works well for a distressed swimmer. To perform a swimming extension rescue, the lifeguard should—

1. Approach the victim from the front (**Fig. 5-16, A**).
2. Extend the end of the rescue tube to the victim (**Fig. 5-16, B**).
3. Tell the victim to hold on to the rescue tube and kick if he or she can.
4. Tow the victim to safety. Be sure to maintain visual contact.
5. Reassure the victim.

Active Drowning Victim Rear Rescue

The active drowning victim rear rescue can be used for either a distressed swimmer or an active drowning victim. To perform an active drowning victim rear rescue, the lifeguard should—

1. Approach the victim from behind (**Fig. 5-17, A**). This may require swimming past and around the victim.
2. Reach under the victim's armpits and grasp the shoulders firmly (**Fig. 5-17, B**).
3. Squeeze the rescue tube between the lifeguard's chest and the victim's back (**Fig. 5-17, C**).
4. Keep the lifeguard's head to one side to avoid being hit by the victim's head if it moves backward.
5. Lean back and pull the victim onto the rescue tube (**Fig. 5-17, D**).

6. Use the rescue tube to support the victim so the victim's mouth is out of the water.
7. Reassure the victim.
8. Tow the victim to safety.

Passive Drowning Victim Rear Rescue

Use the passive drowning victim rear rescue when the victim is at or near the surface, seems unconscious and a head, neck or back injury is not suspected. (If a head, neck or back injury is suspected, use the techniques described in Chapter 10.) A passive drowning victim may be floating face-down at or near the surface in a vertical-to-horizontal position. The goal is to put the rescue tube under the victim's shoulders or back to support him or her face-up. To perform a passive drowning victim rear rescue, the lifeguard should—

1. Approach the victim from behind (**Fig. 5-18, A**).
2. Reach under the victim's armpits and grasp the shoulders firmly (**Fig. 5-18, B**). The lifeguard may be high on the victim's back when doing this.
3. Squeeze the rescue tube between the lifeguard's chest and the victim's back.
4. Keep his or her head to one side to avoid being hit by the victim's head if it moves backward.
5. Roll the victim over by dipping the lifeguard's shoulder and rolling onto the back so that the victim is face-up on top of the rescue tube (**Fig. 5-18, C**).
6. Tow the victim to safety (**Fig. 5-18, D**). For greater distances, use one hand to stroke. Reach the right arm over the victim's right shoulder and grasp the rescue tube. Then use the left hand to stroke. Or reach with the left arm and stroke with the right hand.

RESCUING A SUBMERGED VICTIM

Sometimes a drowning victim is below the surface. This could be in shallow water or in deep water beyond the lifeguard's reach. This may occur when nonswimmers or very weak swimmers enter water over their head. A victim may also submerge after a cardiac arrest, stroke, seizure or other medical emergency resulting in unconsciousness in the water.

Passive Submerged Victim—Shallow Water

To rescue a submerged passive victim in shallow water, the lifeguard should—

1. Swim or quickly walk to the point near the victim's side. Let go of the rescue tube but keep the strap around the shoulders.
2. Face in the same direction as the victim, submerge and reach down to grab the victim under the armpits (**Fig. 5-19, A**).
3. Simultaneously, pick the victim up, move forward and roll the victim face-up upon surfacing (**Fig. 5-19, B**).
4. Grab the rescue tube and position it under the victim's shoulders (**Fig. 5-19, C**).

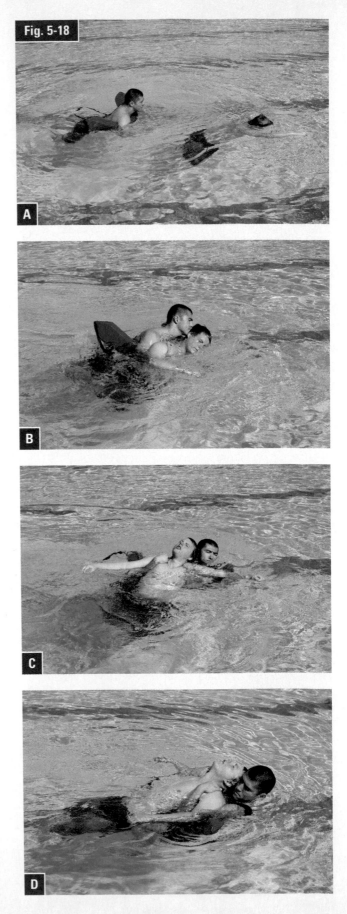

Fig. 5-18

A

B

C

D

Fig. 5-19

5. Move the victim's arm that is closest to the lifeguard down to the side of the victim. Reach the right arm over the victim's right shoulder and grasp the rescue tube or reach with the left arm over the victim's left shoulder and grasp the rescue tube **(Fig. 5-19, D)**.

6. Move the victim quickly to safety **(Fig. 5-19, E)**.

Active or Passive Submerged Victim—Deep Water

Feet-First Surface Dive

In deep water, a lifeguard goes underwater with a feet-first surface dive to rescue or search for a submerged victim. To properly perform a feet-first surface dive, the lifeguard should—

1. Swim to a point near the victim. Release the rescue tube but keep the strap around the shoulders.

2. Position his or her body vertically, then at the same time press both hands down and kick strongly to raise his or her body out of the water **(Fig. 5-20, A)**.

3. Take a breath with the arms at the sides and let his or her body sink underwater. Keep the legs straight and together **(Fig. 5-20, B)**.

4. As downward momentum slows, turn the palms outward and sweep the hands and arms upward and overhead.

5. Repeat this arm movement until deep enough to reach the victim.

Fig. 5-20

A

B

Active or Passive Submerged Victim Rescue—Deep Water

A submerged victim may be passive or active. To perform the following rescue skill in both cases, the lifeguard should—

1. Perform a feet-first surface dive, and position him or herself behind the victim (**Fig. 5-21, A-B**).
2. Reach one arm under the victim's arm (right arm to right side or left arm to left side) and across the victim's chest (**Fig. 5-21, C**). Hold firmly onto the victim's opposite side.
3. When the lifeguard has hold of the victim, he or she should reach up with the free hand and grasp the towline. Pull it down and hold it in the same hand that is holding the victim (**Fig. 5-21, D**). Keep pulling the towline in this way until reaching the surface. Once at the surface, the lifeguard should grasp and position the rescue tube so that it is squeezed between his or her chest and the victim's back (**Fig. 5-21, E**).
4. Reach the free arm over the tube and under the victim's armpit. Grasp his or her shoulder firmly (right arm to right shoulder or left arm to left shoulder) (**Fig. 5-21, F**).
5. Move the other arm from across the victim's chest, and grasp the victim's shoulder firmly.

6. Hold the victim in a face-up position on the rescue tube (**Fig. 5-21, G**).
7. Quickly move the victim to safety.

LIFEGUARDING TIP: Depending on how deep the victim is, the lifeguard should use one of these techniques:

- **If the strap must be removed to descend and reach the victim, hold onto it so that the rescue tube can be used to help bring the victim to the surface.**
- **If the victim is deeper than the strap and towline can extend, release the strap and towline, grasp the victim, push off the bottom (if possible) and kick to the surface. Once at the surface, place the rescue tube in position behind the victim and continue the rescue.**
- **If the strap of the rescue tube is released, it might not be within reach when returning to the surface. The side of the pool or pier may be closer than the rescue tube. In this situation, move to safety without the rescue tube. Support the victim in a face-up position, and if possible, call for help from another lifeguard.**

ESCAPES

A distressed swimmer or an active drowning victim may grab the lifeguard if the rescue technique is faulty or if the rescue tube slips out of position. The lifeguard should always hold onto the rescue tube because it helps both the victim and rescuer stay afloat. If the rescue tube is lost and a drowning victim grabs onto the lifeguard, the front or rear head-hold escape should be used.

To perform a front head-hold escape, the lifeguard should—

1. As soon as the victim grabs hold, take a quick breath, tuck the chin down, turn the head to either side, raise the shoulders and submerge with the victim (**Fig. 5-22, A**).
2. Once underwater, grasp the victim's elbows or the undersides of the victim's arms just above the elbows. Forcefully push up and away. Keep the chin tucked, the arms fully extended and the shoulders raised until free (**Fig. 5-22, B**).
3. Quickly swim underwater out of the victim's reach. Surface and reposition the rescue tube and try the rescue again (**Fig. 5-22, C**).

Fig. 5-21

Fig. 5-22

A

B

C

Fig. 5-23

A

B

C

3. Quickly swim underwater out of the victim's reach. Surface and reposition the rescue tube and try the rescue again (**Fig. 5-23, C**).

MULTIPLE-VICTIM RESCUE

Sometimes two or more victims need to be rescued. A victim may grab a nearby swimmer to try to stay above the water. Several lifeguards should perform a multiple-victim rescue if possible. At least one lifeguard should check the bottom for possible submerged victims while other lifeguards rescue the victims at the surface.

To perform a rear head-hold escape, the lifeguard should—

1. If the victim grabs hold from behind, take a quick breath, tuck the chin down, turn the head to either side, raise the shoulders and submerge with the victim (**Fig. 5-23, A**).
2. Once underwater, grasp the victim's elbows or the undersides of the victim's arms just above the elbows. Forcefully push up and away while twisting the head and shoulders. Keep the chin tucked, the arms fully extended and the shoulders raised until free (**Fig. 5-23, B**).

If there is only one lifeguard rescuing two victims who are clutching each other, the lifeguard should—

1. Approach one victim from behind **(Fig. 5-24, A)**.
2. Reach under the victim's armpits, and grasp the shoulders. Squeeze the rescue tube between his or her chest and the victim's back. Keep the head to one side of the victim's head **(Fig. 5-24, B)**.
3. Use the rescue tube to support both victims with their mouths out of the water. Talk to the victims to help reassure them **(Fig. 5-24, C)**.
4. Support both victims until other lifeguards arrive or the victims calm down enough to help move to safety.

Fig. 5-24

A

B

C

LIFEGUARDING TIP: The buoyancy of the rescue tube will keep the lifeguard and the victims afloat until other lifeguards arrive. The lifeguard should reassure the victims and continue to support them on the rescue tube. Once they calm down, they may be able to help move to safety.

REMOVAL FROM WATER

Sometimes a victim is unconscious or is too exhausted to climb out of the water, even on a ladder. The decision to remove the victim depends on the victim's condition and size, how soon help is expected to arrive and whether anyone can help. If a victim needs first aid, rescue breathing or CPR, remove him or her from the water immediately and make sure EMS personnel have been summoned.

Two-Person Removal from the Water Using a Backboard

To perform the two-person removal from the water using a backboard at the side of a pool or pier:

1. The primary rescuer brings the victim to the side of the pool and turns him or her to face the deck **(Fig. 5-25, A)**. A second rescuer brings a backboard with the head immobilizer and the straps removed if possible.
2. The second rescuer on deck crosses hands to grab the victim's opposite wrist and pulls the victim up slightly to keep the head above the water and away from the pool edge **(Fig. 5-25, B-C)**. Support the victim's head so that it does not fall forward.
3. The primary rescuer climbs out of the water, removes the rescue tube and gets the backboard.
4. The primary rescuer guides the backboard, foot-end first, straight down into the water next to the victim **(Fig. 5-25, D)**. The second rescuer then turns the victim onto the backboard **(Fig. 5-25, E)**. Each rescuer then quickly grasps one of the victim's wrists and one of the handholds of the backboard **(Fig. 5-25, F)**.

LIFEGUARDING TIP: Each rescuer can place his or her foot that is closest to the backboard against the edge of the board to help keep the backboard in-line and vertical.

5. When the primary rescuer gives the signal, both rescuers pull the backboard and victim onto the deck, resting the underside of the board against the edge of the pool **(Fig. 5-25, G)**. (Remember to lift with the legs

Fig. 5-25

A

B

C

D

E

F

G

H

and not with the back.) Step backward and then lower the backboard onto the deck (**Fig. 5-25, H**).

6. Provide immediate care based on the victim's condition. For example, if the victim is unconscious and not breathing, perform rescue breathing. Continue care until EMS personnel arrive and take over.

Do not use the two-person removal from the water using a backboard on a victim with a suspected head, neck or back injury. However, if the victim is unconscious and not breathing and shows no signs of life, immediately remove the victim from the water. See Chapter 10 for information on removing an unconscious victim with a suspected head, neck or back injury.

Walking Assist

Use the walking assist to help a conscious victim walk out of shallow water. To perform a walking assist, the lifeguard should—

1. Place one of the victim's arms around his or her neck and across the shoulder.
2. Grasp the wrist of the arm that is across the shoulder. The lifeguard then wraps his or her free arm around the victim's back or waist to provide support (**Fig. 5-26**).
3. Hold the victim firmly and assist him or her in walking out of the water.

Fig. 5-26

Beach Drag

On a gradual slope from a waterfront beach or a pool with a zero-depth exit, the beach drag is a safe, easy way to remove someone who is unconscious or who cannot walk from the water. This technique should not be used if the victim is suspected to have a head, neck or back injury. To perform a beach drag, the lifeguard should—

1. Stand behind the victim and grasp him or her under the armpits, supporting the victim's head as much as possible with the forearms (**Fig. 5-27, A**). Let the rescue tube trail behind, being careful not to trip on the tube or line.
2. Walk backward and drag the victim to the shore. Use the legs and not the back. A beach drag can also be performed by two rescuers (**Fig. 5-27, B**).
3. Remove the victim completely from the water, or at least until the head and shoulders are out of the water.

For an unconscious victim or a victim in shock, position the victim on a sloping beach parallel to the shore line and provide appropriate care.

Front-and-Back Carry

Use the front-and-back carry in shallow water with a zero-depth exit if the person is unconscious or cannot get out of the water without help. Do not use this method if the victim is suspected to have a head, neck or back injury. To perform a front-and-back carry, the lifeguard should—

1. Call a second rescuer for assistance.
2. From behind the victim, reach under the armpits. Grasp the victim's right wrist with the right hand and left wrist with the left hand. Cross the victim's arms across his or her chest.
3. The second rescuer stands between the victim's legs, facing away from the victim. This rescuer bends down and grasps the victim under the knees.
4. On signal, both rescuers lift the victim and carry him or her out of the water while walking forward (**Fig. 5-20**).

Fig. 5-27

A

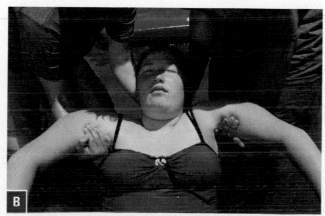

B

Fig. 5-28

ADDITIONAL RESCUE SKILLS AT WATERFRONTS

Using the Rescue Board

At some waterfronts, a rescue board will be used to patrol the outer boundaries of a swimming area. A rescue board also may be kept by the lifeguard stand ready for emergency use. If the facility uses a rescue board, lifeguards should learn how to carry the board effectively, paddle quickly and maneuver it in all conditions. Wind, currents and waves can affect how the board handles. Practice using a rescue board often to maintain skills. Keep the board clean of suntan lotion and body oils, which can make it slippery.

To use a rescue board, the lifeguard should—

1. Hold onto the sides about mid-board when entering the water (**Fig. 5-29, A**).
2. When the water is knee-deep, lay the rescue board on the water and push it forward. Climb on just behind the middle and lie down (**Fig. 5-29, B**).
3. Paddle until reaching the victim. However, to effectively paddle and keep the victim in sight, paddle a few strokes and get into a kneeling position.
4. When patrolling on a rescue board, sit or kneel on it for better visibility.

To approach the victim on a rescue board, the lifeguard should—

1. In calm water, point the bow (front end) of the rescue board toward the victim.
2. From a kneeling position, paddle with both arms moving and recovering at the same time (butterfly arm stroke) (**Fig. 5-30, A**). From the prone position, paddle with either an alternating arm movement (front crawl arm stroke) or with both arms moving and recovering at the same time (**Fig. 5-30, B**).
3. Keep the head up and keep the victim in sight.
4. In rough water or high winds, adjust the angle of approach as needed.

Fig. 5-29

A

B

Fig. 5-30

A

B

Fig. 5-31

To rescue a distressed swimmer or active victim with a rescue board, the lifeguard should—

1. Approach the victim from the side so that the side of the board is next to the victim (Fig. 5-31, A).
2. Grasp the victim's wrist and slide off the rescue board on the opposite side (Fig. 5-31, B).
3. Help the victim reach his or her arms across the rescue board. Encourage the victim to relax and be calm (Fig. 5-31, C).
4. Kick to turn the board toward shore.
5. Hold the rescue board stable and help the victim onto it (Fig. 5-31, D).
6. Tell the victim to lie on his or her stomach facing the bow. Make sure that the bow is not underwater (Fig. 5-31, E).
7. Carefully climb onto the board from the back with the lifeguard's chest between the victim's legs. Be careful not to tip the rescue board, and keep the legs in the water for stability.

8. Paddle the rescue board to shore (Fig. 5-31, F).
9. Slide off the board and help the victim off the board and onto shore with a walking assist.

To rescue someone who is unconscious or cannot hold or climb onto the rescue board, the lifeguard should—

1. Approach the victim from the side (Fig. 5-32, A). Position the board so that the victim is slightly forward of the middle of the board (Fig. 5-32, B).
2. Grasp the victim's hand or wrist and slide off the board on the opposite side, flipping the rescue board over toward the lifeguard (Fig. 5-32, C). Hold the victim's arm across the board with the victim's chest and armpits against the far edge of the board (Fig. 5-32, D).

LIFEGUARDING TIP: Make sure the victim's armpits are along the edges of the board.

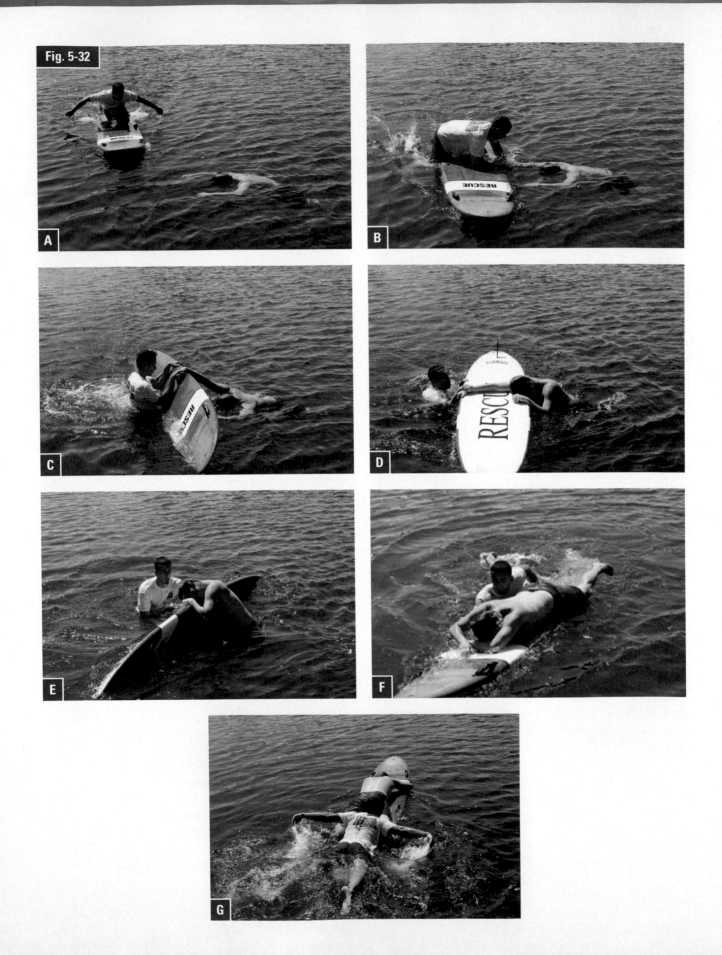

Fig. 5-32

3. Grasp the far edge of the rescue board with the other hand.
4. Kneel on the edge of the rescue board using the lifeguard's own body weight to flip the board toward the lifeguard again, catching the victim's head as the board comes down **(Fig. 5-32, E)**.

LIFEGUARDING TIP: Use caution when flipping the board to ensure that the victim's armpits, and not the upper arms, remain along the edge of the board during the flip.

5. Position the victim lying down lengthwise in the middle of the board with the victim's head toward the bow **(Fig. 5-32, F)**.
6. Kick to turn the board toward shore. Carefully climb onto the board from the back with the chest between the victim's legs. Be careful not to tip the rescue board, and keep the legs in the water for stability.
7. Paddle the rescue board to shore **(Fig. 5-32, G)**.

8. Help the victim to safety with the walking assist, beach drag or other removal technique.

If unable to get the victim onto the rescue board, use the board for flotation and hold the victim face-up to breathe. Call for help and move toward shore.

Using Water Craft for Rescues

If the facility uses water craft for rescues, a lifeguard should practice to become skilled in managing them in all rescue situations and all weather conditions. The facility must train lifeguards in the use of its water craft. To use a water craft for rescues, the lifeguard should follow these basic guidelines:

1. Extend an oar to the victim, and pull him or her to the stern (rear) of the craft **(Fig. 5-33, A)**. It is the most stable area on which to hold.
2. If the victim cannot hold the oar or equipment, move the stern close to the victim. Pull the victim to the stern by the wrist or hand **(Fig. 5-33, B)**.
3. Have the victim hang onto the stern while moving the water craft to safety.

Throw Bags

The throw bag, or rescue bag, is a throwing device often carried by paddlers and swift-water rescue teams. It may also be used at swimming facilities, particularly in rescue water craft. The throw bag is a nylon bag with a foam disk and coiled line inside. The disk gives the bag its shape and keeps it from sinking, but it does not provide flotation for someone in the water. Some bags have attached cord locks that hold the line in the bag. Those should be loosened before use.

To use a throw bag, the lifeguard should hold the loop at the end of the line in one hand and throw the bag underhand with the other. Try to get the attention of the swimmer prior to the toss and throw the bag so the line lands across the victim's shoulder. The line plays out of the bag as it travels through the air. Tell the victim to grab onto the line and hold on. Pull the victim to safety. An overhand toss may be used for more distance or to throw over bushes along the shore. As with

a ring buoy, always consider wind conditions and water current when using a throw bag.

A throw bag is probably the easiest way to throw a line. It has the advantage of always being ready for use. The line is unlikely to tangle during storage or transport. If the first toss misses, then the rope is used as a regular heaving line with weight provided by the bag partially filled with water. It is not easy to quickly restuff a wet line for a second throw.

4. If the victim needs to be brought onto the craft because the water is very cold or the victim is fatigued, help the victim over the stern **(Fig. 5-33, C)**.

When using a motorized water craft, lifeguards should follow these steps:
1. Always approach the victim from downwind and downstream.
2. Shut off the engine about three boat-lengths from the victim, and coast or paddle to the victim.
3. Bring the victim on board before restarting the engine.

SPECIAL SITUATIONS AT WATERFRONTS

Sightings and Cross Bearings

When a drowning victim submerges, the lifeguard should swim or paddle to his or her last seen position. Take a sighting or a cross bearing to keep track of where the victim went underwater.

To take a sighting—
1. Note where the victim went underwater.
2. Line up this place with an object on the far shore, such as a piling, marker buoy, tree, building or anything identifiable. It is best if the first object can be lined up with another object on the shore **(Fig. 5-34)**. This will help maintain a consistent direction when swimming, especially if there is a current.
3. Note the victim's distance from the shore along that line.

Fig. 5-33

A

B

C

Kayaks

Kayaking has become increasingly popular in recent years. Kayaks are used for recreation, touring, competition, sport and as rescue craft at some waterfront facilities. Advances in technology and the growing interest in kayaking have led to a wide variety of kayak designs, shapes and sizes. The kayak is a unique type of craft that requires specialized skills, distinctive from those needed for other small craft. Because of this, if a facility uses rescue kayaks, the facility manager or lifeguard supervisor will provide in-service training in operational skills (boat handling and paddling) and rescue techniques.

Fig. 5-34

With two lifeguards, a cross bearing can be used. To take a cross bearing—

1. Have each lifeguard take a sighting on the spot where the victim was last seen from two different angles (**Fig. 5-35**).
2. Ask other people to help out as spotters from shore.
3. Have both lifeguards swim toward the victim along their sight lines.
4. Have both lifeguards check spotters on shore for directions. Spotters communicate with megaphones, whistles or hand signals.
5. Identify the point where the two sight lines cross. This is the approximate location where the victim went underwater.

Searching Shallow-Water Areas

To search water areas where the bottom cannot be seen:

1. A lifeguard oversees the search.
2. Ask adult volunteers and staff to link their arms and hold hands to form a line in the water. The shortest

person should be in the shallowest water, and the tallest person should be in water no more than chest deep (**Fig. 5-36, A**).

3. Have the whole line slowly move together across the area, starting where the missing person was last seen.
4. As the line moves forward, have searchers sweep their feet across the bottom with each step. If there is a current, walk downstream. A typical search pattern is shown in **Fig. 5-36, B**.
5. Have only trained lifeguards search deeper areas.

Searching Deep-Water Areas
Surface Dives

Surface dives enable lifeguards to submerge to moderate depths to search for a submerged victim. There are two types of surface dives: the feet-first surface dive and the head-first surface dive.

Feet-First Surface Dive During a Line Search. To perform a feet-first surface dive during a line search (a search-

Fig. 5-36

A

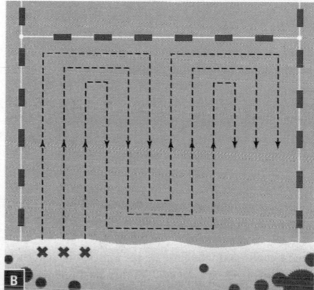

B

Fig. 5-35

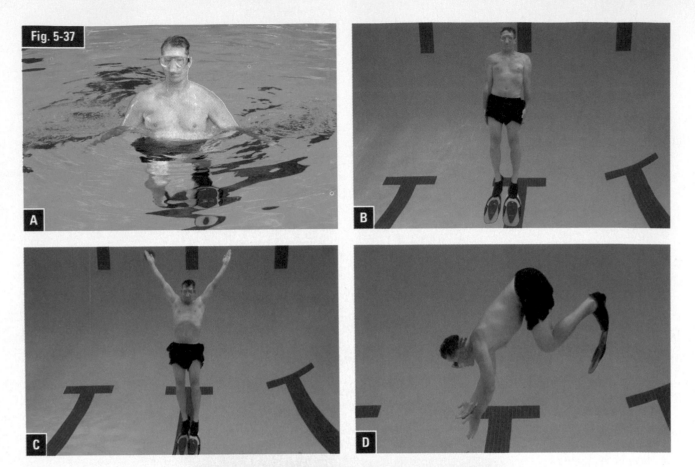

Fig. 5-37

ing pattern that is discussed later), the lifeguard should follow this sequence:

1. When the lead lifeguard gives the command, position the body vertically, then at the same time press down with both hands and kick strongly to raise the body out of the water (**Fig. 5-37, A**).
2. Take a breath with the arms at the sides and let the lifeguard's body sink underwater. Keep the legs straight and together with the toes pointed (**Fig. 5-37, B**).
3. As downward momentum slows, turn the palms outward and sweep the hands and arms upward and overhead (**Fig. 5-37, C**).
4. Repeat this arm movement until deep enough.

5. When deep enough, tuck the body and roll to a horizontal position (**Fig. 5-37, D**).
6. Extend the arms and legs and swim underwater (**Fig. 5-37, E**).

Head-First Surface Dive During a Line Search. To perform a head-first surface dive during a line search, the lifeguard should wait for the lead lifeguard to give the command, then—

1. Gain momentum using a swimming stroke.
2. Take a breath, and sweep the arms backwards to the thighs and turn them palm down (**Fig. 5-38, A**).

Fig. 5-38

A

B

C

D

3. Tuck the chin to the chest and flex at the hip sharply while the arms reach forward and downward toward the bottom **(Fig. 5-38, B).**

4. Lift the legs upward, straight and together so that the weight of the legs helps the descent. The lifeguard's body should be fully extended, streamlined and almost vertical **(Fig. 5-38, C).** The weight of the legs and forward momentum may take the lifeguard deep enough without further movement. But if necessary, the lifeguard should do a simultaneous arm pull with both arms to go deeper, then level out and swim forward underwater **(Fig. 5-38, D).**

LIFEGUARDING TIP: If the depth of the water is unknown or the water is murky, keep one arm extended over the head toward the bottom or use a feet-first surface dive.

Deep-Water Line Search

The deep-water line search is used in water greater than chest deep.

- Wearing masks and fins, several lifeguards form a straight line an arm's length from each other **(Fig. 5-39).**

- One lifeguard is the safety lookout above the water level on a pier, raft or water craft with rescue equipment in case a searcher gets in trouble or the missing person is found.

- On command from the lead lifeguard, all lifeguards do the same type surface dive (feet-first or head-first) to the bottom and swim forward a predetermined number of strokes—usually three. If the water is murky, searchers check the bottom by sweeping their hands back and forth in front of them, making sure to cover

Fig. 5-39

Fig. 5-40

the entire area. To keep the water from becoming cloudier, try to avoid disturbing silt and dirt on the bottom. Do not miss any areas on the bottom when diving and resurfacing.

- Return to the surface as straight up as possible.
- The lead lifeguard accounts for all searchers, reforms the line at the position of the person farthest back and backs up the line one body length. On command, the team dives again.
- Repeat this procedure until the victim is found or the entire area has been searched, by the line moving in one direction (**Fig. 5-40**).
- Repeat the line pattern at a 90-degree angle to the first search pattern.
- If the missing person is not found, expand the search to nearby areas. Consider whether currents may have moved the victim.
- Continue to search until the person is found or emergency personnel take over.
- If a lifeguard finds the victim, the lifeguard should bring the victim up by grasping the victim under the armpit and returning to the surface. Swim the victim to safety, keeping the victim on his or her back, with his or her face out of the water.

Mask and Fins

A mask and fins should be used in an underwater search for a missing person. Use well-maintained equipment that is sized properly and fits well.

Mask

A mask is made up of soft, flexible material, with non-tinted, tempered safety glass and a head strap that is easily adjusted. A mask should be chosen that allows blocking or squeezing of the nose to equalize pressure.

Fig. 5-41

Some masks have additional features such as molded nosepieces or purge valves (**Fig. 5-41**). Regardless of the design, proper fit is the primary concern.

To check that a mask fits properly—

1. Place the mask against the face without using the strap. Keep hair out of the way.
2. Inhale slightly through the nose to create a slight suction inside the mask. This suction should keep the mask in place without being held. A good fit keeps water from leaking into the mask.
3. Adjust the strap so that the mask is comfortable. If it is too tight or too loose, the mask may not seal properly.
4. Try the mask in the water. If it leaks a little, tighten the strap. If it continues to leak, check it again with suction. A different size may be needed.
5. To prevent the mask from fogging, rub saliva on the inside of the face plate, and rinse the mask before putting it on. Commercial defoggers also can be used.

Equalizing Pressure Underwater

When descending into deep water, the pressure may cause pain or injury if it is not equalized. Usually, the pressure is felt in the ears. It is important to equalize the pressure early and often. If unable to equalize the pressure because of a head cold or sinus problem, a rescuer should return to the surface rather than risk an injury. To relieve ear pressure—

1. Place the thumb and finger on the nose or on the nosepiece of a mask, if using a mask.
2. Pinch the nose and keep the mouth shut. Try to exhale gently through the nose until the pressure is relieved.
3. Repeat this as needed to relieve more ear pressure. If the ears hurt, do not attempt to go deeper until successfully equalizing the pressure.
4. If using a mask when descending, the mask squeezes the face because of the increased pressure. To relieve the squeezing, exhale a small amount of air through the nose into the mask.

Fins

Fins provide more speed and allow users to cover greater distances with less effort (**Fig. 5-42**). A good fit is important for efficient movement. Fins come with different sized blades. Larger fins are faster but require more leg strength. Fins should match the user's ability.

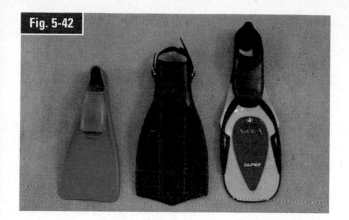

Fig. 5-42

Wetting the feet and fins first makes it easier to put them on. Do not pull the fins on by the heels or straps of the fins. This can cause a break or tear. Push the foot into the fin, and then slide the heel or strap up over the heel.

Use a modified flutter kick that has a kicking action that is deeper and slower, with a little more knee bend, than the usual flutter kick. It is easier to swim underwater using only the legs. Keep the arms relaxed at the side. In murky water, hold the arms out in front to protect the head.

Entering the Water with Mask and Fins

It is important for lifeguards to learn how to enter the water safely while wearing the equipment. Lifeguards should enter using a slide-in entry or with a stride jump when entering from a height of less than 3 feet. Never enter head-first wearing a mask and fins.

To do a stride jump with mask and fins, the lifeguard should—

1. Put one hand over the mask to hold it in place, keeping the elbow close to the chest.
2. Make sure no swimmers or other objects are below.
3. Step out with a long stride over the water, but do not lean forward (**Fig. 5-43**).
4. While entering the water, the fins slow the downward motion.
5. Swim keeping the arms at the side and face in the water.

Fig. 5-43

Cold Water

A serious concern at many waterfront facilities is someone suddenly entering into cold water. Cold water is 70° F (21.° C) or colder. As a general rule, if the water feels cold, consider it cold. Sudden entry into cold water usually occurs if a person accidentally falls in or intentionally enters the water without proper protection. A person may be swimming underwater and enters a thermocline, a sharp change in temperature from one layer of water to another. In any case, cold water can have a serious effect on the victim and on the lifeguard making the rescue.

Sudden entry into cold water may cause the following reactions:

- A gasp reflex, a sudden involuntary attempt to "catch one's breath," may cause the victim to inhale water into the lungs if the face is underwater.
- If the person's face is not underwater, he or she may begin to hyperventilate. This can cause unconsciousness and lead to the risk of breathing in water.
- An increased heart rate and blood pressure can cause cardiac arrest.
- A victim who remains in the cold water may develop hypothermia, which can cause unconsciousness.

In some ways, cold water can be beneficial and may increase a person's chances of survival:

- In cold water, body temperature begins to drop almost as soon as the person enters the water. Swallowing water accelerates this cooling.
- As the core temperature drops, body functions slow almost to a standstill, and the person requires very little oxygen.
- Any oxygen in the blood is diverted to the brain and heart to maintain minimal functioning of these vital organs.

Because of this, some victims have been successfully resuscitated after being submerged in cold water for an extended period.

Rescues in Cold Water

It is important to locate and remove a victim from cold water as quickly as possible. Because a lifeguard also will be affected by cold water, he or she should try to make the rescue without entering the water, if possible. A lifeguard can extend a rescue tube to reach the victim, but the victim might not be able to maintain a hold on the equipment due to the cold.

If a lifeguard must enter the water, he or she should take a rescue tube attached to a towline. A line-and-reel, which is a heavy piece of rope or cord attached to rescue equipment, may be used to tow the lifeguard and the victim to safety. The lifeguard should wear body protection, such as a wetsuit, gloves, booties and hood, if possible.

When the victim is out of the water, the lifeguard should assess his or her condition. Victims who have been submerged in cold water may still be alive even with—

- A decreased or undetectable pulse rate.
- No detectable breathing.
- Bluish skin that is cold to the touch.
- Muscle rigidity.

The lifeguard should begin rescue breathing or cardiopulmonary resuscitation (CPR), as needed, and provide first aid for hypothermia as soon as possible. If not done so already, summon EMS personnel immediately. The sooner the victim receives advanced medical care, the better the chances are for survival.

PUTTING IT ALL TOGETHER

Although rescuing a victim safely is the goal, lifeguards should never jeopardize their own safety when making a rescue. Lifeguards must adapt some skills for moving water and tight spaces of various attractions. At waterfronts, lifeguards should adapt their rescue methods for the specific conditions present. They should always use rescue equipment, such as a rescue tube, to keep themselves and the drowning victim safe. Once the victim has been brought to safety, remove the victim from the water and provide care as needed. Lifeguards should frequently practice rescue skills using equipment specific to the environment in which they will be guarding.

Chapter 6

Before Providing Care and Victim Assessment

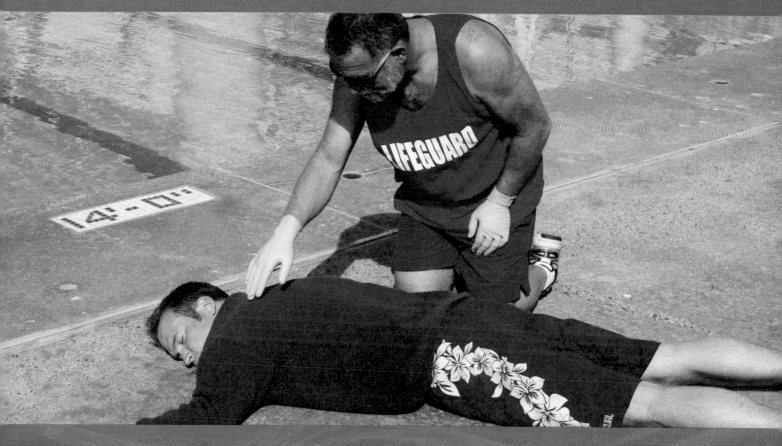

A lifeguard is a professional rescuer—a key link of the emergency medical services (EMS) system. While on duty, a lifeguard is legally obligated, within the bounds of training, to respond and provide care in an emergency

As a professional rescuer, a lifeguard must be able to—

- Support personal, fellow team member and bystander safety.
- Respond in an emergency.
- Take precautions to prevent disease transmission.
- Gain safe access to the victim.
- Get consent before providing care.
- Determine whether any life-threatening conditions are present.
- Provide needed care to the victim.
- Summon more help when needed.
- Use techniques learned in training.

BEFORE PROVIDING CARE

To help prevent disease transmission, a lifeguard needs to understand how infections occur, how diseases are spread from one person to another and what precautions can be taken. Infectious diseases are spread from infected people and from animals, insects or objects that have been in contact with them. Lifeguards must protect themselves and others from infectious diseases.

BLOODBORNE PATHOGENS

Bloodborne pathogens are bacteria and viruses present in blood and body fluids that can cause disease in humans. Bacteria and viruses are the most common forms of pathogens. They are found almost everywhere in our environment. Bacteria can live outside the body and commonly do not depend on other organisms for life. If a person is infected by bacteria, antibiotics and other medications often are used to treat the infection. Viruses depend on other organisms to live. Once viruses are in the body, they are difficult to kill. That is why prevention is so critical. The bloodborne pathogens of primary concern to a professional rescuer are the hepatitis B virus, hepatitis C virus and human immunodeficiency virus (HIV) **(Table 6-1)**.

Hepatitis B
Hepatitis B is a liver infection caused by the hepatitis B virus. Hepatitis B may be severe or even fatal, and it can be in the body for up to 6 months before symptoms ap-

pear. These may include flu-like symptoms such as fatigue, abdominal pain, loss of appetite, nausea, vomiting and joint pain. Later-stage symptoms include jaundice (a yellowing of the skin and eyes).

Medications are available to treat chronic hepatitis B infection, but they do not work for everyone. The most effective means of prevention is the hepatitis B vaccine. This vaccine, which is given in a series of three doses, provides immunity to the disease. Scientific data show that hepatitis B vaccines are very safe for adults, children and infants. There is no confirmed evidence indicating that hepatitis B vaccine causes chronic illnesses.

The hepatitis B vaccination series must be made available to all employees, including lifeguards, who have occupational exposure. It must be made available within 10 working days of initial assignment, after appropriate training has been completed. However, employees may decide not to have the vaccination. If an employee decides not to be vaccinated, he or she must sign a form affirming this decision.

Hepatitis C
Hepatitis C is a liver disease caused by the hepatitis C virus. It is the most common chronic bloodborne infection in the United States. Its symptoms are similar to hepatitis B infection, including fatigue, abdominal pain, loss of appetite, nausea, vomiting and jaundice. There is no vaccine against hepatitis C and no treatment available to prevent infection after exposure. Hepatitis C is the leading cause of liver transplants. For these reasons, hepatitis C is more serious than hepatitis B.

TABLE 6-1	HOW BLOODBORNE PATHOGENS ARE TRANSMITTED		
Disease	**Signs and Symptoms**	**Mode of Transmission**	**Infective Material**
Hepatitis B	Jaundice, fatigue, abdominal pain, loss of appetite, nausea, vomiting, joint pain	Direct and indirect contact	Blood, semen
Hepatitis C	Jaundice, fatigue, dark urine, abdominal pain, loss of appetite, nausea	Direct and indirect contact	Blood, semen
HIV	May or may not be signs and symptoms in early stage. Late-contact-stage symptoms may include fever, fatigue, diarrhea, skin rashes, night sweats, loss of appetite, swollen lymph glands, significant weight loss, white spots in the mouth or vaginal discharge (signs of yeast infection) and memory or movement problems.	Direct and possibly indirect contact	Blood, semen, vaginal fluid, breast milk

HIV

The *human immunodeficiency virus (HIV)* is the virus that causes acquired immunodeficiency syndrome (AIDS). HIV attacks white blood cells and destroys the body's ability to fight infection. This weakens the body's immune system. The infections that strike people whose immune systems are weakened by HIV are called *opportunistic infections*. Some opportunistic infections include severe pneumonia, tuberculosis, Kaposi's sarcoma and other unusual cancers.

People infected with HIV may not feel or look sick. A blood test, however, can detect the HIV antibody. When an infected person has a significant drop in a certain type of white blood cells or shows signs of having certain infections or cancers, he or she may be diagnosed as having AIDS. These infections can cause fever, fatigue, diarrhea, skin rashes, night sweats, loss of appetite, swollen lymph glands and significant weight loss. In the advanced stages, AIDS is a very serious condition. People with AIDS eventually develop life-threatening infections and can die from these infections. Currently, there is no vaccine against HIV.

There are many other illnesses, viruses and infections to which a responder may be exposed. Keep immunizations current, have regular physical check-ups and be knowledgeable about other pathogens. For more information on the illnesses listed above and other diseases and illnesses of concern, contact the Centers for Disease Control and Prevention (CDC) at (800) 342-2437 or visit CDC's Web site at *www.cdc.gov.*

HOW PATHOGENS SPREAD

Exposures to blood and other body fluids occur across a wide variety of occupations. Lifeguards, health-care workers, emergency response personnel, public safety personnel and other workers can be exposed to blood through injuries from needles and other sharps devices, as well as by direct and indirect contact with skin and mucous membranes. For any disease to be spread, including bloodborne diseases, all four of the following conditions must be met:

- A pathogen is present.
- A sufficient quantity of the pathogen is present to cause disease.
- A person is susceptible to the pathogen.
- The pathogen passes through the correct entry site (e.g., eyes, mouth and other mucous membranes; non-intact skin or skin pierced by needlesticks, human bites, cuts, abrasions and other means).

To understand how infections occur, think of these four conditions as pieces of a puzzle **(Fig. 6-1)**. All of the

Disease-Causing Agents

Pathogen	Diseases and Conditions They Cause
Viruses	Hepatitis, measles, mumps, chicken pox, meningitis, rubella, influenza, warts, colds, herpes, HIV (the virus that causes AIDS), genital warts, smallpox, avian flu
Bacteria	Tetanus, meningitis, scarlet fever, strep throat, tuberculosis, gonorrhea, syphilis, chlamydia, toxic shock syndrome, Legionnaires' disease, diphtheria, food poisoning, Lyme disease, anthrax
Fungi	Athlete's foot, ringworm, histoplasmosis
Protozoa	Malaria, dysentery, cyclospora, giardiasis
Rickettsia	Typhus, Rocky Mountain spotted fever
Parasitic Worms	Abdominal pain, anemia, lymphatic vessel blockage, lowered antibody response, respiratory and circulatory complications
Prions	Creutzfeldt-Jakob disease (CJD) or bovine spongiform encephalopathy (mad cow disease), kuru
Yeasts	Candidiasis

For additional information on these or other diseases, visit the CDC Web site at *www.cdc.gov.*

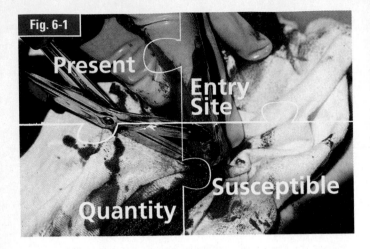

Fig. 6-1

Present

Entry Site

Susceptible

Quantity

Fig. 6-3

pieces must be in place for the picture to be complete. If any one of these conditions is missing, an infection cannot occur.

Bloodborne pathogens, such as hepatitis B, hepatitis C and HIV, are spread primarily through direct or indirect contact with infected blood or other body fluids. While these diseases can be spread by sexual contact through infected body fluids, such as vaginal secretions and semen, these body fluids are not usually involved in occupational transmission. Hepatitis B, hepatitis C and HIV are not spread by food or water or by casual contact such as hugging or shaking hands. The highest risk of occupational transmission is unprotected direct or indirect contact with infected blood.

Direct Contact

Direct contact transmission occurs when infected blood or body fluids from one person enters another person's body at a correct entry site. For example, direct contact transmission can occur through infected blood splashing in the eye or from directly touching the body fluids of an infected person and that infected blood or other body fluid enters the body through a correct entry site **(Fig. 6-2).**

Indirect Contact

Some bloodborne pathogens are also transmitted by indirect contact **(Fig. 6-3)**. *Indirect contact transmission* can occur when a person touches an object that contains the blood or other body fluid of an infected person and that infected blood or other body fluid enters the body through a correct entry site. These objects include soiled dressings, equipment and work surfaces that are contaminated with an infected person's blood or other body fluids. For example, indirect contact can occur when a person picks up blood-soaked bandages with a bare hand and the pathogens enter through a break in the skin on the hand.

Droplet and Vector-Borne Transmission

Other pathogens, such as the flu virus, can enter the body through *droplet transmission.* This occurs when a person inhales droplets from an infected person's cough or sneeze **(Fig. 6-4)**. *Vector-borne transmission* of diseases, such as malaria and West Nile virus, occurs when the body's skin is penetrated by an infectious

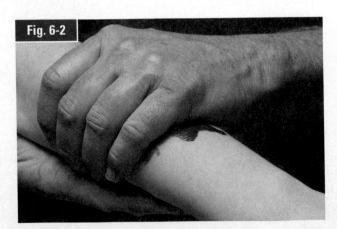

Fig. 6-2

Fig. 6-4

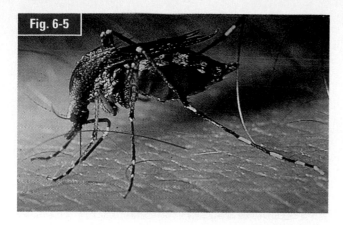

Fig. 6-5

tually no risk for infection by the hepatitis B virus. For an unvaccinated person, the risk for infection from hepatitis B-infected blood from a needlestick or cut exposure can be as high as 30 percent, depending on several factors. In contrast, the risk for infection from hepatitis C-infected blood after a needlestick or cut exposure is about 2 percent and the risk of infection from HIV-infected blood after a needlestick or cut exposure is less than 1 percent.

PREVENTING THE SPREAD OF BLOODBORNE PATHOGENS

OSHA Regulations
The federal Occupational Safety and Health Administration (OSHA) has issued regulations about on-the-job exposure to bloodborne pathogens. OSHA determined that employees are at risk when they are exposed to blood or other body fluids. OSHA therefore requires employers to reduce or remove hazards from the workplace that may place employees in contact with infectious materials.

OSHA regulations and guidelines apply to employees who may come into contact with blood or other body sub-

source, such as an animal or insect bite or sting **(Fig. 6-5)**.

Risk of Transmission
Hepatitis B, hepatitis C and HIV share a common mode of transmission—direct or indirect contact with infected blood or body fluids—but they differ in the risk of transmission. Workers who have received the hepatitis B vaccine and have developed immunity to the virus are at vir-

Employers' Responsibilities

OSHA's regulations on bloodborne pathogens have placed specific responsibilities on employers for protection of employees that include—
- Identifying positions or tasks covered by the standard.
- Creating an exposure control plan to minimize the possibility of exposure and making the plan easily accessible to employees.
- Developing and putting into action a written schedule for cleaning and decontaminating the workplace.
- Creating a system for easy identification of soiled material and its proper disposal.
- Developing a system of annual training for all covered employees.
- Offering the opportunity for employees to get the hepatitis B vaccination at no cost to them.
- Establishing clear procedures to follow for reporting an exposure.

- Creating a system of recordkeeping.
- In workplaces where there is potential exposure to injuries from contaminated sharps, soliciting input from non-managerial employees with potential exposure regarding the identification, evaluation and selection of effective engineering and work-practice controls.
- If a needlestick injury occurs, recording the appropriate information in the sharps injury log, including—
  - Type and brand of device involved in the incident.
  - Location of the incident.
  - Description of the incident.
- Maintaining a sharps injury log in such a way that protects the privacy of employees.
- Ensuring confidentiality of employees' medical records and exposure incidents.

stances that could cause an infection. These regulations apply to lifeguards, as professional rescuers, because lifeguards are expected to provide emergency care as part of their job. OSHA has revised its regulations to include the requirements of the federal Needlestick Safety and Prevention Act. These guidelines can help lifeguards and their employer meet the OSHA bloodborne pathogens standard to prevent transmission of serious diseases. For more information about the OSHA Bloodborne Pathogens Standard 29 CFR 1910.1030, visit OSHA's Web site at *www.osha.gov.*

Exposure Control Plan

OSHA regulations require employers to have an exposure control plan. This is a written program outlining the protective measures that employers will take to eliminate or minimize employee exposure incidents. The exposure control plan should include exposure determination, methods for implementing other parts of the OSHA standard (e.g., ways of meeting the requirements and record-keeping) and procedures for evaluating details of an exposure incident. The exposure control plan guidelines should be made available to lifeguards and should specifically explain what they need to do to prevent the spread of infectious diseases.

Universal, Standard and BSI Precautions

Universal precautions are OSHA-required practices of infection control to protect employees from exposure to blood and other potentially infectious materials. These precautions require that all human blood and certain substances be treated as if known to be infectious for hepatitis B, hepatitis C, HIV or other bloodborne pathogens. Other approaches to infection control are called *standard precautions* and *body substance isolation (BSI) precautions*. These precautions mean that the lifeguard should consider all body fluids and substances as infectious and precautions can be taken through the use of personal protective equipment, good hand hygiene, engineering controls, work practice controls, proper equipment cleaning and spill clean-up procedures.

Personal Protective Equipment

Personal protective equipment that is appropriate for an individual's job duties should be available at any workplace and should be identified in the exposure control plan. Personal protective equipment includes all specialized clothing, equipment and supplies that prevent direct contact with infected materials. These include, but are not limited to, breathing barriers **(Fig. 6-6)**, nonlatex disposable (single-use) gloves, gowns, masks, shields and protective eyewear **(Table 6-2)**.

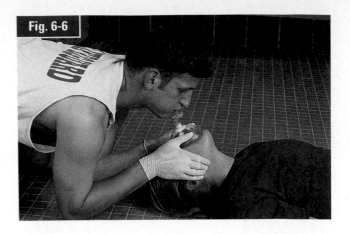

Fig. 6-6

Use nonlatex disposable gloves made of material such as nitrile or vinyl. Wear disposable gloves when providing care to injured or ill people, particularly if there is a risk of coming into contact with blood or body fluids. To remove gloves properly—

1. Partially remove the first glove.
   - Pinch the glove at the wrist, being careful to touch only the glove's outside surface **(Fig. 6-7, A)**.
   - Pull the glove inside-out toward the fingertips without completely removing it **(Fig. 6-7, B)**.
   - The glove is now partly inside out.
2. Remove the second glove.
   - With a partially gloved hand, pinch the outside surface of the second glove.
   - Pull the second glove toward the fingertips until it is inside out, and then remove it completely **(Fig. 6-7, C)**.
3. Finish removing both gloves **(Fig. 6-7, D)**.
   - Grasp both gloves with the free hand.
   - Touching only the clean interior surface of the partially removed glove, with the free hand pull the glove off completely.
4. After removing both gloves—
   - Discard the gloves in an appropriate container.
   - Wash hands thoroughly.

Breathing barriers include resuscitation masks, face shields and bag-valve-mask resuscitators (BVMs). Breathing barriers help protect rescuers against disease transmission when giving rescue breaths to a victim.

To prevent infection, follow these guidelines:
- Avoid contact with blood and other body fluids.
- Use breathing barriers, such as resuscitation masks, face shields and BVMs, when giving rescue breaths to a victim.
- Wear disposable gloves whenever providing care, particularly if there is a risk of coming into contact with blood or body fluids.

TABLE 6-2 RECOMMENDED PROTECTIVE EQUIPMENT AGAINST HEPATITIS B, HEPATITIS C AND HIV TRANSMISSION IN PREHOSPITAL SETTINGS

Task or Activity	Disposable Gloves	Gown	Mask	Protective Eyewear
Bleeding control with spurting blood	Yes	Yes	Yes	Yes
Bleeding control with minimal bleeding	Yes	No	No	No
Emergency childbirth	Yes	Yes	Yes	Yes
Oral/nasal suctioning; manually clearing airway	Yes	No	No, unless splashing is likely	No, unless splashing is likely
Handling and cleaning contaminated equipment and clothing	Yes	No, unless soiling is likely	No	No

U.S. Department of Health and Human Services, Public Health Services (1989, February). *A curriculum guide for public safety and emergency response workers: Prevention of transmission of acquired immunodeficiency virus and hepatitis B virus.* Atlanta, Georgia: U.S. Department of Health and Human Services, Centers for Disease Control and Prevention, with modifications from Nixon, Robert G. (2000). *Communicable diseases and infection control for EMS.* Upper Saddle River, New Jersey: Prentice Hall.

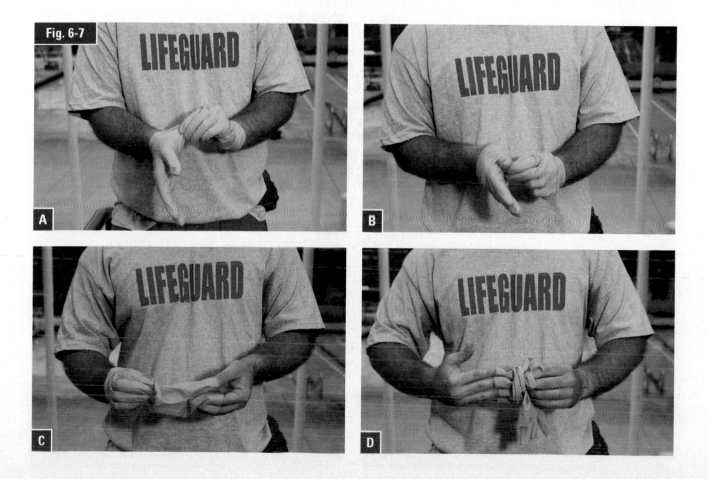

Fig. 6-7

- Use gloves that are appropriate to the task and provide an adequate barrier.
- Remove jewelry, including rings, before wearing disposable gloves.
- Keep any cuts, scrapes or sores covered before putting on protective clothing.
- Do not use disposable gloves that are discolored, torn or punctured.
- Do not clean or reuse disposable gloves.
- Avoid handling items such as pens, combs or radios when wearing soiled gloves.
- Change gloves before providing care to a different victim.
- In addition to gloves, wear protective coverings, such as a mask, eyewear and gown, whenever there is a likelihood of coming in contact with blood or other body fluids that may splash.
- Do not wear gloves and other personal protective equipment away from the workplace.
- Remove disposable gloves without contacting the soiled part of the gloves and dispose of them in a proper container.

Hand Hygiene

Lifeguards should wash their hands before providing care, if possible, so that they do not pass pathogens to the victim. Wash hands frequently and every time after providing care (**Fig. 6-8**). Hand washing is an effective way to help prevent illness. By washing hands often, disease-causing germs that have been picked up from other people, animals or contaminated surfaces are washed away. In addition, jewelry, including rings, should not be worn where the potential for risk of exposure exists.

To ensure correct hand washing, follow these steps:
1. Wet hands with warm water.
2. Apply liquid soap to hands.
3. Rub hands vigorously for at least 15 seconds, covering all surfaces of the hands and fingers. Use soap and warm running water. Scrub nails by rubbing them against the palms.
4. Rinse hands with water.
5. Dry hands thoroughly with a paper towel.
6. Turn off the faucet using the paper towel.

Alcohol-based hand sanitizers and lotions allow hands to be cleansed when soap and water are not readily available. In addition to washing hands frequently, keep fingernails less than $\frac{1}{4}$-inch long and avoid wearing artificial nails.

Engineering Controls and Work Practice Controls

Engineering controls are control measures that isolate or remove a hazard from the workplace. In other words, engineering controls are **the things used** in the workplace to help reduce the risk of an exposure incident. Examples of engineering controls include—
- Sharps disposal containers (**Fig. 6-9**).
- Self-sheathing needles.
- Safer medical devices, such as sharps with engineered injury protections or needleless systems.
- Biohazard bags and labels.
- Personal protective equipment.

Work practice controls reduce the likelihood of exposure by changing the way a task is carried out. These are **the things done** to help reduce the risk of an exposure incident. Examples of work practice controls include—
- Placing sharp items (e.g., needles, scalpel blades) in puncture-resistant, leak-proof and labeled containers and having the containers at the point of use.
- Avoiding splashing, spraying and splattering droplets of blood or other potentially infectious materials when performing all procedures.
- Removing and disposing of soiled protective clothing as soon as possible.

Fig. 6-8

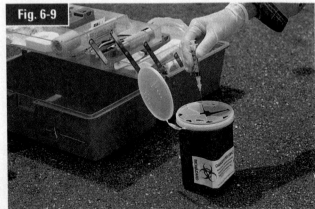
Fig. 6-9

- Cleaning and disinfecting all equipment and work surfaces possibly soiled by blood or other body fluids.
- Washing hands thoroughly with soap and warm water immediately after providing care, using a utility or restroom sink (not one in a food preparation area).
- Not eating, drinking, smoking, applying cosmetics or lip balm, handling contact lenses or touching the eyes, mouth or nose when in an area where exposure to infectious materials is possible.
- Using alcohol-based sanitizers or lotions where handwashing facilities are not available.

Be aware of any areas, equipment or containers that may be contaminated. Biohazard warning labels are required on any container holding contaminated materials, such as used gloves, bandages or trauma dressings. Signs should be posted at entrances to work areas where infectious materials may be present.

Equipment Cleaning and Spill Clean-Up

After providing care, always clean and disinfect the equipment and surfaces that were used **(Fig. 6-10)**. Handle all soiled equipment, supplies and other materials with care until they are properly cleaned and disinfected. Place all used disposable items in labeled containers. Place all soiled clothing in marked plastic bags for disposal or washing **(Fig. 6-11)**. Take the following steps to clean up spills:

- Wear disposable gloves and other personal protective equipment when cleaning up spills.
- Clean up spills immediately or as soon as possible after the spill occurs.

- If the spill is mixed with sharp objects, such as broken glass and needles, do not pick these up with the hands. Use tongs, a broom and dustpan or two pieces of cardboard.

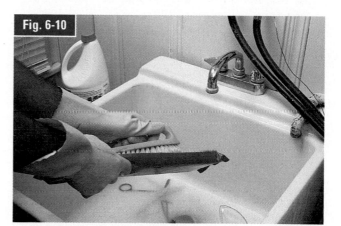

Fig. 6-10

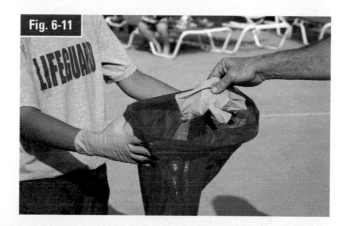

Fig. 6-11

The Needlestick Safety and Prevention Act

Blood and other potentially infectious materials have long been recognized as potential threats to the health of employees who are exposed to these materials through penetration of the skin. Injuries from contaminated needles and other sharps have been associated with an increased risk of disease from more than 20 infectious agents. The most serious pathogens are hepatitis B, hepatitis C and HIV. Needlesticks and other sharps injuries resulting in exposure to blood or other potentially infectious materials are a concern because they happen frequently and can have serious health effects.

In 2001, in response to the federal Needlestick Safety and Prevention Act, OSHA revised the Bloodborne Pathogens Standard 29 CFR 1910.1030. The revised standard clarifies the need for employers to select safer needle devices and to involve employees in identifying and choosing these devices. The updated standard also requires employers to maintain a log of injuries from contaminated sharps.

For information on the Needlestick Safety and Prevention Act, visit OSHA's Web site at *www.osha.gov.*

- Dispose of the absorbent material used to collect the spill in a labeled biohazard container.
- Flood the area with a fresh disinfectant solution of approximately 1½ cups of liquid chlorine bleach to 1 gallon of water (1 part bleach per 10 parts water), and allow it to stand for at least 10 minutes.
- Use appropriate material to absorb the solution, and dispose of it in a labeled biohazard container.
- Scrub soiled boots, leather shoes and other leather goods, such as belts, with soap, a brush and hot water. If a uniform is worn to work, wash and dry it according to the manufacturer's instructions.

IF EXPOSED TO INFECTIOUS MATERIAL

Exposure incidents involve contact with blood or other potentially infectious materials through a needlestick, broken or scraped skin or the mucous membranes of the eyes, mouth or nose. Take these steps immediately:

- Wash needlestick injuries, cuts and exposed skin with soap and warm running water.
- Flush splashes of blood or other potentially infectious materials to the mouth and nose with water.
- Irrigate eyes with clean water, saline or sterile irrigants.

Take the following steps after any exposure incident:

- Report the exposure incident, or have someone else report the incident, to a supervisor immediately. Immediately reporting an exposure incident can be critical to the success of post-exposure treatment.
- Write down what happened.
- Get immediate medical attention. Follow the steps in the exposure control plan for confidential medical evaluation, and follow up with a health-care professional.

GENERAL PROCEDURES FOR INJURY OR SUDDEN ILLNESS ON LAND

When someone suddenly becomes injured or ill, activate the facility's emergency action plan (EAP). Use appropriate first aid equipment and supplies and follow these general procedures:

1. **Size up the scene.**
   - Determine if the scene is safe for lifeguards, other rescuers, the victim(s) and any bystanders.
     - Look for dangers, such as traffic, unstable structures, downed power lines, swift-moving water, violence, explosions or toxic gas exposure.
   - Put on the appropriate personal protective equipment.

Call First or Care First?

If alone when responding to someone who is ill, decide whether to *Call First* or *Care First*.

Call First means to summon emergency medical services (EMS) personnel before providing care. Always *Call First* if a cardiac emergency is suspected—a situation in which time is critical. Examples include sudden cardiac arrest or a witnessed sudden collapse of a child. Next, obtain an automated external defibrillator (AED), if available, and then return to the victim to use the AED or begin cardiopulmonary resuscitation (CPR) if an AED is not available. Also, *Call First* for—

- An unconscious adult (12 years or older).
- An unconscious child or infant known to be at high risk for heart problems.

Care First situations are likely to be related to breathing emergencies rather than cardiac emergencies. In these situations, provide support for airway, breathing and circulation (ABCs) through rescue breaths and chest compressions, as appropriate. *Care First*, that is, provide 2 minutes of care, and then summon EMS personnel for—

- An unconscious infant or child (younger than 12 years old).
- Any victim of a drowning or nonfatal submersion.
- Any victim who has suffered cardiac arrest associated with trauma.
- Any victim who has taken a drug overdose.

- Determine the mechanism of injury or the nature of the illness. Try to find out what happened and what caused the injury or illness.
- Determine the number of victims.
- Determine what additional help may be needed.

2. **Perform an initial assessment**. This is done to identify any life-threatening conditions.
   - Check the victim for consciousness and obtain consent if the victim is conscious.
   - Check for signs of life (movement and breathing).
   - Check for a pulse.
   - Check for severe bleeding.

3. **Summon emergency medical services (EMS) personnel**. Summon EMS personnel by calling 9-1-1 or the local emergency number if any of the following conditions are found:
   - Unconsciousness or disorientation
   - Breathing problems (difficulty breathing or no breathing)
   - Chest discomfort, pain or pressure lasting more than 3 to 5 minutes or that goes away and comes back
   - No pulse
   - Severe bleeding
   - Persistent abdominal pain or pressure
   - Suspected head, neck or back injuries
   - Severe allergic reactions
   - Stroke (weakness on one side of the face, weakness or numbness in one arm, slurred speech or trouble getting words out)
   - Seizures that occur in the water
   - Seizures that last more than 5 minutes or cause injury
   - Repeated seizures (one after another)
   - Seizures involving a victim who is pregnant, diabetic or who does not regain consciousness
   - Vomiting blood or passing blood
   - Severe (critical) burns
   - Suspected broken bones
   - Suspected poisoning
   - Sudden severe headache

4. **Perform a secondary assessment**. Perform a secondary assessment to identify additional conditions. A lifeguard should perform a secondary assessment only if he or she is sure that the victim does not have any life-threatening conditions. The secondary assessment is a method of gathering additional information about injuries or conditions that may need care. These injuries or conditions may not be life threatening, but could become so if not cared for. See Chapter 9 for more information on performing a secondary assessment.

Obtaining Consent

Before providing care to a conscious victim, obtain his or her consent. If the victim is a minor, get consent from a parent or guardian. To get consent, lifeguards should—
- State their name.
- Tell the victim they are trained to help.
- Ask the victim if they may help.
- Explain what may be wrong.
- Explain what they plan to do.

When the victim gives consent, provide care. If the victim does not give consent, do not provide care, but summon EMS personnel. A victim who is unconscious, confused or seriously ill may not be able to give consent. Consent is then implied. Implied consent also applies to a minor whose parents or guardians are not present. This means that the victim would agree to the care if he or she could, so the lifeguard should provide care. Refer to Chapter 1, page 6 for more information on legal considerations.

LIFEGUARDING TIP: Remember to document any refusal of care by the victim(s). If a witness is available, have him or her listen to, and document in writing, any refusal of care.

Initial Assessment

During the initial assessment, check the victim for consciousness, signs of life (movement and breathing), a pulse and severe bleeding. Then provide care based on the conditions found. To conduct an initial assessment—

1. Tap the victim's shoulder and shout, "Are you okay?" **(Fig. 6-12, A)**.
   - For an infant, gently tap the shoulder or flick the foot **(Fig. 6-12, B)**.
2. If no response, summon EMS personnel.
3. Check for signs of life (movement and normal breathing) **(Fig. 6-12, C)**.
   - If the victim is face-down, roll the victim onto his or her back, while supporting the head and neck **(Fig. 6-12, D)**.
   - Tilt the head back and lift the chin to open the airway.
     - Do not tilt a child or infant's head back as far as an adult's. Tilt an infant's head to the neutral position and a child's head slightly past the neutral position.
     - If a head, neck or back injury is suspected, try the jaw-thrust maneuver to open the airway (see p. 109-110).

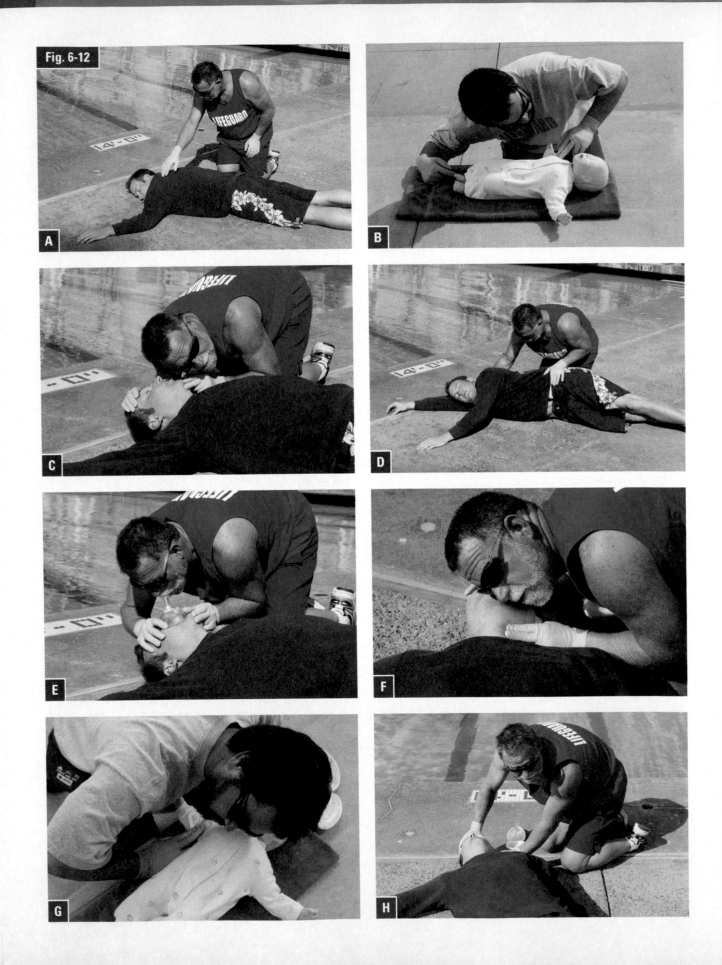

Fig. 6-12

- Look for movement and look, listen and feel for normal breathing for no more than 10 seconds.
  - Irregular, gasping or shallow breathing is not normal breathing.
4. If there is no movement or breathing, give 2 rescue breaths (**Fig. 6-12, E**).
   - Assemble and position the resuscitation mask.
     - Use a pediatric resuscitation mask for a child or infant, if available.
   - Tilt the head back and lift the chin to open the airway.
   - Each rescue breath should last about 1 second and make the chest clearly rise.
5. If the chest clearly rises, check for a pulse for no more than 10 seconds.
   - For a hypothermia victim, check for a pulse for up to 30 to 45 seconds.
   - **Adult and child:** Feel for a pulse at the carotid artery. With one hand on the victim's forehead, the lifeguard should take his or her other hand and place 2 fingers on the front of the neck. Then, slide the fingers down into the groove at the side of the neck (**Fig. 6-12, F**).
   - **Infant:** With one hand on the infant's forehead, use the other hand to find the brachial pulse on the inside of the upper arm, between the infant's elbow and shoulder (**Fig. 6-12, G**).
6. Quickly scan the victim for severe bleeding (**Fig. 6-12, H**).
7. Care for the conditions found.
   - If there is movement, breathing and a pulse—
     - Place the victim in a recovery position (or a modified H.A.IN.E.S. [High Arm in Endangered Spine] recovery position if spinal injury is suspected) and continue to monitor the airway, breathing and circulation (ABCs). For an infant, maintain an open airway and continue to monitor the infant's ABCs.
     - Administer emergency oxygen, if available and trained to do so.
   - If the first 2 rescue breaths do not make the chest clearly rise, provide care for an unconscious choking victim (see Chapter 7).
   - If there is a pulse, but no movement or breathing, perform rescue breathing (see Chapter 7).
   - If there is no movement, breathing or pulse, perform cardiopulmonary resuscitation (CPR) (see Chapter 8).
   - If there is severe bleeding, follow the steps for providing care for a major wound (see Chapter 9).

Recovery Position

If, during the initial assessment, the lifeguard is alone and must leave the victim to summon EMS personnel or finds the victim is moving, breathing and has a pulse but is unconscious, the lifeguard should place the victim in a re-

Fig. 6-13

covery position if a head, neck or back injury is not suspected. This position is used to maintain an open airway for a breathing victim with a decreased level of consciousness (**Fig. 6-13**). To place the victim in a recovery position, the lifeguard should—
1. Kneel at the victim's side.
2. Take the victim's arm farthest away and move it up next to the victim's head and take the victim's other arm and cross it over the chest.
3. Grasp the closest leg and bend it up.
4. Hold the victim's shoulder and hip and gently roll the victim's body as a unit away from the lifeguard, keeping the head, neck and back in a straight line.
5. Carefully angle the victim's head toward the ground, allowing any fluids to drain away from the victim's throat.

Monitor the victim's ABCs. Roll the victim to the opposite side every 30 minutes or if the victim's skin on the lower arm becomes pale, ashen or grayish or is cool to the touch.

Modified H.A.IN.E.S. Recovery Position

If a head, neck or back injury is suspected and a clear, open airway can be maintained, do not move the victim unnecessarily. If the victim must be left to get help, or if a clear airway cannot be maintained, the lifeguard should move the victim to his or her side while keeping the head, neck and back in a straight line by placing the victim in a modified H.A.IN.E.S. recovery position (**Fig. 6-14**). To place a victim in the modified H.A.IN.E.S. recovery position, the lifeguard should—
1. Kneel at the victim's side.
2. Reach across the victim's body and lift the far arm up next to the victim's head with the victim's palm facing up.
3. Then take the victim's nearest arm and place it next to the victim's side.
4. Grasp the victim's leg furthest away and bend it up.
5. Using the lifeguard's hand nearest the victim's head, cup the base of the victim's skull in the palm of the hand

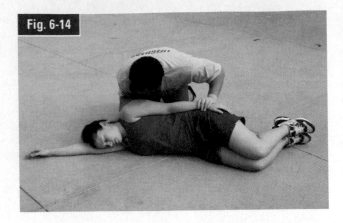

Fig. 6-14

and carefully slide a forearm under the victim's near shoulder. Do not lift or push the victim's head or neck.

6. Place his or her other hand under the victim's closest arm and hip.

7. With a smooth motion, the lifeguard should roll the victim away from him or herself by lifting with his or her hand and forearm. The victim's head must remain in contact with the victim's extended arm. The lifeguard should be sure to support the head and neck with his or her hand.

8. Stop all movement when the victim is on his or her side.

9. Bend the victim's closest knee and place it on top of the victim's other knee. Make sure the victim's arm on top is in line with the upper body.

10. Monitor the victim's ABCs and care for the conditions found.

EMERGENCY MOVES

For emergencies that occur in the water, the victim must be removed from the water for care to be provided. For emergencies on land, lifeguards care for the victim where he or she is found. Do not move the victim unless it is necessary. Moving a victim needlessly can lead to further pain and injury. Move an injured victim on land only if—

- The scene is unsafe or becoming unsafe (e.g., fire, risk of explosion, a hazardous chemical leak or collapsing structure).
- Another victim must be reached who may have a more serious injury or illness.
- To provide proper care (e.g., someone has collapsed on a stairway and needs CPR, which must be performed on a firm, flat surface).

The lifeguard's safety is of the utmost importance. However, if leaving a scene to ensure personal safety, the lifeguard should attempt to move the victim to safety as

One Age Does Not Fit All

Lifeguards may have to provide care to adults, children and infants. When responding to life-threatening emergencies, the specific care a lifeguard provides may be different depending upon the victim's age. For the purpose of the skills presented in this manual, an adult is considered anyone 12 years old or older. A child is considered anyone between 1 and about 12 years old and an infant is anyone under 1 year old. These age categories are used because the recommendations for care differ according to the victim's age and the cause of the emergency.

These age ranges change when operating an AED. For the purpose of operating an AED, a child is considered anyone 1 to 8 years old (or less than 55 pounds) and an adult is considered anyone 9 years old and older.

well. When moving a victim, a lifeguard should consider the following:

- The victim's height and weight
- Physical strength of the lifeguard
- Obstacles, such as stairs and narrow passages
- Distance to be moved
- Whether others are available to assist
- The victim's condition
- Whether aids to transport the victim are readily available

To improve the chances of successfully moving an injured or ill victim without the lifeguard injuring him or herself or the victim—

- Use the legs, not the back, when bending.
- Bend at the knees and hips and avoid twisting the body.
- Walk forward when possible, taking small steps and watching where walking.
- Avoid twisting or bending anyone with a possible head, neck or back injury.
- Do not move a victim who is too large to move comfortably.

There are several ways to move a victim from an unsafe scene or to provide proper care. Use any of the following techniques if it is necessary to move a victim.

Clothes Drag

To move a clothed victim who may have a head, neck or back injury, the lifeguard should—

1. Stand behind the victim's head and gather the victim's clothing behind the victim's neck **(Fig. 6-15)**.
2. Pull the victim to safety, cradling the victim's head with the victim's clothes and the lifeguard's hands.

Two-Person Seat Carry

To carry a conscious victim who cannot walk and has no suspected head, neck or back injury, the lifeguard should—

1. Ask for help from another lifeguard or bystander.
2. Put one arm under the victim's thighs and the other across the victim's back.
3. Interlock his or her arms with those of a second rescuer under the victim's legs and across the victim's back **(Fig. 6-16)**.
4. Carry the victim to safety.

Walking Assist

To help a victim who needs assistance walking to safety, the lifeguard should—

1. Stand at one side of the victim and place the victim's arm across the lifeguard's shoulders and hold onto the victim's forearm.
2. Support the victim's waist with the lifeguard's other hand **(Fig. 6-17)**.

3. Walk the victim to safety. (If the victim begins to fall, this approach will give more control.)

Pack-Strap Carry

The pack-strap carry can be used with conscious and unconscious victims. Using it with an unconscious victim requires a second lifeguard to help position the injured or ill victim on another lifeguard's back.

To move either a conscious or unconscious victim with no suspected head, neck or back injury, the lifeguard should—

1. Have the victim stand or have a second lifeguard support the victim.
2. Position him or herself with his or her back to the victim. The lifeguard should keep his or her back straight and knees bent so that his or her shoulders fit into the victim's armpits.
3. Cross the victim's arms in front of him or herself and grasp the victim's wrists.
4. Lean forward slightly and pull the victim up and onto his or her back.
5. Stand up and walk to safety **(Fig. 6-18)**. Depending on the size of the victim, the lifeguard may be able to hold both of the victim's wrists with one hand, leaving the other hand free to help maintain balance, open doors and remove obstructions.

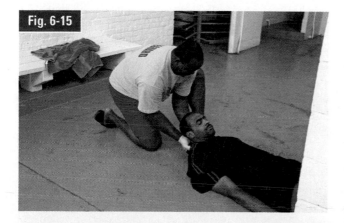

Fig. 6-15

Fig. 6-16

Fig. 6-17

Fig. 6-18

Fig. 6-19

Fig. 6-20

Foot Drag

To move a victim too large to carry or move otherwise, the lifeguard should—

1. Stand at the victim's feet and firmly grasp the victim's ankles and move backward (**Fig. 6-20**).
2. Pull the victim in a straight line, being careful not to bump the victim's head.

Blanket Drag

To move an unconscious victim in an emergency situation when equipment is limited, the lifeguard should—

1. Keep the victim between him or herself and the blanket.
2. Gather half of the blanket and place it against the victim's side.
3. Roll the victim as a unit toward him or herself.
4. Reach over and place the blanket so that it will be positioned under the victim.
5. Roll the victim onto the blanket.
6. Gather the blanket at the head and drag the victim (**Fig. 6-19**).

PUTTING IT ALL TOGETHER

As professional rescuers, lifeguards are an important link in the EMS system and have a duty to act and to meet professional standards. Lifeguards should follow the general procedures for injury or sudden illness on land: size up the scene, perform an initial assessment, summon EMS personnel by calling 9-1-1 or the local emergency number, and, after caring for any life-threatening injuries, perform a secondary assessment. Lifeguards should use standard precautions to protect themselves against disease transmission. Recognizing and caring for emergencies are among the most important skills lifeguards will learn.

Chapter 7

Breathing Emergencies

A lifeguard can be called upon at any time to respond to a breathing emergency. Therefore, it is important for lifeguards to know how to recognize and care for a breathing emergency. Caring for breathing emergencies includes—

- Performing rescue breathing for a victim who is not breathing.
- Giving back blows and abdominal thrusts for a conscious adult or child who is choking.

- Giving back blows and chest thrusts to a conscious infant who is choking.
- Giving chest thrusts, doing a foreign object check/removal and giving rescue breaths to an unconscious adult, child or infant who has an airway obstruction.
- Administering emergency oxygen, if available and trained to do so.

BREATHING EMERGENCIES

A lifeguard may detect a breathing emergency during the initial assessment. A breathing emergency occurs if a victim has difficulty breathing (*respiratory distress*) or stops breathing (*respiratory arrest/failure*). Without adequate oxygen, hypoxia will result. *Hypoxia* is a condition in which insufficient oxygen reaches the cells. Signs and symptoms of hypoxia include increased breathing and heart rates, *cyanosis* (a condition that develops when tissues do not get enough oxygen and turn blue, particularly the lips and nailbeds), changes in the level of consciousness, restlessness and chest pain. Breathing emergencies can be caused by—

- Obstructed airway (choking).
- Injury to the head, chest, lungs or abdomen.
- Illness, such as pneumonia.
- Respiratory conditions, such as emphysema or asthma.
- Heart attack.
- Coronary heart disease, such as angina.
- Allergic reactions (food or insect stings).
- Electrocution.
- Shock.
- Drowning.
- Nonfatal submersion injury.
- Poisoning.
- Drugs.
- Emotional distress.

Respiratory Distress

A victim who is having difficulty breathing is in respiratory distress. Signs and symptoms of respiratory distress include—

- Slow or rapid breathing.
- Unusually deep or shallow breathing.
- Shortness of breath or noisy breathing.
- Dizziness, drowsiness or light-headedness.
- Changes in the level of consciousness.
- Increased heart rate.
- Chest pain or discomfort.
- Skin that is flushed, pale, ashen or bluish.
- Unusually moist or cool skin.
- Gasping for breath.
- Wheezing, gurgling or making high-pitched noises.
- Inability to speak in full sentences.
- Tingling in the hands or feet.

Injuries and other conditions, such as asthma, emphysema and anaphylactic shock, can cause respiratory distress.

Asthma is a condition that narrows the air passages and makes breathing difficult. During an asthma attack, the air passages become constricted by a spasm of the muscles lining the bronchi or by swelling of the bronchi themselves. Asthma may be triggered by an allergic reaction, emotional stress or physical activity. A characteristic sign of asthma is wheezing when exhaling.

Emphysema is a disease in which the lungs lose their ability to exchange carbon dioxide and oxygen efficiently, causing a shortness of breath.

Anaphylactic shock, also known as *anaphylaxis*, is a severe allergic reaction. The air passages may swell and restrict breathing. Anaphylaxis may be caused by insect bites or stings, foods, chemicals, medications or latex allergies. Anaphylactic shock is a life-threatening condition.

Caring for Respiratory Distress

Lifeguards do not need to know the cause of respiratory distress to provide care. Whenever a victim is experiencing difficulty breathing—

- Summon emergency medical services (EMS) personnel by calling 9-1-1 or the local emergency number.
- Help the victim rest in a comfortable position that makes breathing easier.
- Reassure and comfort the victim.
- Assist the victim with any of his or her prescribed medication.
- Keep the victim from getting chilled or overheated.
- Administer emergency oxygen, if it is available and trained to do so.

Someone with asthma or emphysema who is in respiratory distress may try to do pursed lip breathing. Have the person assume a position of comfort. After he or she inhales, have the person slowly exhale out through the lips, pursed as though blowing out candles. This creates back pressure, which can help open airways slightly until EMS personnel arrive.

Respiratory Arrest

A victim who has stopped breathing is in respiratory arrest, or respiratory failure. Respiratory arrest may develop from respiratory distress or may occur suddenly as a result of an obstructed airway, heart attack or other cause. If an unconscious victim is not moving or breathing normally but has a pulse, he or she needs rescue breathing. When checking an unconscious victim, lifeguards may detect an irregular, gasping or shallow breath. This is known as an *agonal breath*. Do not confuse this with normal breathing. Look for movement and check for breathing and a pulse during the initial assessment. If the person is not moving or breathing normally but has a pulse, begin rescue breathing.

Epinephrine Administration

Approximately 2 million people in the United States are at risk for anaphylaxis, and each year 400 to 800 people die from anaphylactic reactions. Insect stings; penicillin; aspirin; food additives, such as sulfites; and certain foods, such as shellfish, fish and nuts, can trigger anaphylaxis in susceptible people. These reactions may be life threatening and require immediate care. A medical ID bracelet should be worn by anyone at risk. Some possible signs and symptoms in anaphylactic victims include—

- Swelling of the face, neck, hands, throat, tongue or other body part.
- Itching of the tongue, armpits, groin or any body part.
- Dizziness.
- Redness or welts on the skin.
- Red, watery eyes.
- Nausea, abdominal pain or vomiting.
- Rapid heart rate.
- Difficulty breathing or swallowing.
- Feelings of constriction in the throat or chest.

Epinephrine is a medication prescribed to treat the signs and symptoms of these reactions. If someone shows any of these signs or symptoms, summon EMS personnel.

LIFEGUARDING TIP: Lifeguards should follow local protocols or medical directives when applicable.

Use an epinephrine auto-injector when a victim—
- Relates a history of allergies or allergic reactions.
- Is having an allergic reaction.
- Requests assistance to administer epinephrine.
- Provides the epinephrine or auto-injector.
- Has a family member who relates a victim's history of allergies or allergic reactions and provides the victim's auto-injector.

Before assisting or administering epinephrine to the victim—
- Summon EMS personnel.
- Check the label to ensure that the prescription is for the victim.
- Ensure that the person has not already taken epinephrine or antihistamine. If so, do not administer another dose unless directed by EMS personnel.
- Ensure that the prescription has not expired.
- Ensure that the medication is clear and not cloudy or discolored.
- Read and follow instructions provided with the auto-injector.

An epinephrine auto-injector is simple and easy to use. However, it needs to be accessed quickly. Assisting the victim with the medication can include getting the pen from a purse, car, home or out of a specially designed carrier on a belt. It may also include taking it out of the plastic tube or assisting the victim with the injection into the thigh.

The standard epinephrine dose is 0.3 mg for an adult or 0.15 mg for a child weighing less than 45 pounds. To administer an intramuscular injection—

1. Locate the middle of the outer thigh or the upper arm to use as the injection site.

Epinephrine Administration *(continued)*

2. Grasp the auto-injector firmly and remove the safety cap.
3. Hold the auto-injector at a 90-degree angle to the victim's outer thigh.
4. Firmly jab the tip straight into the thigh. A click will be heard. Hold the auto-injector firmly in place for 10 seconds.

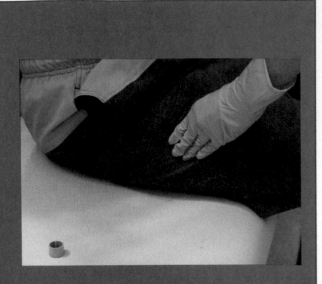

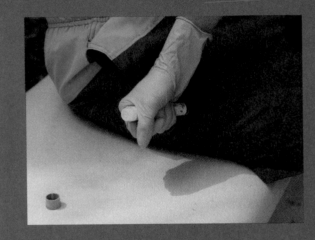

5. Remove it from the thigh and massage the injection site for several seconds.

Continue to check the victim's airway, breathing and circulation (ABCs). Give the used auto-injector to EMS personnel.

In all cases of epinephrine administration, follow-up care and transport to a medical facility is needed. The beneficial effect of epinephrine is relatively short in duration. Someone having a severe allergic reaction may require additional medications that can be administered only in a hospital.

RESCUE BREATHING

Rescue breathing is a technique for breathing air into a victim to give him or her oxygen needed to survive. Exhaled air contains enough oxygen to keep a person alive. When giving rescue breaths, take a normal breath and breathe into the mask. Each breath should last about 1 second and make the chest clearly rise. Give 1 rescue breath about every 5 seconds for an adult. Give 1 rescue breath about every 3 seconds for a child or infant.
  Continue rescue breathing until—
- The victim begins to breathe on his or her own.
- Another trained rescuer takes over.
- Too exhausted to continue.
- The victim has no pulse, in which case cardiopulmonary resuscitation (CPR) should be initiated or an automated external defibrillator (AED) used if one becomes immediately available.
- The scene becomes unsafe.

Rescue Breathing—Adult
If an unconscious adult is not moving or breathing but has a pulse, begin rescue breathing.
1. Conduct an initial assessment.
2. Use a resuscitation mask and give 1 rescue breath about every 5 seconds.
   - Position the resuscitation mask.
   - Tilt the head back and lift the chin to open the airway.
   - Breathe into the mask **(Fig. 7-1)**.
   - Each rescue breath should last about 1 second and make the chest clearly rise.
   - Watch the chest clearly rise when giving each rescue breath.
   - Do this for about 2 minutes.
3. Remove the resuscitation mask, look for movement and recheck for breathing and a pulse **for no more than 10 seconds (Fig. 7-2)**.
   - If there is a pulse, but still no movement or breathing—

Fig. 7-1

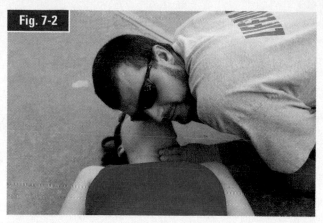

Fig. 7-2

Fig. 7-3

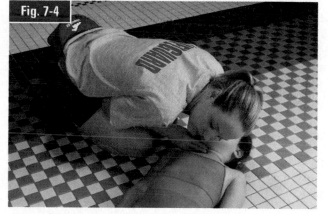

Fig. 7-4

- ● Replace the mask and continue rescue breathing.
- ● Look for movement and recheck for breathing and a pulse about every 2 minutes.
- ■ If there is movement, breathing and a pulse—
  - ● Place the victim in a recovery position (or a modified H.A.IN.E.S. [High Arm in Endangered Spine] position if spinal injury is suspected) and continue to monitor the victim's airway, breathing and signs of circulation (ABCs).
  - ● Administer emergency oxygen, if available and trained to do so.
- ■ If there is no movement, breathing or pulse, begin CPR or two-rescuer CPR.

Rescue Breathing—Child
If an unconscious child is not moving or breathing but has a pulse, begin rescue breathing.
1. Conduct an initial assessment.
2. Use a resuscitation mask and give 1 rescue breath about every 3 seconds.
   - ■ Position the resuscitation mask.
   - ■ Tilt the head slightly past neutral and lift the chin to open the airway.

- ■ Breathe into the mask **(Fig. 7-3)**.
- ■ Each rescue breath should last about 1 second and make the chest clearly rise.
- ■ Watch the chest clearly rise when giving each rescue breath.
- ■ Do this for about 2 minutes.
3. Remove the resuscitation mask, look for movement and recheck for breathing and a pulse **for no more than 10 seconds (Fig. 7-4)**.
   - ■ If there is a pulse, but still no movement or breathing—
     - ● Replace the mask and continue rescue breathing.
     - ● Look for movement and recheck for breathing and a pulse about every 2 minutes.
   - ■ If there is movement, breathing and a pulse—
     - ● Place the child in a recovery position (or a modified H.A.IN.E.S. position if spinal injury is suspected) and continue to monitor the child's ABCs.
     - ● Administer emergency oxygen, if available and trained to do so.
   - ■ If there is no movement, breathing or pulse, begin CPR or two-rescuer CPR.

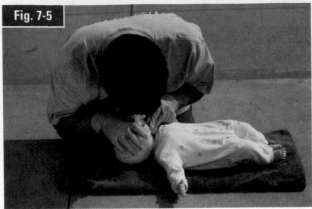

Fig. 7-5

Rescue Breathing—Infant

If an unconscious infant is not moving or breathing but has a pulse, begin rescue breathing.

1. Conduct an initial assessment.
2. Use a resuscitation mask and give 1 rescue breath about every 3 seconds.
   - Position the resuscitation mask.
   - Tilt the head to a neutral position and lift the chin to open the airway.
   - Breathe into the mask **(Fig. 7-5)**.
   - Each rescue breath should last about 1 second and make the chest clearly rise.
   - Watch the chest clearly rise when giving each rescue breath.
   - Do this for about 2 minutes.
3. Remove the resuscitation mask, look for movement and recheck for breathing and a pulse **for no more than 10 seconds (Fig. 7-6)**.
   - If there is a pulse, but still no movement or breathing—
     - Replace the mask and continue rescue breathing.
     - Look for movement and recheck for breathing and a pulse about every 2 minutes.

- If there is movement, breathing and a pulse—
  - Maintain an open airway and continue to monitor the infant's ABCs.
  - Administer emergency oxygen, if available and trained to do so.
- If there is no movement, breathing or pulse, begin CPR or two-rescuer CPR.

Breathing Barriers

Breathing barriers include resuscitation masks, face shields and bag-valve-mask resuscitators (BVMs). Breathing barriers help protect lifeguards against disease transmission when giving rescue breaths. As a professional rescuer, a lifeguard should have a resuscitation mask with a one-way valve or a BVM available in the response gear.

Resuscitation Masks

Resuscitation masks are flexible, dome-shaped devices that cover a victim's mouth and nose and allow lifeguards to breathe air into a victim without making mouth-to-mouth contact. Most employers provide resuscitation masks for lifeguards. Resuscitation masks have several benefits. They—

- Create a seal over the victim's mouth and nose.
- Supply air to the victim more quickly through both the mouth and nose.
- Can be connected to emergency oxygen if they have an oxygen inlet.
- Protect against disease transmission when giving rescue breaths.

A resuscitation mask should have the following characteristics **(Fig. 7-7)**:
- Be easy to assemble and use.
- Be made of transparent, pliable material that creates a tight seal over the victim's mouth and nose.
- Have a one-way valve for releasing exhaled air.

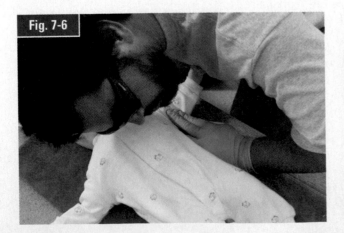

Fig. 7-6

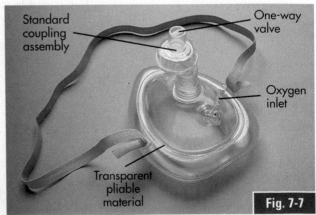

Standard coupling assembly

One-way valve

Oxygen inlet

Transparent pliable material

Fig. 7-7

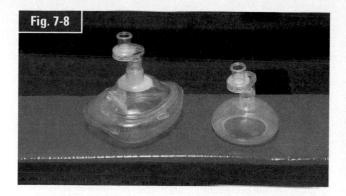

Fig. 7-8

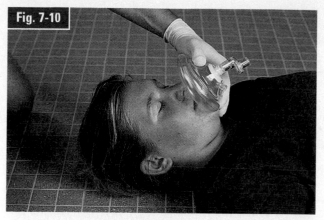

Fig. 7-10

- Have a standard 15-mm or 22-mm coupling assembly (the size of the opening for the one-way valve).
- Have an inlet for delivering emergency oxygen.
- Work well under different environmental conditions, such as extreme heat or cold.

Child and infant resuscitation masks are available and should be used to care for children and infants **(Fig. 7-8)**. If a pediatric resuscitation mask is not available, an adult mask can be used instead by placing the narrow end of the mask over the mouth. Not all resuscitation masks need to be rotated to create an adequate seal.

To use a resuscitation mask to give rescue breaths, take the following steps:

1. Assemble the mask.
   - Attach the one-way valve to the resuscitation mask **(Fig. 7-9)**.
2. Position the mask.
   - Kneel behind or to the side of the victim's head and place the rim of the mask between the lower lip and chin. Lower the resuscitation mask until it covers the victim's mouth and nose **(Fig. 7-10)**.
3. Seal the mask and open the victim's airway and begin rescue breathing.
   - From the back of the victim's head **(Fig. 7-11)**—
     - Place the thumbs along each side of the resuscitation mask.

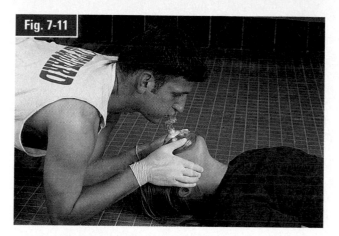

Fig. 7-11

- Slide the fingers into position behind the angles of the victim's jawbone.
- Apply downward pressure with the thumbs.
- Lift the jaw and tilt the head back to open the airway.
- From the side of the victim's head **(Fig. 7-12)**—
  - With the top hand, place the thumb and fingers around the top of the resuscitation mask.
  - With the other hand, slide the first two fingers into position on the bony part of the victim's chin.

Fig. 7-9

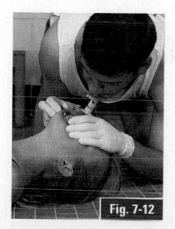

Fig. 7-12

- Apply downward pressure with the top hand and the thumb of the lower hand to seal the top and bottom of the resuscitation mask.
- Lift the chin and tilt the head back to open the airway.
■ If the victim is suspected to have a head, neck or back injury, use the jaw-thrust maneuver on pages 109–110 to open the airway.
■ If using an adult resuscitation mask on an infant—
  - Kneel behind the infant's head.
  - Rotate the mask and position the nose of the mask on the infant's chin.
  - Lower the wide end of the mask to cover the infant's mouth and nose.
  - Place the thumbs along either side of the rim and slide the fingers into position behind the angles of the infant's jawbone.
  - Seal the mask by applying downward pressure with the thumbs.
  - Lift the jaw and tilt the head to a neutral position to open the airway.

LIFEGUARDING TIP: If using a pediatric mask, it is not necessary to rotate the mask. Pediatric masks are specifically designed to fit a child or infant. Seal the pediatric mask and give rescue breaths in the same manner learned for an adult.

Face Shields

One of the most compact and easy-to-use breathing devices is a face shield (**Fig. 7-13**). A face shield is a small sheet of plastic with a filter or one-way valve in the middle. It is placed over a victim's face with the one-way valve covering the mouth. This allows lifeguards to give

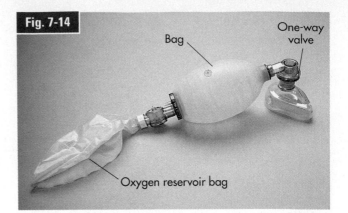

Fig. 7-14

Bag

One-way valve

Oxygen reservoir bag

rescue breaths to a victim while reducing the risk of disease transmission during rescue breathing. A major limitation of face shields is that they cannot be used with emergency oxygen like resuscitation masks and BVMs.

Bag-Valve-Mask Resuscitators

BVMs are hand-held devices used primarily to ventilate a victim in respiratory arrest (**Fig. 7-14**). They can also be used for a victim in respiratory distress. Because it is necessary to maintain a tight seal on the mask, two rescuers should operate a BVM (one rescuer positions and seals the mask, while the second rescuer squeezes the bag).

BVMs have several advantages. They—

- Increase oxygen levels in the blood by using the air in the surrounding environment instead of the air exhaled by the lifeguard.
- Can be connected to emergency oxygen.
- Are more effective at delivering ventilations when used correctly by two rescuers.
- Protect against disease transmission.

BVMs come in various sizes. Pediatric BVMs are available for children and infants. Facilities must have BVMs for adults, children and infants to be appropriately prepared. If a pediatric BVM is not available, an adult mask can be used by placing the narrow end of the mask over the mouth and making sure not to use as much force when squeezing the bag. Using an adult BVM on an infant has the potential for harm and should only be used in an emergency situation when pediatric BVMs are not available.

If an unconscious victim has a pulse but is not moving or breathing, two rescuers can use a BVM to perform rescue breathing. The rescuers should take the following steps:

1. **Rescuer 1** conducts an initial assessment.
2. **Rescuer 2** arrives and assembles the BVM (**Fig. 7-15**).

LIFEGUARDING TIP: Use pediatric BVMs for children and infants.

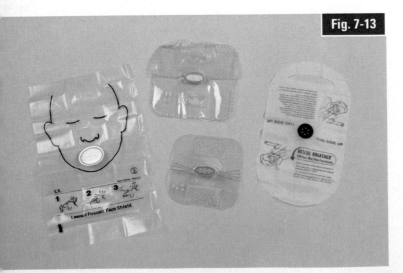

Fig. 7-13

Fig. 7-15

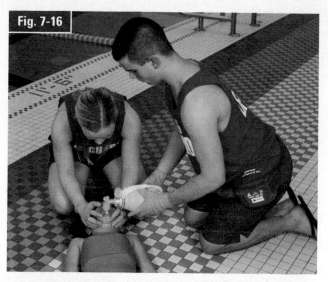

Fig. 7-16

Fig. 7-17

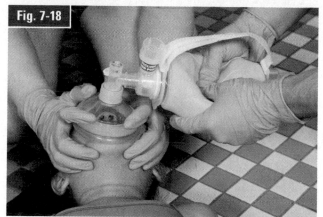

Fig. 7-18

3. **Rescuer 1** kneels behind the victim's head and positions the mask over the victim's mouth and nose **(Fig. 7-16).**

4. **Rescuer 1** seals the mask and opens the airway **(Fig. 7-17).**
   - Kneels behind the victim's head.
   - Places the thumbs along each side of the mask.
   - Slides the fingers behind the angles of the jawbone.
   - Pushes down on the mask with the thumbs, lifts the jaw and tilts the head back.

5. **Rescuer 2** begins ventilations **(Fig. 7-18).**
   - Squeezes the bag slowly for about 1 second using just enough force to make the chest clearly rise with each ventilation.
   - Gives 1 ventilation about every 5 seconds for an adult and 1 ventilation about every 3 seconds for a child or infant.
   - Does this for about 2 minutes.

6. **Rescuer 1** removes the BVM, looks for movement and rechecks for breathing and a pulse **for no more than 10 seconds.**

- If there is a pulse, but still no movement or breathing—
  - Replaces the BVM and continues ventilations.
  - Continues to look for movement and rechecks for breathing and a pulse about every 2 minutes.
- If there is movement, breathing and a pulse—
  - Places the victim in a recovery position (or a modified H.A.IN.E.S. recovery position if spinal injury is suspected) and continues to monitor the ABCs. For an infant, maintain an open airway and continue to monitor the infant's ABCs.
  - Administers emergency oxygen, if available and trained to do so.
- If there is no movement, breathing or pulse, begins CPR or two-rescuer CPR.

Rescue Breathing—Special Situations
Suspected Head, Neck or Back Injury

If an unconscious victim has a suspected head, neck or back injury, remember the priority of care. Airway and breathing take precedence over restricting motion of the head, neck and back. Try to open the airway by lifting the

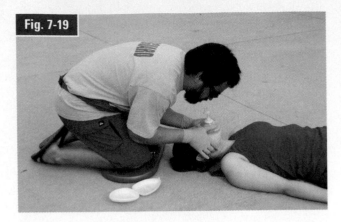

Fig. 7-19

Fig. 7-20

chin without tilting the head, using the jaw-thrust maneuver **(Fig. 7-19)**:

1. From behind the victim's head, position the mask.
2. Place the thumbs along each side of the resuscitation mask.
3. Brace the elbows for support.
4. Slide the fingers into position under the angles of the victim's jawbone.
5. Without moving the victim's head, apply downward pressure with the thumbs to seal the mask and lift the jaw to open the airway.
6. Give rescue breaths.

If the jaw-thrust maneuver does not open the airway, use the head-tilt/chin-lift technique to open the airway. See Chapter 10 for more information on caring for head, neck and back injuries.

Air in the Stomach

When giving rescue breaths, breathe slowly, just enough to make the victim's chest clearly rise. If too much air is pushed into the victim, it will enter the stomach, causing gastric distention. The victim then will likely vomit, which can obstruct the airway and complicate resuscitation efforts.

Vomiting and Drowning

When a lifeguard gives rescue breaths to a victim of a nonfatal submersion injury, the victim will likely vomit. If this occurs, quickly turn the victim onto his or her side. Support the head and neck and turn the body as a unit **(Fig. 7-20)**. Turning the victim onto his or her side keeps vomit from blocking the airway and entering the lungs. After vomiting stops, quickly wipe the victim's mouth clean. Then turn the victim on his or her back, and continue with rescue breathing.

Victims with Dentures

If the victim is wearing dentures, leave them in place unless they become loose and block the airway. Dentures

help support the victim's mouth and cheeks, making it easier to seal the resuscitation mask during rescue breathing.

Mask-to-Nose Breathing

If the victim's mouth is injured, the lifeguard may need to give rescue breathing through the nose. To perform mask-to-nose breathing—

1. Use a resuscitation mask.
2. Maintain the head-tilt position.
3. Place the resuscitation mask over the victim's mouth and nose.
4. Use both hands to close the victim's mouth.
5. Seal the resuscitation mask with both hands.
6. Give rescue breaths.

Mask-to-Stoma Breathing

On rare occasions, a lifeguard may see an opening in a victim's neck as the head is tilted back to check for breathing. This victim may have had an operation to remove part of the windpipe. If so, the victim breathes through this opening, which is called a *stoma*. If a victim with a stoma needs rescue breathing, follow the same steps for mouth-to-mask breathing, except—

1. Look, listen and feel for breathing with an ear over the stoma.
2. Maintain the airway in a neutral position. (This ensures the victim's airway is neither flexed nor extended, as the stoma provides access to the lower airway.)
3. Use a child or infant resuscitation mask over the victim's stoma.
4. If possible, pinch the nose and close the mouth, as some victims with a stoma may still have a passage for air that reaches the mouth and nose in addition to the stoma.
5. Give rescue breaths.

AIRWAY OBSTRUCTION

An airway obstruction is the most common cause of respiratory emergencies. A victim whose airway is blocked can quickly stop breathing, lose consciousness and die. There are two types of airway obstructions: anatomical and mechanical. An *anatomical obstruction* occurs when the airway is blocked by an anatomical structure, such as the tongue or swollen tissues of the mouth and throat. In an unconscious victim, the tongue is a common cause of airway obstruction. This occurs because the tongue relaxes when the body is deprived of oxygen. As a result, the tongue rests on the back of the throat, inhibiting the flow of air to the lungs. A *mechanical obstruction* occurs when foreign objects, such as a piece of food, a small toy or fluids, such as vomit, blood, mucus or saliva, block the airway. A conscious victim who is clutching his or her throat with one or both hands is usually choking. This is considered the universal sign of choking.

Common causes of choking include—

- Poorly chewed food.
- Drinking alcohol before or during meals. (Alcohol dulls the nerves that aid swallowing, making choking on food more likely.)
- Eating too fast or talking or laughing while eating.
- Walking, playing or running with food or objects in the mouth.
- Wearing dentures. (Dentures make it difficult to sense whether food is fully chewed before it is swallowed.)

Caring for Airway Obstructions

Lifeguards must be able to recognize when a victim is choking. The airway may be partially or completely obstructed. A victim who is clutching his or her throat with one or both hands is usually choking. Someone with a partial airway obstruction can still move some air to and from the lungs and may make wheezing sounds. Someone with a complete airway obstruction cannot cough, speak or breathe. Get consent before helping a conscious choking victim. If the choking victim is unconscious, consent is implied.

Conscious Choking—Adult and Child

When caring for a conscious choking adult or child, perform a combination of 5 back blows followed by 5 abdominal thrusts. Each back blow and abdominal thrust should be a distinct attempt to dislodge the object. Use less force when giving back blows and abdominal thrusts to a child. Using too much force may cause internal injuries. Continue back blows and abdominal thrusts until the object is dislodged and the victim can breathe or cough forcefully, or becomes unconscious.

LIFEGUARDING TIP: If a parent or guardian is present, obtain consent before giving care to a conscious choking child. A lifeguard should tell the child's parent or guardian the level of his or her training and the care that will be provided. If the parent or guardian is not available, consent is implied.

To care for a conscious choking adult and child, follow these steps:

1. Ask the victim "Are you choking?" **(Fig. 7-21)**.
   - Identify yourself and ask if you may help.
   - If the victim is coughing forcefully, encourage continued coughing.
2. If the victim cannot cough, speak or breathe, summon EMS personnel.
3. Lean the victim forward and give 5 back blows with the heel of the hand **(Fig. 7-22)**.
   - Position yourself slightly behind the victim.
   - Provide support by placing one arm diagonally across the chest and lean the victim forward.
   - Firmly strike the victim between the shoulder blades with the heel of the hand.
   - Each back blow is a distinct attempt to dislodge the object.

Fig. 7-21

Fig. 7-22

4. Give 5 abdominal thrusts.
  - **For an adult,** stand behind the victim **(Fig. 7-23).**
  - **For a child,** stand or kneel behind the child depending on the child's size. Use less force on a child than would be used on an adult **(Fig. 7-24).**
  - Use one hand to find the navel **(Fig. 7-25).**
  - Make a fist with the other hand and place the thumb side of the fist against the middle of the victim's abdomen, just above the navel.

Fig. 7-23

Fig. 7-24

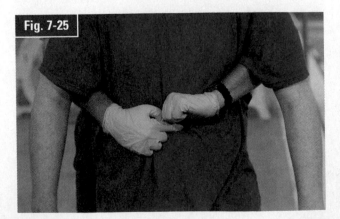

Fig. 7-25

  - Grab the fist with the other hand.
  - Give quick, upward thrusts. Each abdominal thrust should be a distinct attempt to dislodge the object **(Fig. 7-26).**
5. Continue giving 5 back blows and 5 abdominal thrusts until—
  - The object is forced out.
  - The victim begins to cough or breathe on his or her own.
  - The victim becomes unconscious.
    - If the victim becomes unconscious, begin care for an unconscious choking adult or child.

LIFEGUARDING TIP: Some conscious choking victims may need a combination of back blows and chest thrusts instead of abdominal thrusts. Perform chest thrusts if the victim is obviously pregnant, known to be pregnant or too large to reach around.

Conscious Choking—Infant

Abdominal thrusts are not used for a choking infant because of the risk of injury. When caring for a conscious choking infant, use a combination of 5 back blows and 5 chest thrusts. Continue back blows and chest thrusts until the object is dislodged and the infant can breathe or cough forcefully, or becomes unconscious.

LIFEGUARDING TIP: If a parent or guardian is present, obtain consent before providing care to a conscious choking infant. A lifeguard should tell the child's parent or guardian the level of his or her training and the care that will be provided. If the parent or guardian is not available, consent is implied.

Fig. 7-26

To care for a conscious choking infant, follow these steps:

1. If the infant cannot cough, cry or breathe, summon EMS personnel.
2. Carefully position the infant face-down along the forearm.
   - Support the infant's head and neck with the hand.
   - Lower the infant onto the thigh, keeping the infant's head lower than his or her chest.
3. Give 5 back blows **(Fig. 7-27)**.
   - Use the heel of the hand.
   - Give back blows between the infant's shoulder blades.
   - Each back blow should be a distinct attempt to dislodge the object.
4. Position the infant face-up along the forearm.
   - Position the infant between both forearms, supporting the infant's head and neck.
   - Turn the infant face-up.
   - Lower the infant onto the thigh with the infant's head lower than his or her chest.
5. Give 5 chest thrusts **(Fig. 7-28)**.
   - Put 2 or 3 fingers on the center of the chest, just below the nipple line.
   - Compress the chest 5 times about ½ to 1 inch.

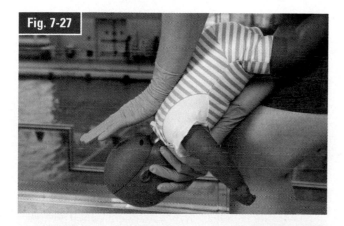

Fig. 7-27

Fig. 7-28

- Each chest thrust should be a distinct attempt to dislodge the object.
6. Continue giving 5 back blows and 5 chest thrusts until—
   - The object is forced out.
   - The infant begins to cough, cry or breathe on his or her own.
   - The infant becomes unconscious.
     - If the infant becomes unconscious, begin care for an unconscious choking infant.

Special Considerations for Choking Victims

In some situations, abdominal thrusts may not be an effective method of care for conscious choking victims. If a rescuer cannot reach far enough around the victim to give effective abdominal thrusts or if the victim is obviously pregnant or known to be pregnant, the rescuer should give 5 back blows followed by 5 chest thrusts.

To perform chest thrusts—

1. Stand behind the victim.
2. Make a fist with one hand and place the thumb side against the center of the victim's chest. If the victim is obviously pregnant or known to be pregnant, position the hands slightly higher on the victim's chest.
3. Grab the fist with the other hand and give quick, inward thrusts **(Fig. 7-29)**. Look over the victim's shoulder so that his or her head does not hit your face when performing the chest thrusts.
4. Repeat the back blows and chest thrusts until the object is forced out, the victim begins to breathe or cough forcefully on his or her own or the victim becomes unconscious.

Unconscious Choking—Adult and Child

If rescue breaths given to an unconscious adult do not make the chest clearly rise, reposition the airway by tilting the head farther back and then try the rescue breaths again. For an unconscious child, if the rescue breaths do not make the

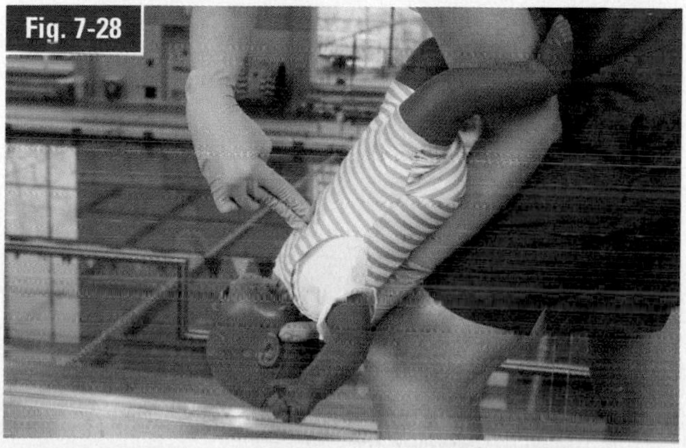

Fig. 7-29

chest clearly rise, reposition the airway by retilting the child's head and attempting the rescue breaths again. If the rescue breaths still do not make the chest clearly rise, give 5 chest thrusts. Repeat cycles of chest thrusts, foreign object check/removal and rescue breaths until the chest clearly rises. If the chest clearly rises, look for movement and check for breathing and a pulse for no more than 10 seconds. Provide care based on the conditions found.

To care for an unconscious choking adult and child, follow these steps:

1. If, during the initial assessment, the first 2 rescue breaths do not make the chest clearly rise, reposition the airway by tilting the victim's head farther back and try 2 rescue breaths again.
   - For a child, reposition the airway by retilting the child's head and try 2 rescue breaths again **(Fig. 7-30)**.
2. If the rescue breaths still do not make the chest clearly rise, give 5 chest thrusts **(Fig. 7-31)**.
   - Place the heel of one hand on the center of the chest.
   - Place the other hand on top of the first hand and compress the chest 5 times.
     - **For an adult,** compress the chest about 1½ to 2 inches.
     - **For a child,** compress the chest about 1 to 1½ inches.

- Each chest thrust should be a distinct attempt to dislodge the object.
- Compress at a rate of about 100 compressions per minute.

LIFEGUARDING TIPS:

- **Keep the fingers off the chest when giving chest thrusts.**
- **Use body weight, not the arms, to compress the chest.**
- **Position the shoulders over the hands with the elbows locked.**
- **If the victim is obviously pregnant or known to be pregnant, adjust hand positions to be slightly higher on the chest.**
- **Take pressure off the chest between chest compressions, but leave the hands in place.**
- **One hand can be used to compress the chest of a child. If using one hand, place it on the center of the child's chest while the other hand is on the child's forehead.**
- **Counting out loud helps keep an even pace.**

3. Look inside the victim's mouth.
   - Grasp the tongue and lower jaw between the thumb and fingers and lift the jaw **(Fig. 7-32)**.
4. If an object is seen, take it out.
   - **For an adult**, remove the object with the index finger by sliding it along the inside of the cheek, using a hooking motion to sweep the object out **(Fig. 7-33)**.
   - **For a child**, remove the object with the little finger by sliding it along the inside of the cheek, using a hooking motion to sweep the object out **(Fig. 7-34)**.

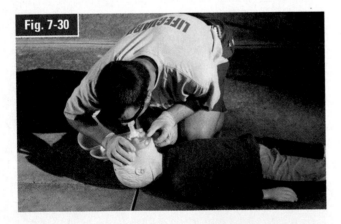
Fig. 7-30

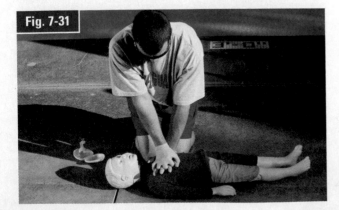
Fig. 7-31

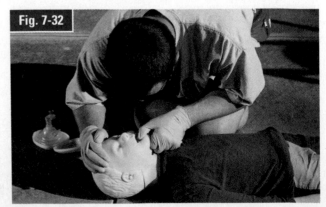
Fig. 7-32

5. Replace the resuscitation mask and give 2 rescue breaths **(Fig. 7-35)**.
- If the rescue breaths still do not make the chest clearly rise—
  - Repeat Steps 2 to 5.
- If the rescue breaths make the chest clearly rise—
  - Remove the mask, look for movement and check for breathing and a pulse **for no more than 10 seconds**.
    - If there is movement, breathing and a pulse—
      - Place the victim in a recovery position (or a modified H.A.IN.E.S. recovery position if

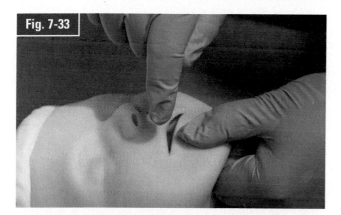

Fig. 7-33

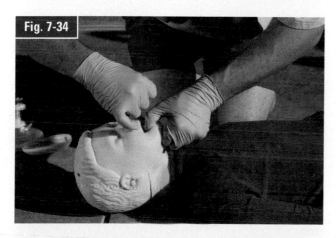

Fig. 7-34

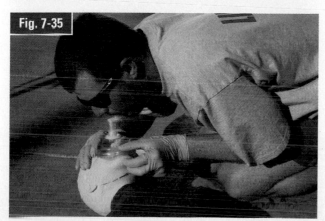

Fig. 7-35

spinal injury is suspected) and continue to monitor the victim's ABCs.
      - Administer emergency oxygen, if available and trained to do so.
- If there is a pulse, but no movement or breathing, perform rescue breathing.
- If there is no movement, breathing or pulse, perform CPR or two-rescuer CPR.

Unconscious Choking—Infant

If a lifeguard gives rescue breaths to an unconscious infant and the rescue breaths do not make the chest clearly rise, reposition the airway by retilting the infant's head and attempt the rescue breaths again. If the rescue breaths still do not make the chest clearly rise, carefully position the infant and give 5 chest thrusts. Repeat cycles of chest thrusts, foreign object check/removal and rescue breaths until the chest clearly rises. If the chest clearly rises, look for movement and check for breathing and a pulse for no more than 10 seconds. Provide care based on the conditions found.

To care for an unconscious choking infant, follow these steps:

1. If, during the initial assessment, the first 2 breaths do not make the chest clearly rise, reposition the airway by retilting the infant's head and try 2 rescue breaths again **(Fig. 7-36)**.

2. If rescue breaths still do not make the chest clearly rise, remove the resuscitation mask and give 5 chest thrusts **(Fig. 7-37)**.
- Keep one hand on the infant's forehead to maintain an open airway.
- Put two or three fingers on the center of the chest, just below the nipple line.
- Compress the chest about ½ to 1 inch.
- Each chest thrust should be a distinct attempt to dislodge the object.
- Compress at a rate of about 100 compressions per minute.

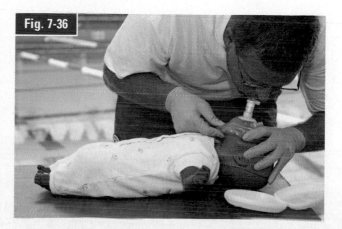

Fig. 7-36

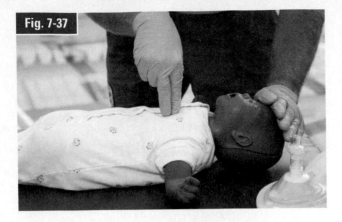

Fig. 7-37

LIFEGUARDING TIP: Take pressure off the chest between chest thrusts, but leave the fingers in place.

3. Look inside the infant's mouth.
   - Grasp the tongue and lower jaw between the thumb and fingers and lift the jaw **(Fig. 7-38)**.
4. If an object is seen, take it out.
   - Remove the object with the little finger by sliding it along the inside of the cheek, using a hooking motion to sweep it out **(Fig. 7-39)**.
5. Replace the resuscitation mask and give 2 rescue breaths **(Fig. 7-40)**.
   - If the rescue breaths still do not make the chest clearly rise—
     - Repeat Steps 2 to 5.
   - If the rescue breaths make the chest clearly rise—
     - Look for movement and check for breathing and a pulse **for no more than 10 seconds (Fig. 7-41)**.
       - If there is movement, breathing and a pulse—
         - Maintain an open airway and continue to monitor the infant's ABCs.
         - Administer emergency oxygen, if available and trained to do so.
       - If there is a pulse, but no movement or breathing, perform rescue breathing.
       - If there is no movement, breathing or pulse, perform CPR or two-rescuer CPR.

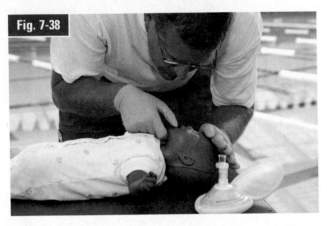

Fig. 7-38

EMERGENCY OXYGEN

When someone has a breathing emergency or cardiac emergency, the flow of oxygen to his or her brain, heart and blood cells is reduced, resulting in *hypoxia*. Hypoxia is a condition in which insufficient oxygen reaches the cells. If breathing stops, the brain and heart will soon be starved of oxygen, resulting in cardiac arrest and then death.

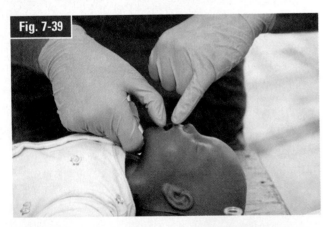

Fig. 7-39

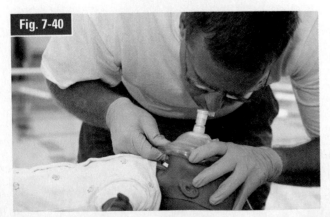

Fig. 7-40

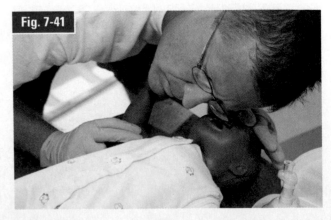

Fig. 7-41

The air a person normally breathes contains about 21 percent oxygen. When a lifeguard gives rescue breaths or provides CPR, the air exhaled into the victim is about 16 percent oxygen. This may not be enough oxygen to save the victim's life. By administering emergency oxygen, a higher percentage of oxygen is delivered, thus increasing the victim's chance of survival. It also helps reduce the pain and breathing discomfort caused by hypoxia.

Emergency oxygen can be given for just about any breathing or cardiac emergency. If a person is breathing but has no obvious signs or symptoms of injury or illness, emergency oxygen should be considered if—

- An adult is breathing fewer than 12 breaths per minute or more than 20 breaths per minute.
- A child is breathing fewer then 15 breaths per minute or more than 30 breaths per minute.
- An infant is breathing fewer than 25 breaths per minute or more than 50 breaths per minute.

Oxygen should be delivered with properly sized equipment for the respective victim and appropriate flow rates for the delivery device.

Variable-Flow-Rate Oxygen

Many EMS systems use variable-flow-rate oxygen. Variable-flow-rate oxygen systems allow the lifeguard to vary the flow of oxygen and the type of delivery device used. Because of the large amount of oxygen EMS systems deliver and the variety of equipment and emergency situations to which they respond, variable-flow-rate oxygen is practical. To deliver variable-flow-rate emergency oxygen, the following pieces of equipment need to be assembled:

- An oxygen cylinder
- A regulator with pressure gauge and flowmeter
- A delivery device

Emergency oxygen units are available without prescription for first aid use provided they contain at least a 15-minute supply of oxygen and are designed to deliver a preset flow rate of at least 6 liters per minute (LPM). Oxygen cylinders are labeled "U.S.P." and marked with a yellow diamond that says "Oxygen" (**Fig. 7-42, A**). The U.S.P. stands for United States Pharmacopeia and indicates the oxygen is medical grade. Oxygen cylinders come in different sizes and have various pressure capacities. In the United States, oxygen cylinders typically have green markings. However, the color scheme is not regulated, so different manufacturers and other countries may use different color markings. Oxygen cylinders are under high pressure and should be handled carefully. The regulator

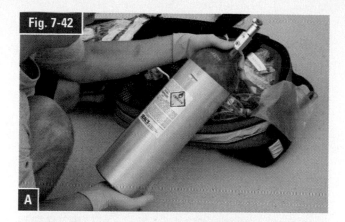

Fig. 7-42

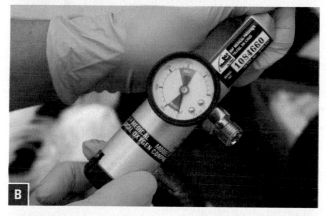

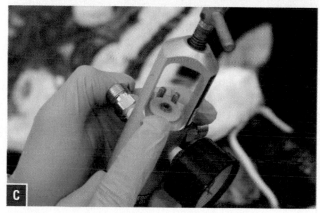

lowers the pressure coming out of the cylinder so that the oxygen can be used safely (**Fig. 7-42, B**). The regulator also has a pressure gauge that shows the pressure in the cylinder. The pressure gauge shows if the cylinder is full (2,000 pounds per square inch [psi]), nearly empty or in between. The regulator must be carefully attached to the oxygen cylinder. An "O-ring" gasket makes the seal tight (**Fig. 7-42, C**). The flowmeter controls how rapidly the oxygen flows from the cylinder to the victim. The flow can be set from 1–25 LPM.

Fig. 7-43

Fixed-Flow-Rate Oxygen

Some emergency oxygen systems have the regulator set at a fixed-flow rate. The flow rate is set at 6 LPM, 12 LPM or another rate. In some cases, the fixed-flow-rate systems may have a dual (high/low) flow setting. Fixed-flow-rate oxygen systems typically come with the delivery device, regulator and cylinder already connected to each other **(Fig. 7-43)**. This eliminates the need to assemble the equipment, which makes it quick and very simple to deliver emergency oxygen.

To operate this type of device, the lifeguard simply turns it on, checks that oxygen is flowing and places the mask over the victim's face. The drawback to using fixed-flow-rate oxygen systems is that the flow rate cannot be adjusted to different levels. This limits both the type of delivery device that can be used and the concentration of oxygen that can be delivered. A fixed-flow-rate unit with a preset flow of 6 LPM can be used with a nasal cannula or resuscitation mask. With a preset flow rate of 12 LPM, the unit can be used with a resuscitation mask or non-rebreather mask.

Because of the simplicity of the preconnected fixed-flow-rate systems and the life-saving benefits of oxygen, these systems are becoming increasingly popular in the workplace, schools and other places where professional rescuers may have to respond to on-site emergencies.

OXYGEN DELIVERY DEVICES

An oxygen delivery device is the piece of equipment a victim breathes through when receiving emergency oxygen. Tubing carries the oxygen from the regulator to the delivery device on the victim's face **(Table 7-1)**. These devices include nasal cannulas, resuscitation masks, non-rebreather masks and BVMs. Various sizes of masks, BVMs and nasal cannulas are available for adults, children and infants. Appropriate sizing is important to ensure adequate airway management.

Nasal Cannulas

A *nasal cannula* delivers oxygen to someone who is breathing **(Fig. 7-44)**. It has two small prongs that are inserted into the nose. Nasal cannulas are not used often in an emergency because they do not give as much oxygen as a resuscitation mask, a non-rebreather mask or a BVM. They are used mostly for victims with minor breathing problems rather than for life-threatening conditions. If a victim will not accept having a mask on his or her face, a nasal cannula can be used. With a nasal cannula, set the flow rate at 1–6 LPM.

Resuscitation Masks

A resuscitation mask with an oxygen inlet can be used with emergency oxygen to give rescue breaths to a nonbreathing victim. It also can be used for someone who is breathing but still needs emergency oxygen. Some resuscitation masks come with elastic straps to put over the victim's head to

TABLE 7-1   OXYGEN DELIVERY DEVICES

Delivery Device	Common Flow Rate	Oxygen Concentration	Function
Nasal Cannula	1–6 LPM	24–44 percent	Breathing victims only
Resuscitation Mask	6–15 LPM	35–55 percent	Breathing and nonbreathing victims
Non-Rebreather Mask	10–15 LPM	90 percent or more	Breathing victims only
BVM	15 LPM or more	90 percent or more	Breathing and nonbreathing victims

Fig. 7-44

Fig. 7-45

side of the mask. The reservoir bag should be inflated by covering the one-way valve with the thumb before placing it on the victim's face. The oxygen reservoir bag should be sufficiently inflated (about ⅔ full) so as not to deflate when the victim inhales. If it begins to deflate, increase the flow rate of the oxygen to refill the reservoir bag. With non-rebreather masks, the flow rate should be set at 10–15 LPM. When using the non-rebreather mask with a high flow rate of oxygen, up to 90 percent or more oxygen can be delivered to the victim. If children or infants do not want the mask over their faces, use the blow-by oxygen method. Hold the mask close to their mouth and nose so oxygen is still being delivered.

Bag-Valve-Mask Resuscitators AKA BVM

A BVM can be used on a person who is breathing or not breathing. By using a BVM with emergency oxygen attached to an oxygen reservoir bag, up to 100 percent oxygen can be delivered to the victim (**Fig. 7-47**). The BVM can be held by a breathing victim to inhale the oxygen, or the lifeguard can squeeze the bag as the victim inhales to help deliver more oxygen. If a BVM is used without emergency oxygen, the nonbreathing victim receives 21 percent oxygen—the amount in the air. With a BVM, the flow rate should be set at 15 LPM or more.

keep the mask in place (**Fig. 7-45**). If the mask does not have a strap, the lifeguard or the victim can hold it in place. With a resuscitation mask, set the flow rate at 6–15 LPM.

Non-Rebreather Masks

A non-rebreather mask is an effective method for delivering high concentrations of oxygen to breathing victims (**Fig. 7-46**). The *non-rebreather mask* consists of a face mask with an attached oxygen reservoir bag and a one-way valve between the mask and bag to prevent the victim's exhaled air from mixing with the oxygen in the reservoir bag. The victim inhales oxygen from the bag and exhaled air escapes through flutter valves on the

OXYGEN ADMINISTRATION

To deliver emergency oxygen:
1. Make sure the oxygen cylinder is labeled "U.S.P." and marked with a yellow diamond that says "Oxygen" (**Fig. 7-48**).
2. Clear the valve.
   - Remove the protective covering and save the O-ring gasket.
   - Turn the cylinder away from you and others before opening.
   - Open the cylinder valve for 1 second to clear the valve (**Fig. 7-49**).

Fig. 7-46

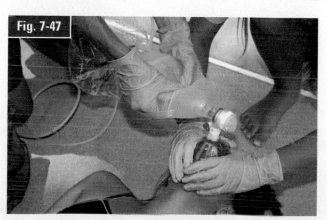

Fig. 7-47

3. Attach the regulator.
- Put the O-ring gasket into the valve on top of the cylinder, if necessary **(Fig. 7-50)**.
- Make sure that it is marked "Oxygen Regulator" **(Fig. 7-51)**.
- Secure the regulator on the cylinder by placing the three metal prongs into the valve.
- Hand-tighten the screw until the regulator is snug **(Fig. 7-52)**.

4. Open the cylinder valve one full turn **(Fig. 7-53)**.
- Check the pressure gauge **(Fig. 7-54)**.
- Determine that the cylinder has enough pressure.
5. Attach the delivery device.
- Attach the plastic tubing between the flowmeter and the delivery device **(Fig. 7-55)**.
6. Adjust the flowmeter.
- Turn the flowmeter to the desired flow rate **(Fig. 7-56)**.

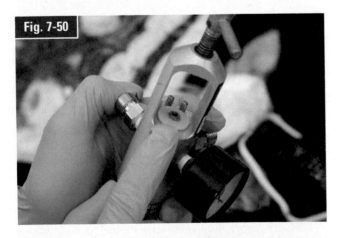

Fig. 7-48

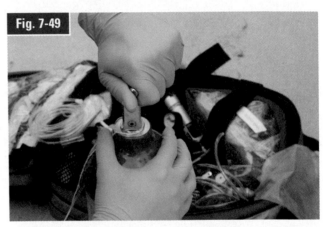

Fig. 7-49

Fig. 7-50

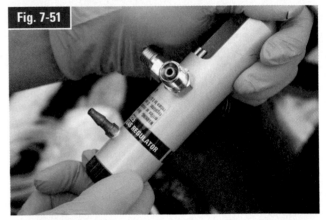

Fig. 7-51

Fig. 7-52

Fig. 7-53

Fig. 7-54

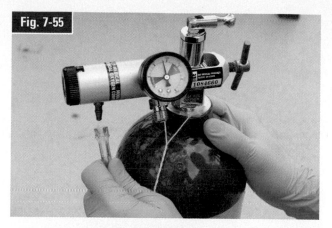

Fig. 7-55

Fig. 7-56

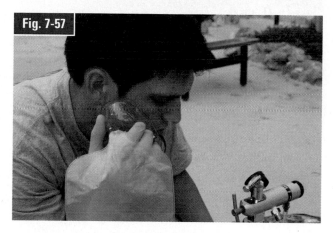

Fig. 7-57

Fig. 7-58

7. Verify the oxygen flow.
- Listen and feel for oxygen flow through the delivery device (**Fig. 7-57**).

8. Place the delivery device on the victim and continue care until EMS personnel arrive and take over (**Fig. 7-58**).

Oxygen Safety Precautions

When preparing and administering oxygen, safety is a concern. Use emergency oxygen equipment according to the manufacturer's instructions and in a manner consistent with federal and local regulations. Also follow these recommended guidelines:

- Be sure that oxygen is flowing before putting the delivery device over the victim's face.
- Do not use oxygen around flames or sparks. Oxygen causes fire to burn more rapidly.
- Do not use grease, oil or petroleum products to lubricate or clean the regulator. This could cause an explosion.
- Do not stand oxygen cylinders upright unless they are well secured. If the cylinder falls, the regulator or valve could become damaged or cause injury.
- Do not drag or roll cylinders.
- Do not carry a cylinder by the valve or regulator.

- With a nasal cannula, set the rate at 1–6 LPM.
- With a resuscitation mask, set the rate at 6–15 LPM.
- With a non-rebreather mask, set the rate at 10–15 LPM.
  - Ensure that the oxygen reservoir bag is inflated by placing the thumb over the one-way valve at the bottom of the mask until the bag is sufficiently inflated.
- With a BVM, set the rate at 15 LPM or more.

- Do not hold on to protective valve caps or guards when moving or lifting cylinders.
- Do not deface, alter or remove any labeling or markings on the oxygen cylinder.
- Do not attempt to mix gases in an oxygen cylinder or transfer oxygen from one cylinder to another.
- If defibrillating, make sure that no one is touching or in contact with the victim or the resuscitation equipment.
- Do not defibrillate someone when around flammable materials, such as gasoline or free-flowing oxygen.

PUTTING IT ALL TOGETHER

As a lifeguard, recognizing the signs and symptoms of respiratory distress and respiratory arrest is important. Lifeguards need to know how to give rescue breaths to a victim who has a pulse but is not moving or breathing normally, and how to care for a conscious or unconscious victim who is choking. Lifeguards should also know how to use a resuscitation mask and BVM properly. If there is emergency oxygen available, lifeguards should know how to use the equipment to deliver a higher concentration of oxygen to victims of respiratory distress and respiratory arrest.

Administering emergency oxygen to the victim of a cardiac or breathing emergency can help improve the victim's chances of survival. It also helps reduce the pain and breathing discomfort caused by hypoxia. It is important to follow safety precautions and use the equipment according to the manufacturer's instructions when using emergency oxygen. Variable-flow-rate oxygen systems allow the lifeguard to vary the concentration of oxygen and the type of delivery device used. Preconnected fixed-flow-rate systems eliminate the need to assemble the equipment, which makes it quick and very simple to deliver emergency oxygen.

Chapter 8

Cardiac Emergencies

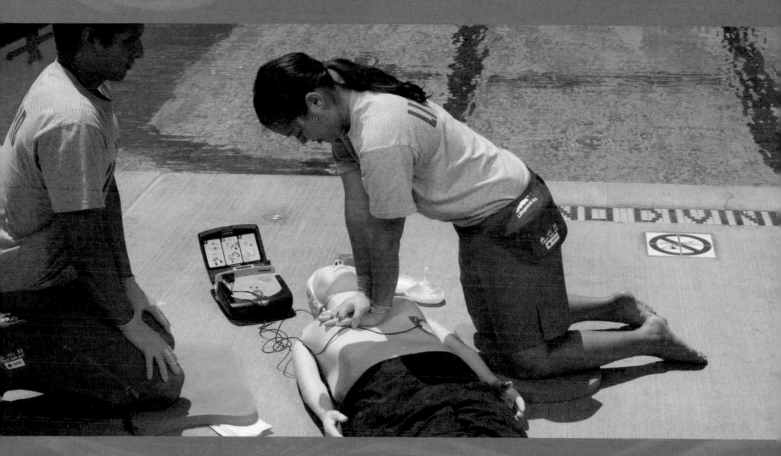

A cardiac emergency is a life-threatening emergency that can occur at any time to a victim of any age. Lifeguards may be called upon to care for a victim of a cardiac emergency. This care includes performing cardiopulmonary resuscitation (CPR) and using an automated external defibrillator (AED). By following the Cardiac Chain of Survival, a lifeguard can increase a victim's chance of survival.

CARDIAC CHAIN OF SURVIVAL

The initial assessment section in Chapter 6 explained how to identify and care for life-threatening conditions. A lifeguard's priorities focused on the victim's airway, breathing and circulation (ABCs). As professional rescuers, lifeguards must learn how to provide care for cardiac emergencies, such as heart attacks and cardiac arrest. To effectively respond to cardiac emergencies, it helps to understand the importance of the Cardiac Chain of Survival. The four links in the Cardiac Chain of Survival are—

1. **Early recognition of the emergency and early access to emergency medical services (EMS)**. The sooner 9-1-1 or the local emergency number is called, the sooner EMS personnel arrive and take over.

2. **Early CPR**. CPR helps supply oxygen to the brain and other vital organs to keep the victim alive until an AED is used or advanced medical care is provided.
3. **Early defibrillation**. An electrical shock called defibrillation may restore a normal heart rhythm. Each minute defibrillation is delayed reduces the victim's chance of survival by about 10 percent.
4. **Early advanced medical care**. EMS personnel who provide more advanced care and transport the victim to the hospital.

Common Causes of a Heart Attack

Heart attacks usually result from cardiovascular disease. Cardiovascular disease is the leading cause of death for adults in the United States. Cardiovascular disease develops slowly when deposits of cholesterol, a fatty substance made by the body, and other material may gradually build up on the inner walls of the arteries (**Fig. 8-1**). This condition, called *atherosclerosis*, causes these vessels to progressively narrow. When coronary arteries narrow, a heart attack may occur. Other common causes of heart attack include respiratory distress, electrocution and traumatic injury.

Recognizing a Heart Attack

When the muscle of the heart suffers a loss of oxygenated blood, the result is a *myocardial infarction*, or heart attack. The sooner a lifeguard recognizes the signs

Fig. 8-1

Arteries of the heart

Unblocked   Partially   Completely
                   blocked   blocked

and symptoms of a heart attack and acts, the better chance a lifeguard has to save a life. While many people will deny they are having a heart attack, it is important that a lifeguard summon EMS personnel by calling 9-1-1 or the local emergency number if the victim shows some or all of the following signs and symptoms:

- **Discomfort, pressure or pain.** The major signal is persistent discomfort, pressure or pain in the chest that does not go away. Unfortunately, it is not always easy to distinguish heart attack pain from the pain of indigestion, muscle spasms or other conditions. This often causes people to delay getting medical care. Brief, stabbing pain or pain that gets worse when the person bends or breathes deeply is not usually caused by a heart problem.

  The pain associated with a heart attack can range from discomfort to an unbearable crushing sensation in the chest. The victim may describe it as pressure, squeezing, tightness, aching or heaviness in the chest. Many heart attacks start slowly, as mild pain or discomfort. Often the victim feels discomfort or pain in the center of the chest (**Fig. 8-2**). It may spread to the shoulder, arm, neck, jaw or back. The discomfort or pain becomes constant. It is usually not relieved by resting, changing position or taking medicine. When interviewing the victim, a lifeguard should ask open-ended questions, such as "Can you describe the pain

for me?" and allow the victim to respond in his or her own words.

Any chest pain that is severe, lasts longer than 3 to 5 minutes, goes away and comes back or persists even during rest requires medical care at once. Even people who have had a previous heart attack may not recognize the signs and symptoms because each heart attack can have entirely different signs and symptoms.

- **Pain that comes and goes.** Some people with coronary heart disease may have chest pain or pressure that comes and goes. This type of pain is called *angina pectoris*, a medical term for pain in the chest. It develops when the heart needs more oxygen than it gets because the arteries leading to it are too narrow. When a person with angina is exercising, excited or emotionally upset, the heart might not get enough oxygen. This lack of oxygen can cause chest discomfort or pain.

  A person who knows he or she has angina may tell a lifeguard about the condition. People with angina usually have medicine to take to stop the pain. Stopping physical activity or easing the distress and taking the medicine usually ends the discomfort or pain of angina.

- **Trouble breathing.** Another signal of a heart attack is trouble breathing. The victim may be breathing faster than normal because the body tries to get much-needed oxygen to the heart.

- **Other signs and symptoms.** The victim's skin may be pale or ashen, especially around the face. The face also may be damp with sweat. Some people suffering from a heart attack sweat heavily or feel dizzy. These signs and symptoms are caused by the stress put on the body when the heart does not work as it should. Both men and women experience the most common signs and symptoms of a heart attack—chest pain or discomfort. But women are somewhat more likely to experience some of the other warning signals, particularly shortness of breath, nausea or vomiting and back or jaw pain. Women also tend to delay telling others about their signs and symptoms to avoid bothering or worrying them.

Care for a Heart Attack

If someone is having a heart attack—

- Take immediate action and summon EMS personnel.
- Have the victim stop what he or she is doing and rest. Assist the victim out of the water, if needed.
- Loosen any tight or uncomfortable clothing.
- Closely monitor the victim until EMS personnel arrive. Notice any changes in the victim's appearance or behavior.

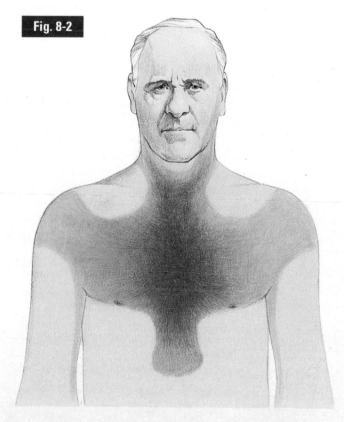

Fig. 8-2

Aspirin Administration

A conscious victim who is showing early signs and symptoms of a heart attack can be helped by offering him or her an appropriate dose of aspirin when the signs and symptoms first begin. However, offer aspirin only if medically appropriate and local protocols allow, and never delay summoning EMS personnel. Always summon EMS personnel as soon as the signs and symptoms of a heart attack are recognized, and then help the victim to be comfortable before giving him or her aspirin.

Then, if the victim is able to take medicine by mouth, ask the victim—

- Are you allergic to aspirin?
- Do you have a stomach ulcer or stomach disease?
- Are you taking any blood thinners, such as Coumadin™ or Warfarin™?
- Have you been told by a doctor not to take aspirin?

If the victim answers no to all of these questions, offer him or her two chewable (162 mg) baby aspirins, or up to one 5-grain (325 mg) adult aspirin tablet with a small amount of water. Be sure that only aspirin is used and not Tylenol™, acetaminophen, Motrin™, Advil™ or ibuprofen, which are painkillers. Likewise, do not use coated aspirin products or products meant for multiple uses such as cold, fever and headache.

Doses of aspirin may be offered if the victim has been under a rescuer's care, has regained consciousness and is able to take the aspirin by mouth.

LIFEGUARDING TIP: Lifeguards should follow local protocols or medical directives when applicable.

- Comfort the victim.
- If medically appropriate and local protocols or medical direction permit, give aspirin if the victim can swallow and has no known contraindications.
- Assist the victim with his or her prescribed medication.
- Administer emergency oxygen if available and trained to do so.
- Be prepared to perform CPR or use an AED.

Cardiac Arrest

Cardiac arrest is a life-threatening emergency. It may be caused by a heart attack, electrocution, respiratory arrest, drowning or other conditions. *Cardiac arrest* occurs when the heart stops beating or is beating too irregularly or weakly to circulate blood effectively. It can occur suddenly and without warning. In many cases, the victim may already be experiencing the signs and symptoms of a heart attack.

The signs of cardiac arrest include—

- Unconsciousness.
- No movement or breathing.
- No pulse.

CPR

A victim who is unconscious, not moving or breathing and has no pulse is in cardiac arrest and needs CPR. CPR is a combination of rescue breaths and chest compressions. Summoning EMS personnel immediately is critical for the victim's survival. If an AED is available, use the AED according to local protocols and in combination with CPR until more EMS personnel arrive and take over.

Effective chest compressions are essential for quality CPR. Effective chest compressions circulate blood to the victim's brain and other vital organs. Chest compressions can also increase the likelihood that a successful shock from an AED can be delivered to a victim suffering a sudden cardiac arrest, especially if more than 4 minutes have elapsed since the victim's collapse. To ensure quality CPR (Table 8-1)—

- Compress the chest at a rate of about 100 compressions per minute for any victim.
- Chest compressions should be deep. Compress the chest of an adult about 1½ to 2 inches, a child about 1 to 1½ inches and an infant about ½ to 1 inch.

TABLE 8-1   SUMMARY OF TECHNIQUES FOR CPR—ADULT, CHILD AND INFANT

	Adult	Child	Infant
Hand Position:	Two hands on the center of the chest	Two hands or one hand on the center of the chest	Two or three fingers on the center of the chest (just below the nipple line)
Compress:	About 1½ to 2 inches	About 1 to 1½ inches	About ½ to 1 inch
Breathe:	Until chest clearly rises (about 1 second per breath)	Until chest clearly rises (about 1 second per breath)	Until chest clearly rises (about 1 second per breath)
Cycle: (1 rescuer)	30 compressions 2 breaths	30 compressions 2 breaths	30 compressions 2 breaths
Cycle: (2 rescuers)	30 compressions 2 breaths	15 compressions 2 breaths	15 compressions 2 breaths
Rate:	About 100 compressions per minute	About 100 compressions per minute	About 100 compressions per minute

- Let the chest fully recoil to its normal position after each compression before starting the next compression.

A lifeguard should continue CPR until another trained rescuer arrives and takes over, an AED becomes available and ready to use, he or she is too exhausted to continue, the scene becomes unsafe or an obvious sign of life is detected. When performing CPR, it is not unusual for the victim's ribs to break or cartilage to separate. The victim may vomit and the scene may be chaotic. As professional rescuers with a duty to respond, lifeguards need to understand that despite their best efforts to provide quality care, not all victims of cardiac arrest survive.

CPR—Adult

If an unconscious adult is not moving or breathing and has no pulse, begin CPR.

To perform CPR for an adult—

1. Conduct an initial assessment.
2. Find the correct hand position to give compressions **(Fig. 8-3)**.
   - Place the heel of one hand on the center of the chest.
   - Place the other hand on top.
3. Give 30 chest compressions **(Fig. 8-4)**.
   - Compress the chest about 1½ to 2 inches.
   - Let the chest fully recoil to its normal position after each compression.

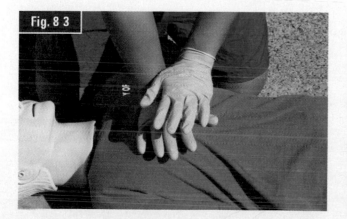

Fig. 8-3

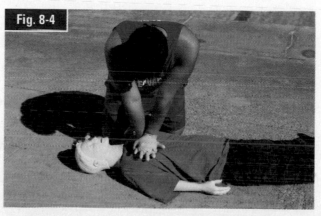

Fig. 8-4

■ Compress at a rate of about 100 compressions per minute.

LIFEGUARDING TIPS:
- Keep the fingers off the chest when giving chest compressions.
- Use body weight, not the arms, to compress the chest.
- Position the shoulders over the hands with the elbows locked.
- If the victim is obviously pregnant or known to be pregnant, adjust hand positions to be slightly higher on the chest.
- Take pressure off the chest between chest compressions, but leave the hands in place.
- Counting out loud helps keep an even pace.

4. Replace the resuscitation mask and give 2 rescue breaths **(Fig. 8-5)**.
   ■ Each rescue breath should last about 1 second.
   ■ Give rescue breaths that make the chest clearly rise.
5. Perform cycles of 30 compressions and 2 rescue breaths **(Fig. 8-6)**.
   ■ Continue CPR until—
     • Another trained rescuer arrives and takes over.
     • An AED becomes available and is ready to use.
     • The lifeguard is too exhausted to continue.
     • The scene becomes unsafe.
     • An obvious sign of life is detected.

LIFEGUARDING TIP: An AED should be used as soon as one becomes available.

Fig. 8-6

CPR—Child and Infant

CPR for children and infants is similar to the technique used for adults but is modified because of their smaller body sizes. Cardiac arrest in children and infants is usually caused by a respiratory emergency. If a lifeguard recognizes a child or infant is in respiratory distress or arrest, provide care immediately. If cardiac arrest occurs, begin CPR.

CPR—Child

To perform CPR for a child—
1. Conduct an initial assessment.
2. Find the correct hand position to give compressions **(Fig. 8-7)**.
   ■ Place the heel of one hand on the center of the chest.
   ■ Place the other hand on top.
3. Give 30 chest compressions **(Fig. 8-8)**.
   ■ Compress the chest about 1 to 1½ inches.
   ■ Let the chest fully recoil to its normal position after each compression.
   ■ Compress at a rate of about 100 compressions per minute.

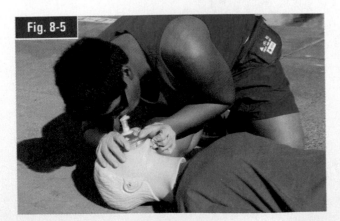

Fig. 8-5

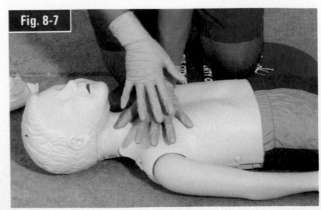

Fig. 8-7

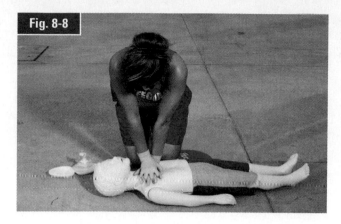

Fig. 8-8

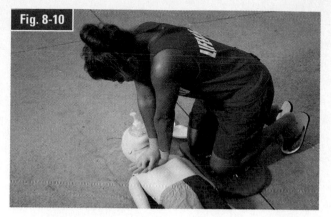

Fig. 8-10

LIFEGUARDING TIPS:

- **Keep the fingers off the chest when giving chest compressions.**
- **Use body weight, not the arms, to compress the chest.**
- **Position the shoulders over the hands with the elbows locked.**
- **Counting out loud helps keep an even pace.**
- **A one-handed technique can be used to compress the chest of a child. If using only one hand for compressions, place it on the center of the child's chest while the other hand is on the child's forehead.**

4. Replace the resuscitation mask and give 2 rescue breaths (**Fig. 8-9**).
   - Each rescue breath should last about 1 second.
   - Give rescue breaths that make the chest clearly rise.
5. Perform cycles of 30 compressions and 2 rescue breaths (**Fig. 8-10**).

- Continue CPR until—
  - Another trained rescuer arrives and takes over.
  - An AED becomes available and is ready to use.
  - The lifeguard is too exhausted to continue.
  - The scene becomes unsafe.
  - An obvious sign of life is detected.

LIFEGUARDING TIP: An AED should be used as soon as one becomes available.

CPR—Infant
To perform CPR for an infant—
1. Conduct an initial assessment.

LIFEGUARDING TIP: Place the infant on his or her back on a firm, flat surface, such as the floor or a table.

2. Find the correct hand position to give compressions (**Fig. 8-11**).
   - Put 2 or 3 fingers on the center of the chest just below the nipple line.
   - Keep one hand on the infant's forehead to maintain an open airway.

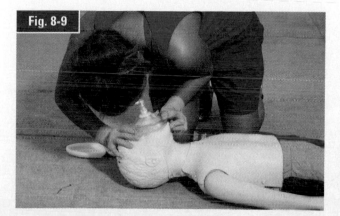

Fig. 8-9

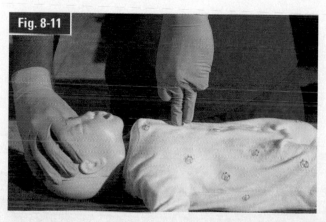

Fig. 8-11

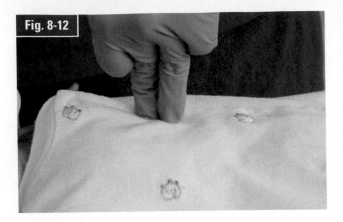

Fig. 8-12

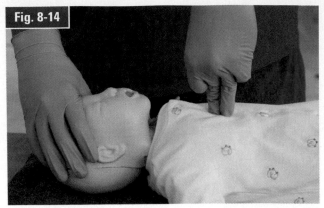

Fig. 8-14

3. Give 30 chest compressions (**Fig. 8-12**).
- Compress the chest about ½ to 1 inch.
- Let the chest fully recoil to its normal position after each compression.
- Compress at a rate of about 100 compressions per minute.

LIFEGUARDING TIPS:
- **Take the pressure off the chest between compressions, but leave the fingers in place.**
- **Counting out loud helps keep an even pace.**

4. Replace the resuscitation mask and give 2 rescue breaths (**Fig. 8-13**).
- Each rescue breath should last about 1 second.
- Give rescue breaths that make the chest clearly rise.

5. Perform cycles of 30 compressions and 2 rescue breaths (**Fig. 8-14**).
- Continue CPR until—
  - Another trained rescuer arrives and takes over.
  - The lifeguard is too exhausted to continue.
  - The scene becomes unsafe.
  - An obvious sign of life is detected.

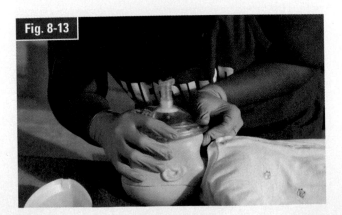

Fig. 8-13

Two-Rescuer CPR

When an additional rescuer is available, provide two-rescuer CPR. One rescuer gives rescue breaths and the other rescuer gives chest compressions. When providing two-rescuer CPR to an adult, rescuers should perform 30 compressions and 2 rescue breaths during each cycle. When performing two-rescuer CPR on a child or infant, rescuers should change the compression-to-rescue breaths ratio to 15:2. This provides more frequent respirations for children and infants. Rescuers should change positions (alternate turns giving compressions and breaths) about every 2 minutes. Changing positions should take less than 5 seconds.

Perform two-rescuer CPR in the following situations:
- Two rescuers arrive on the scene at the same time and begin CPR together
- One rescuer is performing CPR and a second rescuer becomes available

When CPR is being performed by one rescuer and a second rescuer arrives, the second rescuer should ask whether EMS personnel have been summoned. If EMS personnel have not been summoned, the second rescuer should do so before getting the AED or assisting with care. If EMS personnel have been summoned, the second rescuer should get the AED, or if an AED is not available, the second rescuer should help perform two-rescuer CPR.

Two-Rescuer CPR—Adult and Child

To perform two-rescuer CPR on an adult or child, follow these steps:

1. Rescuer 1 conducts an initial assessment.
2. Rescuer 2 finds the correct hand position to give compressions.
- Place the heel of one hand on the center of the chest.
- Place the other hand on top.

3. Rescuer 2 gives chest compressions (**Fig. 8-15**).
- Give compressions when **Rescuer 1** says, "Victim has no pulse. Begin CPR."

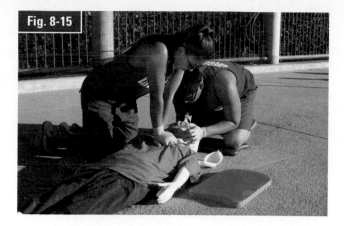

Fig. 8-15

- **Adult**: 30 compressions, compress the chest about 1½ to 2 inches
- **Child**: 15 compressions, compress the chest about 1 to 1½ inches
- Let the chest fully recoil to its normal position after each compression.
- Compress at a rate of about 100 compressions per minute.

4. **Rescuer 1** replaces the mask and gives 2 rescue breaths **(Fig. 8-16)**.
   - Each rescue breath should last about 1 second.
   - Rescue breaths should make the chest clearly rise.

5. Rescuers do about 2 minutes of compressions and breaths.
   - **Adult**: cycles of 30 chest compressions and 2 rescue breaths
   - **Child**: cycles of 15 chest compressions and 2 rescue breaths

6. Rescuers change positions.
   - **Rescuer 2** calls for a position change by using the word "change" at the end of the last compression cycle.
   - **Rescuer 1** gives 2 rescue breaths.
   - **Rescuer 2** moves to the victim's head with his or her own mask.

- **Rescuer 1** moves into position at the victim's chest and locates the correct hand position on the victim's chest.
- Changing positions should take less than 5 seconds.

7. **Rescuer 1** gives chest compressions **(Fig. 8-17)**.
   - Continue cycles of chest compressions and rescue breaths.

Rescuers should continue performing two-rescuer CPR until—

- Another trained rescuer arrives and takes over.
- An AED is available and ready to use.
- The rescuers are too exhausted to continue.
- The scene becomes unsafe.
- An obvious sign of life is detected.

When providing two-rescuer CPR to an infant, rescuers should perform the two-thumb-encircling-hands chest compression technique with thoracic squeeze. To perform two-rescuer CPR on an infant, follow these steps:

1. **Rescuer 1** conducts an initial assessment.
2. **Rescuer 2** finds the correct hand position to give compressions **(Fig. 8-18)**.

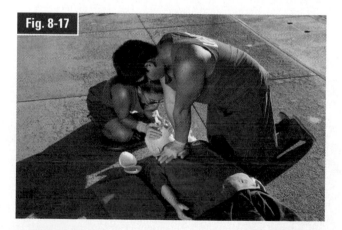

Fig. 8-17

Fig. 8-16

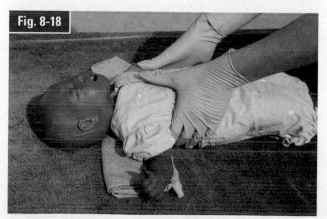

Fig. 8-18

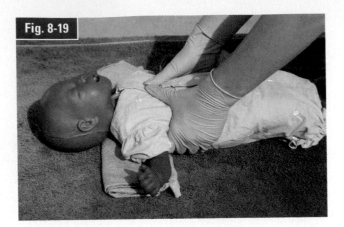

Fig. 8-19

- If available, place a towel or padding underneath the infant's shoulders to help maintain the head in the neutral position.
- Place the thumbs next to each other on the center of the chest just below the nipple line.
- Place both hands underneath the infant's back and support the infant's back with the fingers.
- Ensure that the hands do not compress or squeeze the side of the ribs.

3. **Rescuer 2** gives 15 chest compressions **(Fig. 8-19)**.
   - Give compressions when **Rescuer 1** says, "Victim has no pulse, begin CPR."
   - Use both thumbs to compress the chest about ½ to 1 inch at a rate of about 100 compressions per minute.
   - Let the chest fully recoil to its normal position after each compression.

4. **Rescuer 1** replaces the mask and gives 2 rescue breaths **(Fig. 8-20)**.
   - Each rescue breath should last about 1 second.
   - Give rescue breaths that make the chest clearly rise.

5. Rescuers do about 2 minutes of 15 chest compressions and 2 rescue breaths.
6. Rescuers change positions.
   - **Rescuer 2** calls for a position change by using the word "change" in place of the word "15" in the last compression cycle.
   - **Rescuer 1** gives 2 rescue breaths.
   - **Rescuer 2** moves to the infant's head with his or her own mask.
   - **Rescuer 1** moves into position and locates the correct finger placement on the infant's chest.
   - Changing positions should take less than 5 seconds.
7. **Rescuer 1** gives chest compressions **(Fig. 8-21)**.
   - Continue cycles of 15 chest compressions and 2 rescue breaths.

Rescuers should continue performing two-rescuer CPR on an infant until—
- Another trained rescuer arrives and takes over.
- The rescuers are too exhausted to continue.
- The scene becomes unsafe.
- An obvious sign of life is detected.

CPR—Special Situations

Lifeguards should continue CPR without interruptions for as long as possible. They should attempt to limit any interruptions to only seconds, except for specific interventions, such as insertion of an advanced airway device or use of a defibrillator.

Sometimes lifeguards may have to move a victim to perform CPR. For example, in a stairwell, lifeguards should move the victim to a flat area at the head or foot of the stairs to perform CPR (do not interrupt CPR for longer than about 30 seconds). If a victim is being transferred to an ambulance or into the emergency department, do not interrupt CPR.

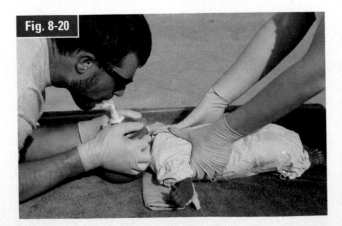

Fig. 8-20

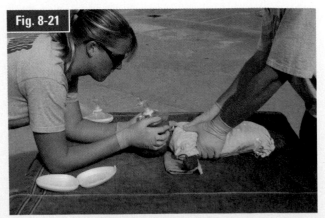

Fig. 8-21

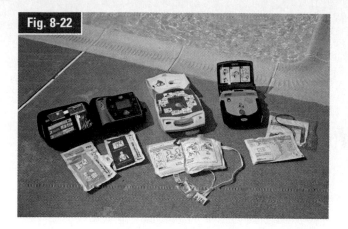

Fig. 8-22

AEDs

Each year, approximately 500,000 Americans die of cardiac arrest. CPR started promptly can help by keeping blood that contains oxygen flowing to the brain and other vital organs. However, in many cases, CPR alone cannot correct the underlying heart problem and return the heart to a normal rhythm. An AED is needed to correct the problem (**Fig. 8-22**). An AED is an automated device that recognizes a heart rhythm that requires a shock. AEDs provide an electrical shock to the heart, called *defibrillation*. The sooner the shock is administered, the greater the likelihood of the victim's survival. Lifeguards must assess victims quickly and be prepared to use an AED in cases of cardiac arrest.

The Heart's Electrical System

The heart's electrical system controls the pumping action of the heart. Under normal conditions, specialized cells of the heart initiate and transmit electrical impulses. These cells make up the *conduction system*. Electrical impulses travel through the upper chambers of the heart, called the *atria*, to the lower chambers of the heart, called the *ventricles* (**Fig. 8-23**).

The normal point of origin of the electrical impulse is the *sinoatrial (SA) node* above the atria. This impulse travels to a point midway between the atria and ventricles. This point is called the *atrioventricular (AV) node*. The pathway divides after the AV node into two branches, then into the right and left ventricles. These right and left branches become a network of fibers, called *Purkinje fibers*, which spread electrical impulses across the heart. Under normal conditions, this impulse reaches the muscular walls of the ventricles and causes the ventricles to contract. This contraction forces blood out of the heart to circulate through the body. The contraction of the left ventricle results in a pulse. The pauses between the pulse beats are the periods between contractions. When the heart muscles contract, blood is forced out of the heart. When they relax, blood refills the chambers.

Electrical activity of the heart can be evaluated with a cardiac monitor or electrocardiograph. Electrodes attached to an electrocardiograph pick up electrical impulses and transmit them to a monitor. This graphic record is referred to as an *electrocardiogram (ECG)*. Heart rhythms appear on an ECG as a series of peaks and valleys.

When the Heart Stops

Any damage to the heart from disease or injury can disrupt the heart's electrical system. This disruption can result in an abnormal heart rhythm that can stop circulation. The two most common abnormal rhythms initially present in

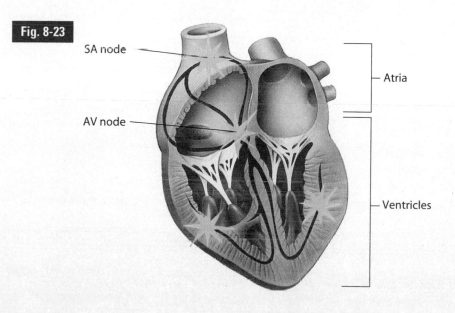

Fig. 8-23

SA node

AV node

Atria

Ventricles

sudden cardiac arrest victims are *ventricular fibrillation (V-fib)* and *ventricular tachycardia (V-tach)*. V-fib is a state of totally disorganized electrical activity in the heart. It results in *fibrillation*, or quivering, of the ventricles. In this state, the ventricles cannot pump blood and there is no movement or breathing and no pulse. V-tach is a very rapid contraction of the ventricles. Though there is electrical activity resulting in a regular rhythm, the rate is often so fast that the heart is unable to pump blood properly. As with V-fib, there is no movement or breathing and no pulse.

Defibrillation

In many cases, V-fib and V-tach rhythms can be corrected by early defibrillation. Delivering an electrical shock with an AED disrupts the electrical activity of V-fib and V-tach long enough to allow the heart to spontaneously develop an effective rhythm on its own. If V-fib or V-tach is not interrupted, all electrical activity will eventually cease, a condition called *asystole*. Asystole cannot be corrected by defibrillation. Remember that feeling for a pulse will not help determine what, if any, rhythm the heart has. CPR, started immediately and continued until defibrillation, helps maintain a low level of circulation in the body until the abnormal rhythm can be corrected by defibrillation.

Using an AED—Adult

When a cardiac arrest occurs, an AED should be used as soon as it is available and ready to use.

To use an AED on an adult—

1. Conduct an initial assessment.
2. Turn on the AED **(Fig. 8-24)**.
3. Wipe the victim's chest dry **(Fig. 8-25)**.
4. Attach the pads **(Fig. 8-26)**.
   - Place one pad on the victim's upper right chest.
   - Place the other pad on the victim's lower left side.
5. Plug the connector into the AED, if necessary **(Fig. 8-27)**.
6. Make sure that no one, including you, is touching the victim **(Fig. 8-28)**.
   - Look to see that no one is touching the victim.
   - Say, "EVERYONE STAND CLEAR."
7. Push the "analyze" button, if necessary. Let the AED analyze the heart rhythm.
8. If a shock is advised, push the "shock" button **(Fig. 8-29)**.
   - Look to see that no one is touching the victim.
   - Say, "EVERYONE STAND CLEAR."
9. After the shock, or if no shock is indicated—
   - Perform 5 cycles (about 2 minutes) of CPR before analyzing the heart rhythm again **(Fig. 8-30)**.

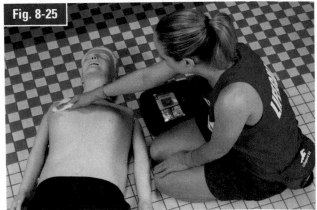

Fig. 8-24

Fig. 8-25

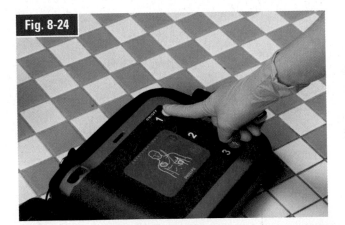

Fig. 8-26

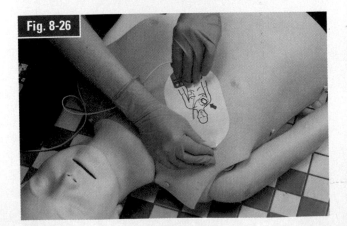

Fig. 8-27

- If at any time an obvious sign of life is detected, stop CPR and monitor the victim's ABCs.
- Administer emergency oxygen, if available and trained to do so.

If a second rescuer arrives with an AED while CPR is in progress, **Rescuer 1** should continue CPR until **Rescuer 2** is finished preparing the AED for use.

Rescuer 2 should complete the following steps:

1. Turn on the AED **(Fig. 8-31)**.
2. Wipe the victim's chest dry **(Fig. 8-32)**.

3. Attach the pads **(Fig. 8-33)**.
   - Place one pad on the victim's upper right chest.
   - Place the other pad on the victim's lower left side.
4. Plug the connector into the AED, if necessary **(Fig. 8-34)**.
5. Make sure that no one, including Rescuer 1, is touching the victim **(Fig. 8-35)**.
   - Look to see that nobody is touching the victim.
   - Say, "EVERYONE STAND CLEAR."
6. Push the "analyze" button, if necessary. Let the AED analyze the heart rhythm.

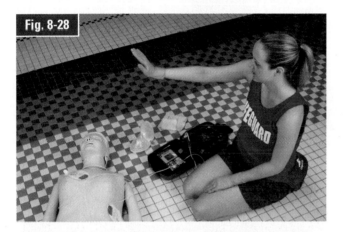
Fig. 8-28

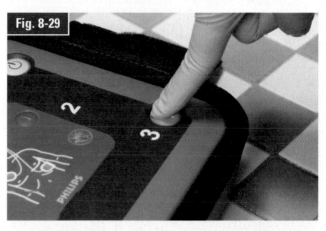
Fig. 8-29

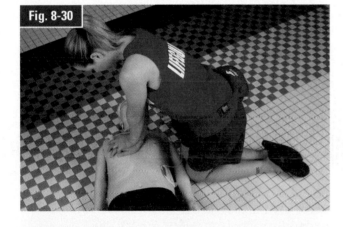
Fig. 8-30

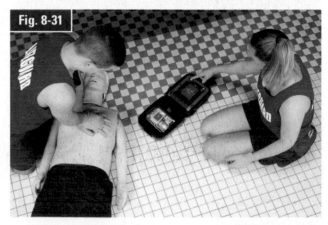
Fig. 8-31

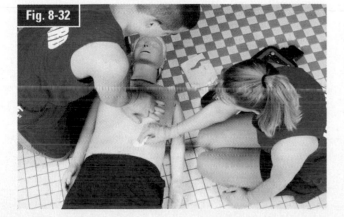
Fig. 8-32

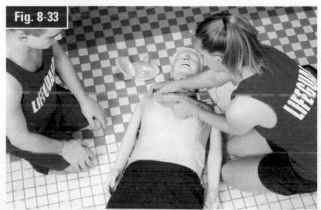
Fig. 8-33

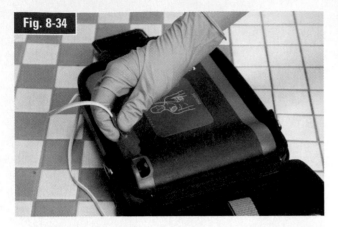
Fig. 8-34

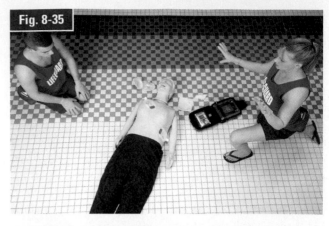
Fig. 8-35

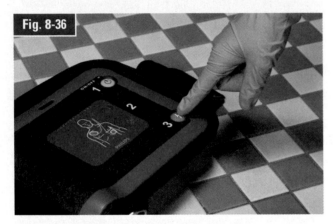
Fig. 8-36

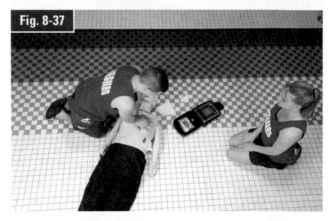
Fig. 8-37

7. If a shock is advised, push the "shock" button (**Fig. 8-36**).
   - Look to see that no one is touching the victim.
   - "Say, "EVERYONE STAND CLEAR."
8. After the shock, or if no shock is indicated—
   - **Rescuer 1** should perform 5 cycles (about 2 minutes) of CPR before analyzing the heart rhythm again (**Fig. 8-37**).
   - If at any time an obvious sign of life is detected, stop CPR and monitor the victim's ABCs.
   - Administer emergency oxygen, if available and trained to do so.

Using an AED—Child

While the incidence of cardiac arrest in children is relatively low compared with adults, cardiac arrest resulting from V-fib does happen to young children. Most cardiac arrests in children are not sudden. The most common causes of cardiac arrest in children are—
- Airway and breathing problems.
- Traumatic injuries or accidents (e.g., automobile, drowning, electrocution or poisoning).
- A hard blow to the chest.
- Congenital heart disease.

AEDs equipped with pediatric AED pads are capable of delivering appropriate levels of energy to children between 1 and 8 years of age or weighing less than 55 pounds. Use pediatric AED pads and/or equipment, if available. If pediatric-specific equipment is not available, an AED designed for adults may be used on a child. Always follow local protocols and manufacturer's instructions.

For a child in cardiac arrest, follow the same general steps and precautions that are used when using an AED on an adult.

To use an AED on a child—
1. Conduct an initial assessment.
2. Turn on the AED.
3. Wipe the child's chest dry.
4. Attach the pads.
   - Use pediatric AED pads, if available.
   - Place one pad on the child's upper right chest.
   - Place the other pad on the child's lower left side.
   - Make sure the pads are not touching. If the pads risk touching each other on a child, place one pad on the child's chest (**Fig. 8-38, A**) and the other pad on the child's back (between the shoulder blades) (**Fig. 8-38, B**).
5. Plug the connector into the AED, if necessary.
6. Make sure that no one, including you, is touching the child.
   - Look to see that no one is touching the child.
   - Say, "EVERYONE STAND CLEAR."
7. Push the "analyze" button, if necessary. Let the AED analyze the heart rhythm.

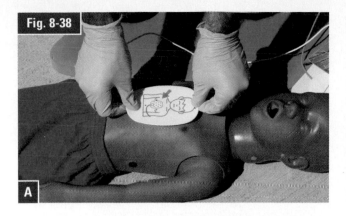

Fig. 8-38

A

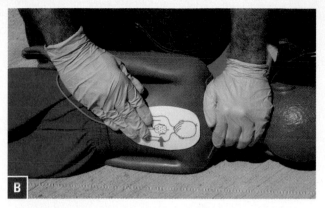

Fig. 8-38

B

8. If a shock is advised, push the "shock" button.
 ■ Look to see that nobody is touching the child.
 ■ Say, "EVERYONE STAND CLEAR."
9. After the shock, or if no shock is indicated—
 ■ Perform 5 cycles (about 2 minutes) of CPR before analyzing the heart rhythm again.
 ■ If at any time an obvious sign of life is detected, stop CPR and monitor the child's ABCs.
 ■ Administer emergency oxygen, if available and trained to do so.

If a second rescuer arrives with an AED while CPR is in progress, **Rescuer 1** should continue CPR until **Rescuer 2** is finished preparing the AED for use.

Rescuer 2 should complete the following steps:
1. Turn on the AED.
2. Wipe the child's chest dry (**Fig. 8-39**).
3. Attach the pads (**Fig. 8-40**).
 ■ Use pediatric AED pads, if available.
 ■ Place one pad on the child's upper right chest.
 ■ Place the other pad on the child's lower left side.
 ■ Make sure the pads are not touching. If the pads risk touching each other on a child, place one pad on the child's chest (**Fig. 8-41, A**) and the other pad on the child's back (between the shoulder blades) (**Fig. 8-41, B**).
4. Plug the connector into the AED, if necessary.

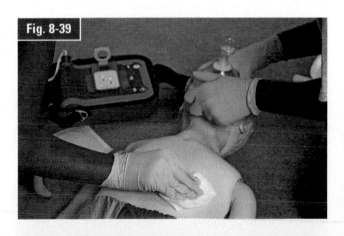

Fig. 8-39

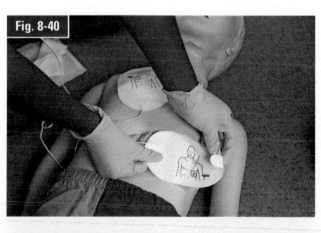

Fig. 8-40

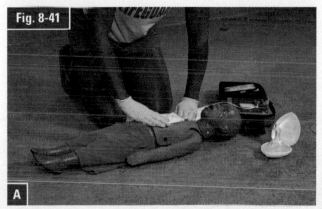

Fig. 8-41

A

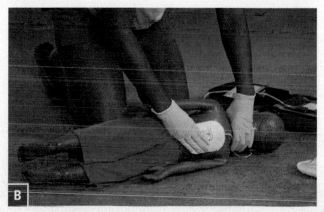

B

5. Make sure that nobody, including **Rescuer 1,** is touching the child.
   - Look to see that nobody is touching the child.
   - Say, "EVERYONE STAND CLEAR."
6. Push the "analyze" button, if necessary. Let the AED analyze the heart rhythm.
7. If a shock is advised, push the "shock" button.
   - Look to see that no one is touching the child.
   - Say, "EVERYONE STAND CLEAR."
8. After the shock, or if no shock is indicated—
   - **Rescuer 1** performs 5 cycles (about 2 minutes) of CPR before analyzing the heart rhythm again **(Fig. 8-42)**.
   - If at any time an obvious sign of life is detected, stop CPR and monitor the child's ABCs.
   - Administer emergency oxygen, if available and trained to do so.

AED Precautions

Take the following precautions when using an AED:
- Do not touch the victim while defibrillating. Someone could be shocked.
- Before shocking a victim with an AED, make sure that no one is touching or is in contact with the victim or the resuscitation equipment.
- Do not touch the victim while the AED is analyzing. Touching or moving the victim may affect the analysis.
- Do not use alcohol to wipe the victim's chest dry. Alcohol is flammable.
- Do not defibrillate someone when around flammable or combustible materials such as gasoline or free-flowing oxygen.
- Do not use an AED in a moving vehicle. Movement may affect the analysis.
- Do not use an AED on a victim who is in contact with water. Move the victim away from puddles of water, swimming pools or out of the rain, before defibrillating.
- Do not use an AED and/or pads designed for adults on a child under age 8 or less than 55 pounds, unless pediatric pads specific to the device are not available. Local protocols may differ on this and should be followed.
- Do not use pediatric AED pads on an adult, as they may not deliver enough energy for defibrillation.

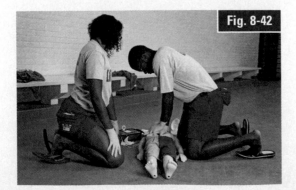

Fig. 8-42

- Do not use an AED on a victim wearing a nitroglycerin patch or other patch on the chest. With a gloved hand, remove any patches from the chest before attaching the device.
- Do not use a mobile phone or radio within 6 feet of the AED. This may interrupt analysis.

AEDs—Special Situations

Some situations require lifeguards to pay special attention when using an AED. These include using AEDs around water, using AEDs on victims with implantable devices or nitroglycerin patches and using AEDs on victims of trauma or hypothermia. Be familiar with these situations and know how to respond appropriately. Always use common sense when using an AED and follow the manufacturer's recommendations.

AEDs Around Water

If the victim was removed from the water, be sure there are no puddles of water around rescuers, the victim or the AED. Remove wet clothing for proper pad placement if necessary. Dry the victim's chest and attach the AED.

If it is raining, ensure that the victim is as dry as possible and sheltered from the rain. Wipe the victim's chest dry. Minimize delaying defibrillation when taking steps to provide for a dry environment. The electrical current of an AED is directional between the pads. AEDs are very safe, even in rain and snow, when all precautions and manufacturer's operating instructions are followed.

AEDs and Implantable Devices

Sometimes people may have had a pacemaker implanted if they have a weak heart, a heart that skips beats or a heart that beats too slow or fast. These small implantable devices are sometimes located in the area below the right collarbone. There may be a small lump that can be felt under the skin. Sometimes the pacemaker is placed somewhere else. Other people may have an implantable cardioverter defibrillator (ICD), a miniature version of an AED, which acts to automatically recognize and restore abnormal heart rhythms. Sometimes a victim's heart beats irregularly, even if the victim has a pacemaker or ICD.

If the implanted device is visible or the rescuer knows that the victim has an implanted device, do not place the defibrillation pad directly over the device **(Fig. 8-43)**. This may interfere with the delivery of the shock. Adjust pad placement, if necessary, and continue to follow the established protocol. If unsure, use the AED if needed. It will not harm the victim or rescuer.

Nitroglycerin Patches

People with a history of cardiac problems may have nitroglycerin patches on their chests. Since nitroglycerin can be absorbed by a rescuer, remove the patch with a gloved

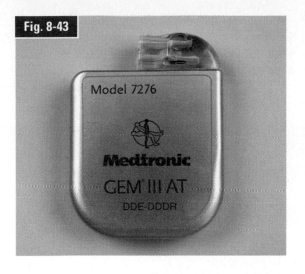

Fig. 8-43

Model 7276

Medtronic

GEM III AT

DDE-DDDR

hand before defibrillation. Nicotine patches used to stop smoking look similar to nitroglycerin patches. In order not to waste time trying to identify patches, remove any patch seen on the victim's chest with a gloved hand (**Fig. 8-44**).

Hypothermia

Some people who have experienced hypothermia have been resuscitated successfully even after prolonged exposure to the cold. It will take longer to perform a check or an assessment of a victim suffering from hypothermia because looking for movement and checking for breathing and a pulse can take up to 30 to 45 seconds. If no pulse is detected, begin CPR until an AED becomes available. If the victim is wet, dry his or her chest and attach the AED. If a shock is indicated, deliver a shock and follow the instructions of the AED. If there are no obvious signs of life, continue CPR. Follow local protocols as to whether additional shocks should be delivered. Continue CPR and protect the victim from further heat loss. Wet garments should be removed, if possible. The victim should not be defibrillated in water. CPR or defibrillation should not be withheld to rewarm the victim. Rescuers should take care not to shake a hypothermia victim unnecessarily, as this could result in V-fib.

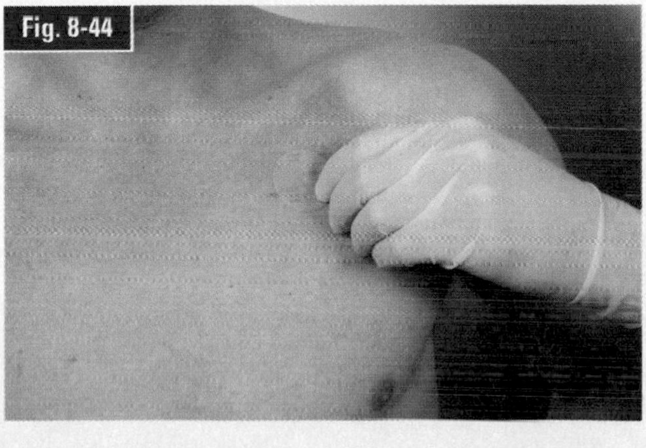

Fig. 8-44

Trauma

If a victim is in cardiac arrest resulting from traumatic injuries, an AED may still be used. Defibrillation should be administered according to local protocols.

Chest Hair

Some men have a lot of hair on their chest, which can make getting a good pad-to-skin contact difficult. Since time to first shock is critical, attach the pads and analyze as soon as possible. Press firmly on the pads to attach them to the victim's chest. If a "check pads" message comes from the AED, remove the pads and replace with new ones. The pad adhesive will pull out some of the chest hair, which may solve the problem. If the "check pads" message continues, remove the pads, shave the victim's chest and attach new pads to the victim's chest. A safety surgical razor should be included in the AED kit. Be careful not to cut the victim while shaving.

AED Maintenance

For defibrillators to perform optimally, they must be maintained like any other machine. AEDs require minimal maintenance. These devices have various self-testing features. However, it is important that operators be familiar with any visual or audible prompts the AED may have to warn of malfunction or a low battery. It is important to read the operator's manual thoroughly and check with the manufacturer to obtain all necessary information regarding maintenance.

In most instances, if the AED detects any malfunction, contact the manufacturer. The device may need to be returned to the manufacturer for service. While AEDs require minimal maintenance, it is important to remember the following:

- Follow the manufacturer's specific recommendations for periodic equipment checks.
- Make sure that the batteries have enough energy for one complete rescue. (A fully charged back-up battery should be readily available.)
- Make sure that the correct defibrillator pads are in the package and are properly sealed.
- Check any expiration dates on defibrillation pads and batteries and replace as necessary.
- After use, make sure that all accessories are replaced and that the machine is in proper working order.
- If at any time the machine fails to work properly or warning indicators are recognized, discontinue use and contact the manufacturer immediately.

PUTTING IT ALL TOGETHER

As professional rescuers, lifeguards should be able to recognize and respond to cardiac emergencies. Understand the importance of the four links of the Cardiac

Chain of Survival: early recognition of the emergency and early access to EMS, early CPR, early defibrillation and early advanced medical care. Be able to recognize and care for the signs and symptoms of a heart attack. Know how to recognize and care for a victim of cardiac arrest.

When using an AED, be sure to follow local protocols. AEDs are relatively easy to operate and generally require minimal training and retraining. When using an AED at an aquatic facility, be sure that the victim is placed on a dry surface, such as a backboard, and moved away from the pool's or water's edge.

AED Algorithm for the Professional Rescuer

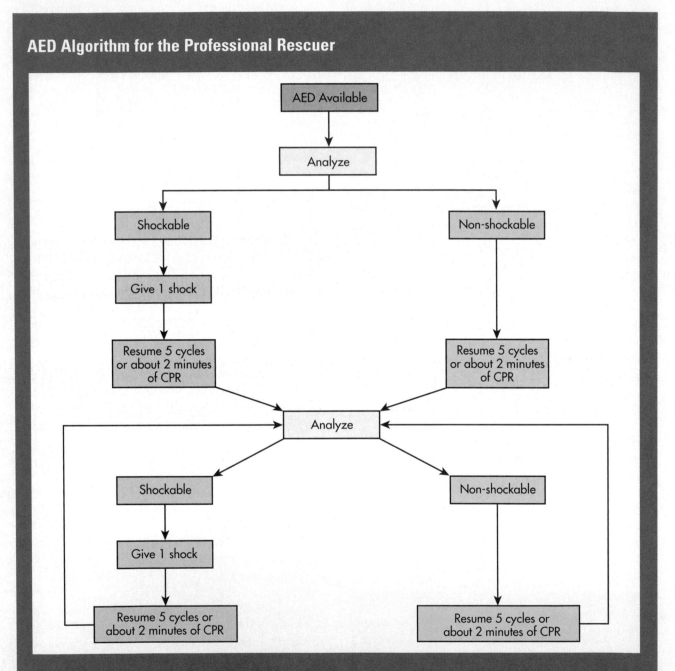

Note: As long as there is no obvious sign of life and the AED still indicates a need to shock, continue repeating sets of 1 shock to the maximum your local protocols allow, with 5 cycles (about 2 minutes) of CPR between each set. Also, as long as there is no obvious sign of life and the AED indicates that no shock is advised, you should still continue to give 5 cycles (about 2 minutes) of CPR before the AED reanalyzes. Be thoroughly familiar with your local protocols, which may vary from this example.

Chapter 9

First Aid

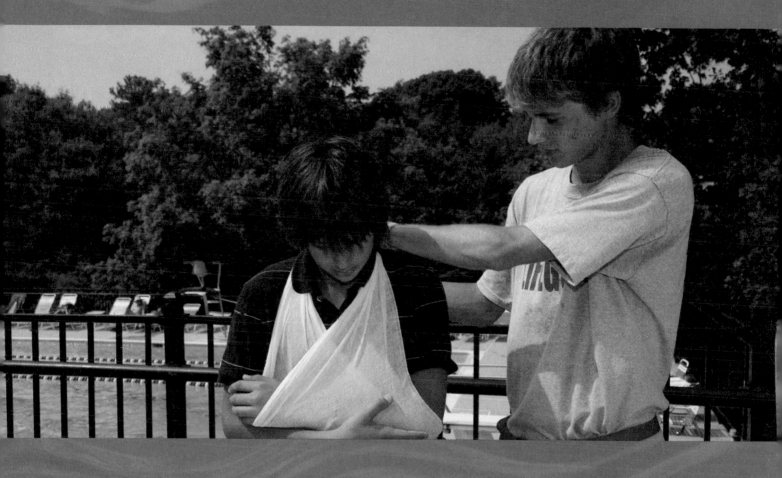

Even when everyone works to prevent emergencies, injuries and illnesses do occur at aquatic facilities. Every facility needs a first aid area or room where an injured or ill person can be provided first aid and can rest. First aid supplies should also be kept here (Fig. 9-1). Some facilities may staff the first aid area or room with personnel that have more advanced training, such as an emergency medical technician (EMT). Know where first aid areas are, what first aid equipment and supplies are there,

what additional staff resources are available and how to provide first aid correctly.

Remember to follow the general procedures for injury or sudden illness on land: size up the scene, perform an initial assessment, summon emergency medical services (EMS) personnel by calling 9-1-1 or the local emergency number and perform a secondary assessment. Use appropriate personal protective equipment, such as disposable gloves and breathing barriers. Carry a few first aid supplies in a hip pack (Fig. 9-2).

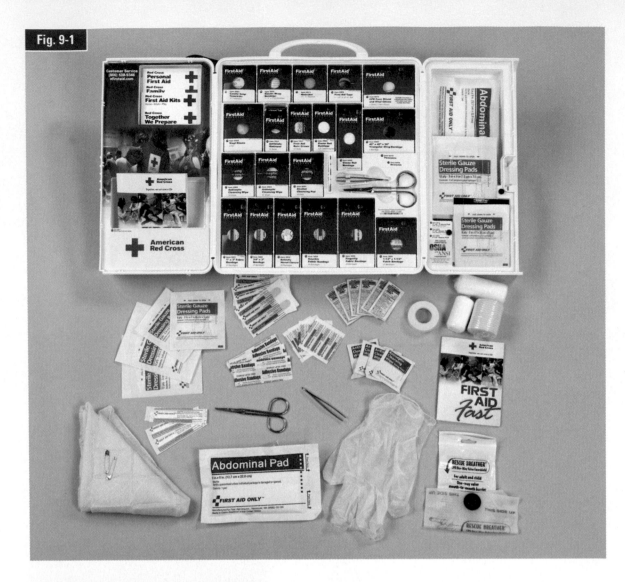

Fig. 9-1

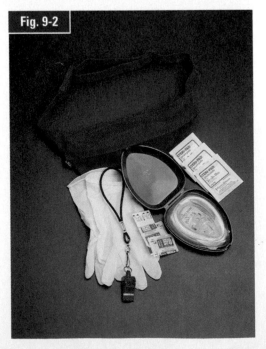

Fig. 9-2

SECONDARY ASSESSMENT

After completing the initial assessment and determining that there are no life-threatening conditions, perform a secondary assessment. During the secondary assessment, perform a quick head-to-toe examination for an adult or a toe-to-head examination for a child or infant and take a brief history **(Fig 9-3)**.

Using SAMPLE to Take a Brief History

Use the mnemonic SAMPLE as an easy way to remember the questions that should be asked when taking a brief history. When talking to children, get down at eye level with the child, talk slowly and in a friendly manner, use simple words and ask questions that the child can answer easily. Also, a lifeguard should ask if the child's parents are nearby to seek their permission to examine the child.

- **Signs and symptoms**—What happened? Where do you feel any pain or discomfort? Do you have any numbness or loss of sensation? If so, where?

- **Allergies**—Do you have any allergies to medications, food, etc.? If so, what type of reactions have you experienced when you were exposed?
- **Medications**—Do you have any medical conditions or are you taking any medications? If so, what conditions do you have or what medications are you taking? Have you taken any medications in the past 12 hours?
- **Pertinent past medical history**—Have you experienced any recent falls, accidents or blows to the head? Have you ever been in any medical, surgical or trauma incidents?
- **Last oral intake**—When did you last eat or drink? What did you last eat or drink?
- **Events leading up to the incident**—What were you doing before the incident occurred? What were you doing when the incident occurred?

Checking a Conscious Adult

After taking a brief history, check the victim by performing a head-to-toe examination. Before beginning the examination, tell the victim what you are going to do. Visually inspect the victim's body looking carefully for any bleeding, cuts, bruises and obvious deformities (**Fig. 9-4**). Look for a medical identification necklace or bracelet on the victim's wrist, neck or ankle (**Fig. 9-5**). A necklace or bracelet will provide medical information about the person, explain how to care for certain conditions and list whom to call for help. Do not ask the victim to move any areas in which he or she has discomfort or pain or if head, neck or back injury is suspected. The lifeguard then performs the examination by checking—

- The head (**Fig. 9-6**).
  - Look at the scalp, face, ears, eyes, nose and mouth for cuts, bumps, bruises and depressions.
  - Note if the victim has any changes in the level of consciousness, such as dizziness, or feels light-headed.
- Skin appearance and temperature (**Fig. 9-7**).
  - Feel the victim's forehead with the back of the hand and note if the skin is cold or hot.
  - Look at the coloring of the victim's face and lips.
  - Look at the victim's skin and note if it is moist or dry; or if it is red, pale, flushed or ashen.
- The neck (**Fig. 9-8**).
  - Ask the victim to move his or her head from side-to-side if there is no discomfort and if an injury to the neck is not suspected.
  - Note pain, discomfort or inability to move.

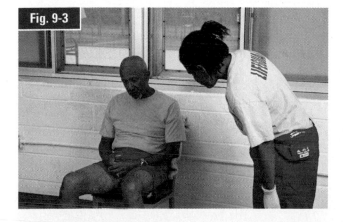

Fig. 9-3

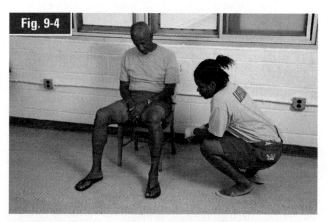

Fig. 9-4

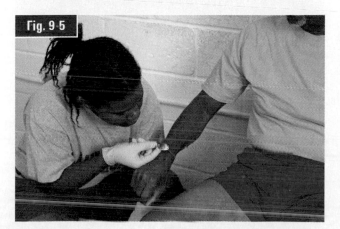

Fig. 9-5

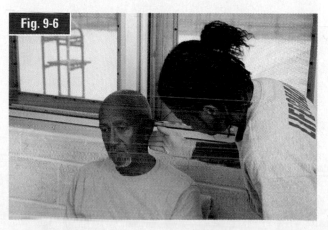

Fig. 9-6

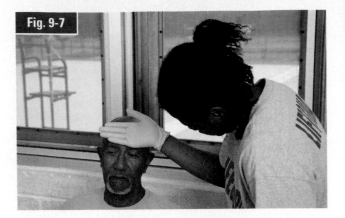

Fig. 9-7

Fig. 9-8

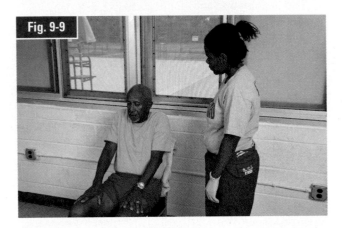

Fig. 9-9

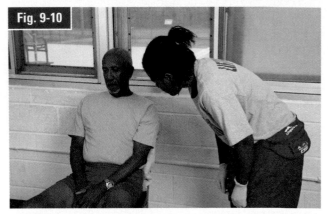

Fig. 9-10

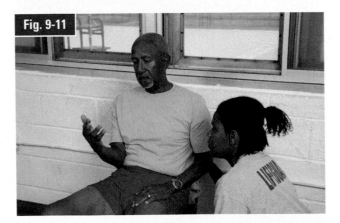

Fig. 9-11

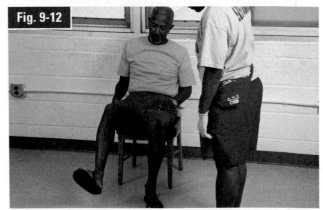

Fig. 9-12

- The shoulders (**Fig. 9-9**).
  - Ask the victim to shrug his or her shoulders.
- The chest and abdomen (**Fig. 9-10**).
  - Ask the victim to take a deep breath and blow air out.
  - Listen for difficulty or changes in breathing.
  - Ask the victim if he or she is experiencing pain during breathing.
- The arms (**Fig. 9-11**).
  - Check one arm at a time.
  - Ask the victim to move his or her hand and fingers and to bend the arm.

- The legs (**Fig. 9-12**).
  - Check one leg at a time.
  - Ask the victim to move his or her foot and toes and to bend the leg.

After completing the check, care for any conditions found. Have the victim rest in a comfortable position if he or she can move all body parts without pain or discomfort and has no other apparent signs or symptoms of injury or illness. Continue to watch for changes in consciousness and breathing.

If the victim is unable to move a body part or is experiencing dizziness or pain on movement—

- Help the victim rest in a comfortable position.

- Keep the victim from getting chilled or overheated.
- Reassure the victim.
- Determine whether to summon EMS personnel.
- Continue to watch for changes in the level of consciousness and breathing.

Checking a Conscious Child or Infant

When checking a child or infant for nonlife-threatening conditions, observe the child or infant before touching him or her. Look for signs and symptoms that indicate changes in the level of consciousness, trouble breathing and any apparent injuries or conditions. When beginning the check, start the examination at the toes so the child or infant can become familiar with the process and see what is happening. Look and check for the same things that would be examined for an adult or unconscious child or infant.

LIFEGUARDING TIP: If any life-threatening conditions develop when performing the secondary assessment, stop the assessment and provide appropriate care immediately.

SUDDEN ILLNESS

Sudden illness can happen to anyone, anywhere. A lifeguard may not know what the illness is, but he or she can still provide care. Victims of sudden illness usually look and feel ill. If something is suspected to be wrong, check the victim and look for a medical identification necklace or bracelet on the person's wrist, neck or ankle **(Fig. 9-13).** A tag will provide medical information about the person, explain how to care for certain conditions and list whom to call for help. The victim may try to say nothing is seriously wrong, but the victim's condition can worsen rapidly. Do not be afraid to ask the victim questions.

Fig. 9-13

There are many types of sudden illness, such as—
- A diabetic emergency.
- Fainting.
- A seizure.
- A stroke.
- An allergic reaction.
- Poisoning.

Signs and Symptoms of Sudden Illness

Many different sudden illnesses have similar signs and symptoms. These include—
- Changes in the level of consciousness, such as feeling light-headed, dizzy or becoming unconscious.
- Nausea or vomiting.
- Difficulty speaking or slurred speech.
- Numbness or weakness.
- Loss of vision or blurred vision.
- Changes in breathing; the person may have trouble breathing or may not be breathing normally.
- Changes in skin color (pale, ashen or flushed skin).
- Sweating.
- Persistent pressure or pain.
- Diarrhea.
- Seizures.
- Paralysis or an inability to move.
- Severe headache.

General Care Steps for Sudden Illness

When providing care for sudden illness, follow the general procedures for injury or sudden illness on land and—
- Care for any life-threatening conditions first.
- Monitor the victim's airway, breathing and circulation (ABCs).
- Watch for changes in the level of consciousness.
- Keep the victim comfortable and reassure him or her.
- Keep the victim from getting chilled or overheated.
- Do not give the victim anything to eat or drink unless the victim is fully conscious and is not in shock.
- Care for any other problems that develop, such as vomiting.
- Administer emergency oxygen, if available and trained to do so.

Diabetic Emergency

Victims who are diabetic sometimes become ill because there is too much or too little sugar in their blood. Many diabetics use diet, exercise or medication to control their diabetes. The victim may disclose that he or she is diabetic or it may be learned from the information on a medical identification tag or from a bystander. Often, diabetics know what is wrong and will ask for something with sugar in it or may carry some form of sugar with them.

If the diabetic victim is conscious and can safely swallow food or fluids, give him or her sugar, preferably in liquid form. Most fruit juices and nondiet soft drinks have enough sugar to be effective. A lifeguard can also give table sugar dissolved in a glass of water. If the victim's problem is low blood sugar, sugar will help quickly. If the problem is too much sugar, the sugar will not cause any further harm.

Always summon EMS personnel if—

- The victim is unconscious or about to lose consciousness.
- The victim is conscious and unable to swallow.
- The victim does not feel better within about 5 minutes after taking sugar.
- Sugar cannot be found immediately. Do not spend time looking for it.

Fainting

When a victim suddenly loses consciousness and then reawakens, he or she may simply have fainted. Fainting is not usually harmful and the victim will usually quickly recover. Lower the victim to the ground or other flat surface and position the victim on his or her back. If possible, raise the victim's legs 8 to 12 inches. Loosen any tight clothing, such as a tie or collar. Make sure the victim is breathing. Do not give the victim anything to eat or drink. If the victim vomits, position the victim on his or her side.

Seizures

Provide care to a person who has had a seizure in the same manner as for any unconscious victim. To protect the victim from being injured, remove any nearby objects that might cause injury. Protect the victim's head by placing a thin cushion under it. Folded clothing makes an adequate cushion. If there is fluid in the victim's mouth, such as saliva, blood or vomit, roll him or her on one side so that the fluid drains from the mouth.

When the seizure is over, the victim will usually begin to breathe normally. He or she may be drowsy and disoriented or unresponsive for a period of time. Check to see if the victim was injured during the seizure. Be reassuring and comforting. If the seizure occurred in public, the victim may be embarrassed and self-conscious. Ask bystanders not to crowd around the victim. He or she will be tired and want to rest. Stay with the victim until he or she is fully conscious and aware of his or her surroundings.

If the victim is known to have periodic seizures, there is no need to summon EMS personnel. He or she will usually recover from a seizure in a few minutes. However, summon EMS personnel if—

- The seizure lasts more than 5 minutes.
- The victim has multiple seizures.
- The victim appears to be injured.
- The victim is pregnant.
- The victim is a diabetic.
- The victim fails to regain consciousness.
- The seizure occurs in the water.

Fig. 9-14

Seizures in the Water

If the victim has a seizure in the water—

1. Summon or have someone else summon EMS personnel.
2. Support the victim with his or her head above water until the seizure ends (**Fig. 9-14**).
3. Remove the victim from the water as soon as possible after the seizure (since he or she may have inhaled or swallowed water).
4. Place the victim face-up on the deck and perform an initial assessment. Perform rescue breathing or cardiopulmonary resuscitation (CPR) if needed. If the victim vomits, turn the victim on his or her side to drain fluids from the mouth. Sweep out the mouth (or suction out the mouth if trained to do so).

Stroke

As with other sudden illnesses, the signs and symptoms of a stroke or mini-stroke are a sudden change in how the body is working or feeling. This may include sudden weakness or numbness of the face, arm or leg. Usually, weakness or numbness occurs only on one side of the body. In addition, the victim may—

- Have difficulty talking or being understood when speaking.
- Have blurred or dimmed vision.
- Experience a sudden, severe headache; dizziness; or confusion.

To care for a victim of stroke, think **FAST**—

- **F**ace—Weakness on one side of the face.
  - Ask the victim to smile. This will show if there is drooping or weakness in the muscles on one side of the face.
- **A**rm—Weakness or numbness in one arm.
  - Ask the victim to raise both arms to find out if there is weakness in the limbs.
- **S**peech—Slurred speech or trouble speaking.
  - Ask the victim to speak a simple sentence to listen for slurred or distorted speech. Example: "I have the lunch orders ready."

- **T**ime—Time to summon EMS personnel if any of these signs or symptoms is seen.
    - Note the time that the signs and symptoms began and summon EMS personnel immediately.

BITES AND STINGS

Spider Bites/Scorpion Stings

Only two spiders in the United States are poisonous—the black widow and the brown recluse. Their bite can make a person very sick or can be fatal. Spider bites at aquatic facilities usually occur on the hands and arms when people reach or rummage in dark areas, such as lockers or storage areas. In addition, some scorpion stings can cause death.

If someone has been bitten by a black widow or brown recluse or stung by a scorpion—

- Summon EMS personnel.
- Wash the wound.
- Apply a cold pack to the site.
- If it is available, give the victim anti-venom—a medication that blocks the effects of the spider's poisonous venom.
- Care for life-threatening conditions.
- Monitor the victim's ABCs.
- Keep the victim comfortable.

Snakebites

Snakebites kill very few people in the United States. Of the 7000 people bitten each year in the United States, less than five die.

To care for someone bitten by a pit viper, such as a rattlesnake, copperhead or cotton mouth—

- Summon EMS personnel.
- Wash the wound. Keep the injured area still and lower than the heart.

To care for someone bitten by an *elapid snake,* such as a coral snake **(Fig. 9-15)**—

- Summon EMS personnel.
- Wash the wound.
- Apply an elastic roller bandage. Use a narrow bandage to wrap a hand or wrist, a medium-width bandage to wrap an arm or ankle and a wide bandage to wrap a leg.
    - Check the circulation of the limb beyond where the bandage will be placed by noting changes in skin color and temperature.
    - Place the end of the bandage against the skin and use overlapping turns.
    - Gently stretch the bandage while wrapping. The wrap should cover a long body section, such as an arm or a calf, beginning at the point farthest from

Fig. 9-15

the heart. For a joint like a knee or ankle, use figure-eight turns to support the joint.

- Always check the area above and below the injury site for warmth and color, especially fingers and toes, after applying an elastic roller bandage. By checking before and after bandaging, any tingling or numbness that is noticed can be determined to be from the bandaging or the injury.
- Check the snugness of the bandage—a finger should easily, but not loosely, pass under the bandage.
- Keep the injured area still and lower than the heart.

For any snakebite, **DO NOT**—
- Apply ice.
- Cut the wound.
- Apply suction.
- Apply a tourniquet.
- Use electric shock.

Stings

Insect stings are painful. They can be fatal for people who have severe allergic reactions. This allergic reaction may result in a breathing emergency. If someone is having a breathing emergency, summon EMS personnel.

To care for an insect sting—

- Examine the sting site to see if the stinger is in the skin (if there is one). If it is, scrape the stinger away from the skin with a fingernail or a plastic card, such as a credit card.
- Wash the wound with soap and water.
- Cover the site and keep it clean.
- Apply a cold pack to the site to reduce pain and swelling.
- Watch the victim for signals of an allergic reaction.
- Care for life-threatening conditions.
- Monitor the victim's ABCs.
- Keep the victim comfortable.

Marine Life

Many marine creatures, including spiny urchins, stingrays and some types of coral and jellyfish, can sting people in the water. The supervisor of the aquatic facility should inform lifeguards about the kinds of marine life around the facility with which facility staff should be concerned.

If someone has been stung by marine life—

- Summon EMS personnel if the victim does not know what stung him or her, was stung on the face or neck, is known to be allergic to marine life or starts to have trouble breathing.
- Wash the wound with soap and water.
- For a jellyfish, sea anemone or Portuguese man-of-war sting, soak the area with household vinegar, baking soda mixed in water or rubbing alcohol as soon as possible. Do not rub the wound or apply fresh water or ammonia because this increases pain.
- For a stingray, sea urchin or spiny fish sting, flush the wound with tap water. Ocean water also may be used. Immobilize the injured area and soak it in nonscalding hot water, as hot as the victim can stand, for about 30 minutes or until the pain goes away. If hot water is not available, packing the area in hot sand may have a similar effect if the sand is hot enough. Then carefully clean the wound and apply a bandage.
- Care for life-threatening conditions.
- Monitor the victim's ABCs.
- Keep the victim comfortable.

POISONING

Ingested Poison

A *poison* is any substance that can cause injury, illness or death when introduced into the body. If a person is showing signals of poisoning, call the Poison Control Center at 1-800-222-1222. If the person is unconscious, if there is a change in the level of consciousness or if another life-threatening condition is present, summon EMS personnel.

Inhaled Poison

Poisonous fumes can come from a variety of sources. They may or may not have an odor. Common inhaled poisons include—

- Carbon monoxide (car exhaust, fires, charcoal grills).
- Chlorine gas (highly toxic, requires training on how to recognize and deal with it).

If someone has inhaled poisonous fumes—
- Size up the scene to be sure it is safe to help the victim.

- Summon EMS personnel.
- Move the victim to fresh air.
- Care for life-threatening conditions.
- Monitor the victim's ABCs.
- If conscious, keep the victim comfortable.

Poisonous Plants

Poison ivy, poison oak and poison sumac are the most common poisonous plants (**Fig. 9-16, A-C**). Some people are allergic to these plants and have life-threatening reactions after contact, while others may not even get a rash.

Fig. 9-16

A

B

C

If someone has come in contact with a poisonous plant—
- Remove exposed clothing and wash the exposed area thoroughly with soap and water as soon as possible after contact.
- If rash or wet blisters develop, advise the victim to see his or her health-care professional.
- If the condition spreads to large areas of the body or face, have the victim seek medical attention.

WOUNDS

Soft tissues are the layers of skin and the fat and muscle beneath the skin's outer layer. A physical injury to the body's soft tissue, such as the skin, fat and muscles, is called a *wound*. Any time the soft tissues are damaged or torn, the body is threatened. Injuries may damage the soft tissues at or near the skin's surface or deep in the body. Germs can get into the body through a scrape, cut, puncture or burn and cause infection. Severe bleeding can occur at the skin's surface and under it, where it is harder to detect. Burns are a special kind of soft tissue injury. Like other types of soft tissue injury, burns can damage the top layer of skin or the skin and the layers of fat, muscle and bone beneath. Soft tissue injuries are typically classified as either closed or open wounds.

Closed Wounds
Closed wounds occur beneath the surface of the skin. Internal bleeding may occur when the skin's surface is not broken and damage to soft tissue and blood vessels happens below the surface. Most closed wounds, such as a bruise (contusion), do not require special medical care. However, a significant violent force can cause injuries involving larger blood vessels and the deeper layers of muscle tissue. These injuries can result in severe bleeding beneath the skin. In this case, medical care is needed quickly.

Caring for Internal Bleeding
Summon EMS personnel immediately if—
- The victim complains of severe pain or cannot move a body part without pain.
- The force that caused the injury was great enough to cause serious damage.
- An injured extremity is blue or extremely pale.
- The victim has excessive thirst, becomes confused, faint, drowsy or unconscious.
- The victim is vomiting blood or coughing up blood.
- The victim has skin that feels cool or moist or looks pale or bluish.
- The victim has a rapid, weak pulse.

- The victim has tender, swollen, bruised or hard areas of the body, such as the abdomen.

While waiting for EMS personnel to arrive—
1. Care for any life-threatening conditions first.
2. Monitor the victim's ABCs.
3. Watch for changes in the level of consciousness.
4. Keep the victim comfortable and reassure the victim.
5. Keep the victim from getting chilled or overheated.
6. Care for any other problems that develop, such as vomiting.

If the closed wound is not serious—
1. Apply direct pressure on the area to decrease bleeding under the skin.
2. Elevate the injured part to reduce swelling if a muscle, bone or joint injury is not suspected and it does not cause more pain.
3. Apply ice or a cold pack on the area to help control swelling and pain.
   - When applying ice or a chemical cold pack, place a gauze pad, towel or other cloth between the source of cold and the victim's skin.
   - Leave the ice or cold pack on for no more than 20 minutes. If continued icing is needed, remove the pack for 20 minutes and then replace it.

Open Wounds
In an open wound, the break in the skin can be as minor as a scrape of the surface layers or as severe as a deep penetration. The amount of bleeding depends on the location and severity of the injury.

The following are the four main types of open wounds:
- **Abrasion (Fig. 9-17)**
  - Skin has been rubbed or scraped away (e.g., scrape, road rash, rug burn). The area usually is painful.
  - Dirt and other matter can enter the wound. Cleaning the wound is important to prevent infection.

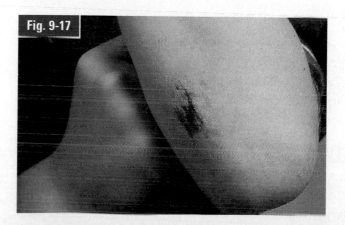

Fig. 9-17

- **Laceration (Fig. 9-18)**
  - Cuts bleed freely, and deep cuts can bleed severely.
  - Deep cuts can damage nerves, large blood vessels and other soft tissues.
- **Avulsion (Fig. 9-19)**
  - A cut in which a piece of soft tissue or even part of the body, such as a finger, is torn loose or is torn off entirely (e.g., amputation).
  - Often, deeper tissues are damaged, causing significant bleeding.
- **Puncture (Fig. 9-20)**
  - Puncture wounds often do not bleed a lot and can easily become infected.

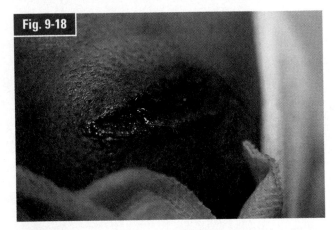

Fig. 9-18

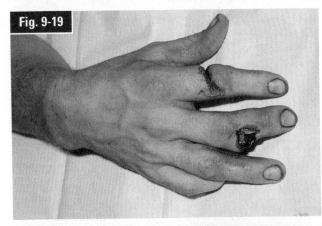

Fig. 9-19

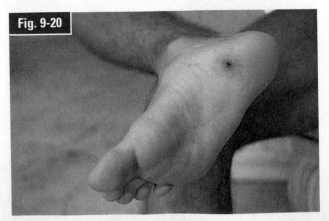

Fig. 9-20

- Bleeding can be severe with damage to major blood vessels or internal organs.
- An embedded object in the wound should be removed only by EMS personnel.

External Bleeding

External bleeding occurs when there is a break in the skin's surface. Most externally bleeding injuries a lifeguard will encounter will be minor, such as a small cut that can be cared for by applying an adhesive bandage. Minor bleeding, such as a small cut, usually stops by itself within 10 minutes when the blood clots. However, sometimes the cut is too large or the blood is under too much pressure for effective clotting to occur. In these cases, recognition and care needs to happen quickly.

Caring for External Bleeding. To care for a minor wound, follow these general guidelines:

- Cover the wound with a dressing, such as a sterile gauze pad.
- Apply direct pressure firmly against the wound for a few minutes to control any bleeding **(Fig. 9-21)**.
- Wash the wound thoroughly with soap and water. If possible, irrigate an abrasion for about 5 minutes with clean, running tap water.
- Apply triple-antibiotic ointment or cream to a minor wound if the person has no known allergies or sensitivities to the medication.
- Cover the wound with a sterile dressing and bandage (or with an adhesive bandage) if it is still bleeding slightly or if the area of the wound is likely to come into contact with dirt or germs **(Fig. 9-22)**.

To care for a major wound, follow the general procedures for injury or sudden illness on land and—

- Cover the wound with a dressing, such as a sterile gauze pad.
- Apply direct pressure firmly against the wound until bleeding stops.
- Cover the dressing with a roller bandage and tie the knot directly over the wound.

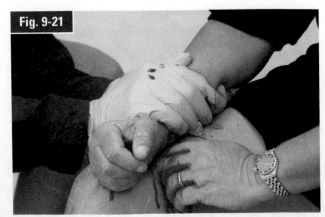

Fig. 9-21

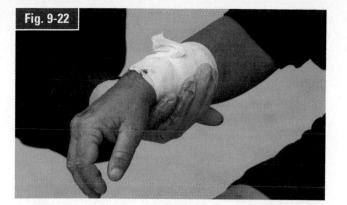

Fig. 9-22

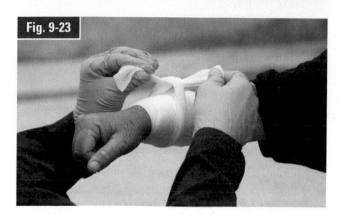

Fig. 9-23

- If the bleeding does not stop—
  - Apply additional dressings and bandages on top of the first ones **(Fig. 9-23)**.
  - Take steps to minimize shock.
  - Summon, or have someone else summon, EMS personnel if not already done.
- Wash hands immediately after providing care.

Shock

Any serious injury or illness can cause the condition known as *shock*. Shock is a natural reaction by the body. It usually means the victim's condition is very serious. Signs and symptoms of shock include—
- Restlessness or irritability.
- Altered level of consciousness.
- Pale or ashen, cool, moist skin.
- Nausea or vomiting.
- Rapid breathing and pulse.
- Excessive thirst.

To minimize the effects of shock—
- Make sure that EMS personnel have been summoned.
- Monitor the victim's ABCs.
- Control any external bleeding.
- Keep the victim from getting chilled or overheated.
- Have the victim lie down and elevate the legs about 12 inches if a head, neck or back injury or if broken bones in the hips or legs are not suspected.

- Comfort and reassure the victim until EMS personnel arrive and take over.
- Administer emergency oxygen, if available and trained to do so.

LIFEGUARDING TIP: *DO NOT GIVE FOOD OR DRINK TO A VICTIM OF SHOCK.*

Care for Wounds—Special Situations
Many kinds of wounds can occur at aquatic facilities, such as severed body parts, embedded objects or injuries to the mouth. In such situations, remain calm and follow the general procedures for injury or sudden illness on land.

Eye Injury
Care for open or close wounds around the eyeball as for any soft tissue injury. Never put direct pressure on the eyeball. For embedded objects in the eye—
- Summon EMS personnel.
- Help the victim into a comfortable position.
- Do not try to remove any object from the eye.
- Bandage loosely and do not put pressure on the injured eyeball.
- Stabilize the object as best as possible. A paper cup can be placed around the object to stabilize it **(Fig. 9-24)**.

For small foreign bodies in the eye, such as sand or other small debris—
- Tell the victim to blink several times to try to remove the object.
- Gently flush the eye with water.
- Seek medical attention if the object remains.

For chemicals in the eye—
- Flush the eye continuously with water for 10 minutes or until EMS personnel arrive. Always flush away from the uninjured eye.

Injuries to the Mouth and Teeth
If a head, neck or back injury is not suspected—
- Rinse out the mouth with cold tap water, if available.

Fig. 9-24

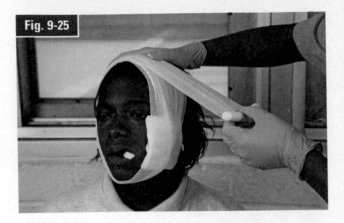

Fig. 9-25

Fig. 9-26

- Have the victim lean slightly forward or place the victim on his or her side.
- Try to prevent the victim from swallowing the blood, which may cause nausea or vomiting.
- Apply a dressing.
  - For inside the cheek, place folded sterile dressings inside the mouth against the wound.
  - For outside of the cheek, apply direct pressure using a sterile dressing (**Fig. 9-25**).
  - For the tongue or lips, apply direct pressure using a sterile dressing. Apply cold to reduce swelling and ease pain.
- If a tooth is knocked out—
  - Rinse out the mouth with cold tap water, if available.
  - Have the victim bite down on a rolled sterile dressing in the space left by the tooth (or teeth).
  - Save any displaced teeth.
    - Carefully pick up the tooth by the crown (white part), not the root.
    - Rinse off the root of the tooth in water if it is dirty. Do not scrub it or remove any attached tissue fragments.
    - Place the tooth in milk, if possible, or water and keep it with the victim.
  - Advise the victim to get to a dentist with the tooth as soon as possible.

Injuries to the Abdomen
- Summon EMS personnel.
- Wounds through the abdomen can cause internal organs to push out.
- Carefully remove clothing from around the wound.
- Do not attempt to put the organs back into the abdomen.
- Cover the organs with a moist, sterile dressing and cover the dressing with plastic wrap.
- Place a folded towel or cloth over the dressing to keep the organs warm.
- Care for shock.

Nosebleed
- Have the victim sit leaning slightly forward (**Fig. 9-26**).
- Pinch the nostrils together for about 10 minutes or until bleeding stops.
  - Other methods of controlling bleeding include applying an ice pack to the bridge of the nose or putting pressure on the upper lip just beneath the nose.
- After the bleeding stops, have the victim avoid rubbing, blowing or picking the nose, which could restart the bleeding.
- Medical attention is needed if the bleeding persists or recurs or if the victim says it results from high blood pressure.
- If the victim loses consciousness, place the victim on his or her side to allow blood to drain from the nose. Summon EMS personnel immediately.

Severed Body Parts
- Summon EMS personnel.
- Control the bleeding.
- Wrap and bandage the wound to prevent infection.
- Wrap the severed body part(s) in sterile gauze (or clean material) (**Fig. 9-27**).

Fig. 9-27

- Place the severed body part(s) in a plastic bag.
- Put the plastic bag on ice (but do not freeze it).
- Care for shock.
- Be sure the body part is taken to the hospital with the victim immediately.

Animal and Human Bites

An animal or human bite may be serious because of the wound and the risk of infection.
- Summon EMS personnel if the wound bleeds severely or if the animal is suspected to have rabies.
- For severe bleeding, control the bleeding first. Do not clean the wound. It will be properly cleaned at the hospital.

If the bleeding is minor—
- Wash the wound with soap and water.
- Control the bleeding.
- Cover with a sterile bandage.

Emergency Childbirth

If a pregnant woman is about to give birth, summon EMS personnel. Important information to give to the dispatcher includes—
- The pregnant woman's name, age and expected due date.
- How long she has been having labor pains.
- If this is her first child.

The lifeguard should also—
- Talk with the woman to help her remain calm.
- Place layers of newspaper or other absorbent material covered with layers of towels or blankets on a flat surface for the woman to lie on.
- Control the scene so that the woman will have privacy.
- Position the woman on her back with her knees bent, feet flat and legs spread apart.

Remember, the woman delivers the baby, so be patient and let it happen naturally. The baby will be slippery, so take care to avoid dropping the newborn. After delivery, wrap the newborn in a clean, warm blanket or towel and place the newborn next to the mother.

LIFEGUARDING TIPS:
- **Do not let the woman get up or leave to find a restroom (most women at this moment feel a desire to use the restroom).**
- **Do not hold the woman's knees together, this will not slow the birth process and may complicate the birth or harm the baby.**

- **Do not place fingers in the vagina for any reason.**
- **Do not pull on the baby.**

Continue to meet the needs of the newborn while caring for the mother. Help the mother to begin nursing the newborn, if possible. This will stimulate the uterus to contract and help slow bleeding. The placenta will still be in the uterus, attached to the newborn by the umbilical cord. Contractions of the uterus will usually expel the placenta within 30 minutes. Do not pull on the umbilical cord. Catch the placenta in a clean towel or container. It is not necessary to separate the placenta from the newborn.

Scalp Injuries

Scalp injuries often bleed heavily. Putting pressure on the area around the wound can control the bleeding.
- Apply gentle pressure at first because there may be a skull fracture **(Fig. 9-28)**. If a depression, spongy areas or bone fragments are felt, do not put direct pressure on the wound.
- Summon EMS personnel if the seriousness of the scalp injury is unknown.
- For an open wound with no sign of a fracture, control the bleeding with several dressings secured with a bandage.

Embedded Objects

An object that remains in an open wound is called an *embedded object*. Take the following steps to care for an embedded object:
- Summon EMS personnel.
- Place several dressings around the object to keep it from moving.
- Bandage the dressings in place around the object **(Fig. 9-29)**.
- Do not remove the object.

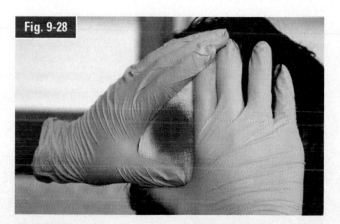
Fig. 9-28

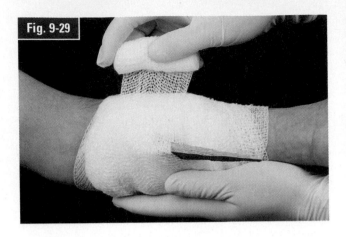

Fig. 9-29

Burns

There are four sources of burns: heat, radiation, chemical and electrical. Burns can be superficial (first degree), partial thickness (second degree) or full thickness (third degree) **(Fig 9-30, A-C)**. How severe a burn is depends on—

- The temperature or strength of the heat or other source.
- The length of exposure to the burn source.
- The location of the burn.
- The area and size of the burn.
- The victim's age and general medical condition.

The following burns can lead to shock and need immediate medical attention:

- Burns that cause a victim to have difficulty breathing
- Burns covering more than one body part or a large surface area
- Burns to the head, neck, hands, feet or genitals
- Burns to the airway (burns to the mouth and nose may be a signal of this)
- Burns (other than a very minor one) to a child younger than age 5 or an elderly person older than age 60
- Burns from chemicals, explosions or electricity

Caring for Burns

To care for burns, follow the general procedures for a land emergency. If the scene is safe, check the victim for life-threatening conditions. Summon EMS personnel if the condition is life threatening.

To care for burns—

- Stop the burning by removing the person from the source of the burn.
- Cool the burned area with cool, running water until pain is relieved.
- Cover the burned area loosely with a sterile dressing.
- Prevent infection.
- Take steps to minimize shock.
- Keep the victim from getting chilled or overheated.
- Comfort and reassure the victim.

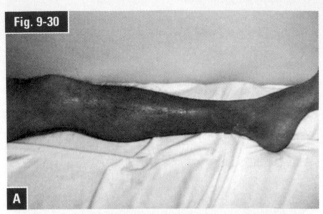

Fig. 9-30

A

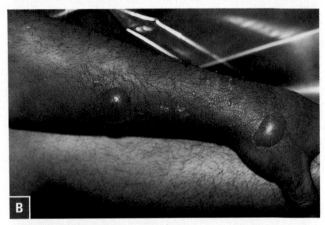

B

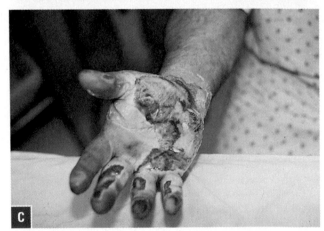

C

To care for electrical burns—

- Summon EMS personnel.
- Check the scene for safety, and check for life-threatening injuries. If a power line is down, wait for the fire department or the power company to disconnect the power source.
- Cool the burn.
- Be aware that electrocutions can cause cardiac and breathing emergencies. Be prepared to perform CPR or defibrillation.

- Cover the burn with a dry, sterile dressing.
- Take steps to minimize shock.

To care for chemical burns—
- Summon EMS personnel.
- Brush off dry chemicals with a gloved hand, being careful not to get the chemical on oneself or to brush it into the victim's eyes. Flush the affected area continuously with large amounts of water.
- Keep flushing the area for at least 20 minutes or until EMS personnel arrive.
- If a chemical gets into an eye, flush the eye with cool, clean running water until EMS personnel arrive. Always flush the affected eye from the nose outward and downward to prevent washing the chemical into the other eye.
- If possible, have the person remove contaminated clothes to prevent further contamination while continuing to flush the area.

To care for radiation (sun) burns—
- Care is the same as for any other burn.
- Cool the burned area and protect the area from further damage by keeping it out of the sun.

INJURIES TO MUSCLES, BONES AND JOINTS

Injuries to muscles, bones and joints can happen from accidents, such as falls. There are four types of muscle, bone and joint injuries:
- Fractures—A complete break, a chip or a crack in a bone.
- Dislocations—The movement of a bone away from its normal position at a joint. They are usually more obvious than fractures.
- Sprains—The tearing of ligaments at a joint.
- Strains—The stretching and tearing of muscles or tendons.

It is difficult to know whether a muscle, bone or joint injury is a fracture, dislocation, sprain or strain, but it is not necessary to know what type of injury the victim has because the care that is provided is the same.

Caring for Muscle, Bone and Joint Injuries
When caring for muscle, bone and joint injuries, use the general procedures for a land emergency and—
- Summon EMS personnel if the victim cannot move or use the injured area.
- Support the injured area above and below the site of the injury.
- Check for feeling, warmth and color below the injured area.

- Immobilize and secure the injured area if the victim must be moved and it does not cause further pain or injury.
- Recheck for feeling, warmth and color below the injured area.

Immobilizing Muscle, Bone and Joint Injuries
Immobilizing a muscle, bone or joint injury helps keep the injured body part from moving. This may also help reduce any pain. Splinting is a method of immobilizing an injured extremity and should be used **ONLY** if moving or transporting a person to seek medical attention and if splinting does not cause more pain.

If splinting is necessary—
- Splint the injury in the position in which the injured area was found.
- Splint the injured area and the joints or bones above and below the injury site.
- Check for circulation (i.e., feeling, warmth and color) before and after splinting.

Following are ways to immobilize common muscle, bone and joint injuries:
- **Anatomic splints.** The person's body is the splint. For example, an arm can be splinted to the chest or an injured leg to the uninjured leg.
- **Soft splints.** Soft materials, such as a folded blanket, towel, pillow or folded triangular bandage, can be splint materials. A sling is a specific kind of soft splint that uses a triangular bandage tied to support an injured arm, wrist or hand.
- **Rigid splints.** Boards, folded magazines or newspapers or metal strips that do not have any sharp edges can serve as splints.
- **The ground.** An injured leg may be immobilized by being stretched out on the ground.

Arm Injuries
To care for injuries to the arm—
- Leave the arm in the position in which it was found or in the position in which the victim is holding it (**Fig. 9-31**).

Fig. 9-31

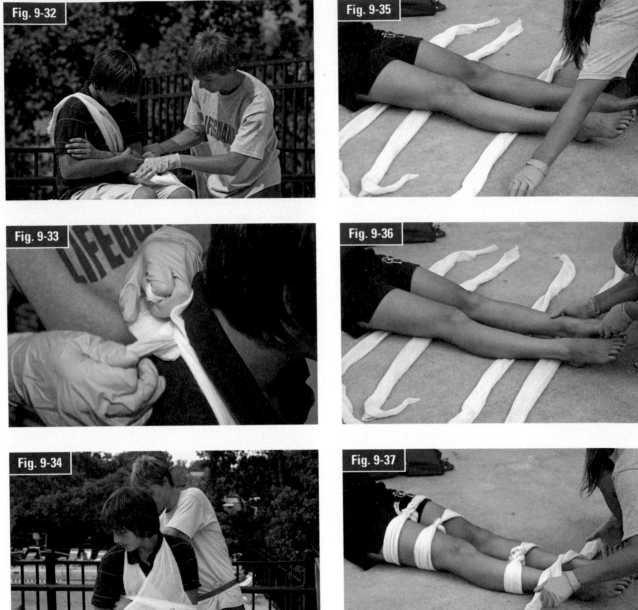

- Place a triangular bandage under the injured arm and over the uninjured shoulder to form a sling (**Fig. 9-32**).
- Tie the ends of the sling at the side of the neck. Place gauze pads under the knots to make it more comfortable for the victim (**Fig. 9-33**).
- Secure the arm to the chest with a folded triangular bandage (**Fig. 9-34**).

Leg Injuries
To care for injuries to the leg—
- Immobilize an injured leg by binding it to the uninjured leg:
  - Place several folded triangular bandages above and below the injured body area (**Fig. 9-35**).

- Place the uninjured body part next to the injured body area (**Fig. 9-36**).
- Tie triangular bandages securely with knots (**Fig. 9-37**).

Foot Injuries
To care for injuries to the foot—
- Immobilize the ankle and foot using a soft splint, such as a pillow or folded blanket. Do not remove the victim's shoes.
  - Place several folded triangular bandages above and below the injured area (**Fig. 9-38**).
  - Gently wrap a soft object (pillow or folded blanket) around the injured area (**Fig. 9-39**).
  - Tie bandages securely with knots (**Fig. 9-40**).

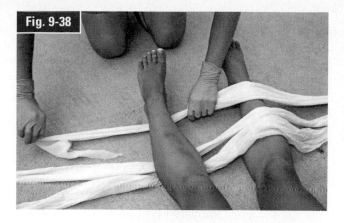

Fig. 9-38

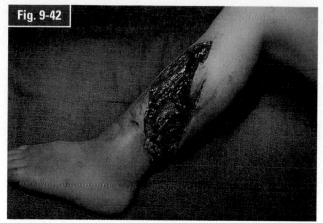

Fig. 9-42

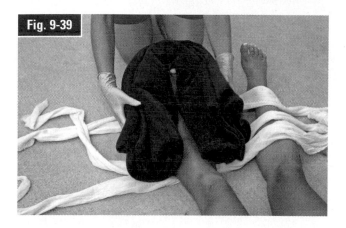

Fig. 9-39

Rib/Breastbone Injuries
- Place a pillow or folded towel between the victim's injured ribs and arm.
- Bind the arm to the body to help support the injured area.

Hand and Finger Injuries
- For a hand injury, place a bulky dressing in the palm of the victim's hand and wrap with a roller bandage.
- For a possible fractured or dislocated finger, tape the injured finger to the finger next to it **(Fig. 9-41)**.

Caring for Open Fractures
An open fracture occurs when a broken bone tears through the skin and surrounding soft tissue **(Fig. 9-42)**. To care for a victim with an open fracture—
- Summon EMS personnel.
- Place sterile dressings around the open fracture as would be done for an embedded object.
- Bandage the dressings in place around the fracture.
- Do not move the exposed bone and limb. This may cause the victim great pain and may worsen the injury.

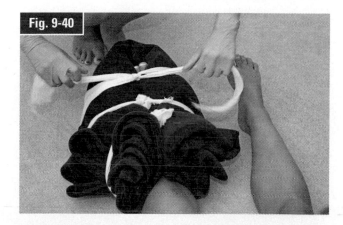

Fig. 9-40

HEAT- AND COLD-RELATED EMERGENCIES

Exposure to extreme heat or cold can make a person ill. A person can develop a heat or cold-related illness even when temperatures are not extreme. Whether such emergencies occur depends on the wind and humidity and the victim's physical activity, general working or living conditions, age and state of health.

Once the signs and symptoms of a heat- or cold-related illness appear, the victim's condition can quickly get worse and even lead to death.

Heat-Related Emergencies
Heat-related emergencies are progressive conditions caused by overexposure to heat. If recognized in the early stages, heat-related emergencies can usually be

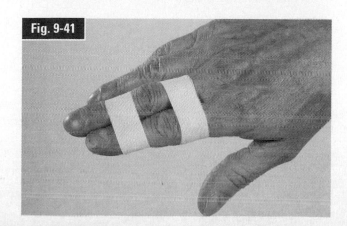

Fig. 9-41

reversed. If not recognized early, they may progress to heat stroke, a life-threatening condition. There are three types of heat-related emergencies.

- *Heat cramps* are painful muscle spasms that usually occur in the legs and abdomen. Heat cramps are the least severe of the heat-related emergencies.
- *Heat exhaustion* (early stage) is an early indicator that the body's cooling system is becoming overwhelmed. Signs and symptoms of heat exhaustion include—
  - Cool, moist, pale, ashen or flushed skin.
  - Headache, nausea, dizziness.
  - Weakness, exhaustion.
  - Heavy sweating.
- *Heat stroke* (late stage) is when the body's systems are overwhelmed by heat and stop functioning. Heat stroke is a life-threatening condition. Signs and symptoms of heat stroke include—
  - Red, hot, dry skin.
  - Changes in the level of consciousness.
  - Vomiting.

Caring for Heat-Related Emergencies

Take the following steps to care for someone suffering from a heat-related emergency:

- Move the victim to a cool place.
- Loosen tight clothing.
- Remove perspiration-soaked clothing.
- Apply cool, wet towels to the skin.
- Fan the victim.
- If the victim is conscious, give him or her small amounts of cool water to drink.

If the victim refuses water, vomits or starts to lose consciousness—

- Send someone to summon EMS personnel.
- Place the victim on his or her side.
- Continue to cool the victim by using ice or cold packs on his or her wrists, ankles, groin and neck and in the armpits.
- Continue to check for breathing and a pulse.

Cold-Related Emergencies

It does not have to be extremely cold for someone to suffer a cold-related emergency, especially if the victim is wet or if it is windy.

Hypothermia

Hypothermia occurs when a victim's entire body cools because he or she is unable to keep warm. The victim will die if not provided care. The signs and symptoms of hypothermia include—

- Shivering, numbness or a glassy stare.
- Apathy, weakness or impaired judgment.
- Loss of consciousness.

To care for hypothermia—

- Gently move the victim to a warm place.
- Monitor the victim's ABCs.
- Give rescue breathing or CPR if needed.
- Remove any wet clothing and dry the victim.
- Warm the victim by wrapping him or her in blankets or by putting dry clothing on the victim (passive rewarming).
- If the victim is alert, give him or her warm liquids to drink that do not contain alcohol or caffeine.
- Hot water bottles and chemical hot packs may be used when first wrapped in a towel or blanket before applying.
  - Do not warm the victim too quickly, such as by immersing him or her in warm water. Rapid warming may cause dangerous heart rhythms.

Frostbite

Frostbite is the freezing of body parts exposed to the cold. Severity depends on the air temperature, length of exposure and the wind. Frostbite can cause the loss of fingers, hands, arms, toes, feet and legs. The signs and symptoms of frostbite include—

- A lack of feeling in an affected area.
- Skin that appears waxy, cold to the touch or discolored (flushed, white, yellow or blue).

To care for frostbite—

- Get the victim out of the cold.
- Do not attempt to rewarm the frostbitten area if there is a chance that it might refreeze or if close to a medical facility.
- Handle the area gently; never rub the affected area.
- Warm gently by soaking the affected area in warm water (100°–105° F or 37°–40° C) until normal color returns and the area feels warm.
- Loosely bandage the area with dry, sterile dressings.
- If the victim's fingers or toes are frostbitten, place dry, sterile gauze between them to keep them separated.
- Avoid breaking any blisters.
- Take precautions to prevent hypothermia.
- Summon EMS personnel to seek emergency medical care as soon as possible.

PUTTING IT ALL TOGETHER

A variety of injuries and illnesses may be seen in an aquatic environment. People can be injured and become ill in many ways, and part of a lifeguard's job is to provide effective care. Follow general procedures for injury or sudden illness on land until EMS personnel arrive and take over. Remember that a lifeguard has a duty to respond, and this role is important for the safety and well-being of patrons.

Chapter 10

Caring for Head, Neck and Back Injuries

Every year, there are approximately 11,000 spinal cord injuries in the United States. Approximately 9 percent of these injuries occur during sports and recreation, some from diving into shallow water.[1]

Head, neck and back injuries rarely happen during supervised diving into deep water. Most injuries occur during unsupervised activity. In pools, head, neck and back injuries most often occur at the shallow end, in a corner or where the bottom slopes from shallow to deep water. They also occur when someone strikes

a floating object, like an inner tube or person, while diving. Head, neck or back injuries also occur out of the water when a person trips or falls on a pool deck or in a locker room.

At lakes, rivers and oceans, head, neck and back injuries usually occur in areas where depths change with the tide or current. At beaches, these injuries often occur mainly when someone plunges head-first into shallow water or a breaking wave. These injuries also result from collisions with an underwater hazard, such as a rock, tree stump or sandbar.

This chapter describes how to recognize and care for possible head, neck or back injuries.

[1] The Spinal Cord Injury Information Network, June 2006.

CAUSES OF HEAD, NECK AND BACK INJURIES

Lifeguards should suspect that a head, neck or back injury occurred in the following situations:

- Any injury caused by entry into shallow water
- Injury as a result of a fall greater than a standing height
- An injury involving a diving board, water slide or a person entering water from a height, such as an embankment, cliff or tower
- A person holding his or her neck or head and complaining of pain
- A person complaining of neck or back pain, tingling in the extremities or weakness
- Someone who appears to be frail or over 65 years of age
- A person who is not fully alert
- Someone who appears to be intoxicated
- Someone with a head or neck injury
- Injury by a force to the head

Signs and symptoms of possible head, neck or back injury include—

- Changes in the level of consciousness.
- Severe pain or pressure in the head, neck or back.
- Loss of balance.
- Partial or complete loss of movement of any body area.
- Tingling or loss of sensation in the hands, fingers, feet or toes.
- Persistent headache.
- Unusual bumps, bruises or depressions on the head, neck or back.
- Seizures.
- Blood or other fluids in the ears or nose.
- Heavy external bleeding of the head, neck or back.
- Impaired breathing or vision as a result of injury.
- Nausea or vomiting.
- Bruising of the head, especially around the eyes and behind the ears.

CARING FOR HEAD, NECK AND BACK INJURIES

Caring for a head, neck or back injury is similar to caring for other serious bone or muscle injuries. A lifeguard must stabilize and restrict motion of the head, neck and back. Because movement can cause further damage, keep the victim as still as possible until emergency medical services (EMS) personnel arrive and take over. If unsure whether the victim has a serious injury, always provide care as if the head, neck or back is injured. The care provided to a victim with a head, neck or back injury depends on—

- The victim's condition, including whether he or she is breathing and shows signs of life (movement and normal breathing).
- The location of the victim (shallow or deep water, at the surface of the water, submerged or not in the water).
- The availability of additional help, such as other lifeguards, bystanders, fire fighters, police or EMS personnel.
- The facility's specific procedures.
- The air and water temperature.

CARING FOR HEAD, NECK AND BACK INJURIES IN THE WATER

If a head, neck or back injury is suspected, follow these general rescue procedures:

1. **Activate the facility's emergency action plan (EAP).** Alert other lifeguards that a victim has a possible head, neck or back injury in addition to any other problems identified. The other lifeguards will perform their responsibilities as indicated in the facility's EAP for head, neck and back injuries. These responsibilities may include:
   - Providing backup coverage.
   - Clearing the water of patrons.
   - Getting the backboard and head immobilizer.
   - Summoning EMS personnel by calling 9-1-1 or the local emergency number.
2. **Assess the victim's condition.** Determine if the victim's condition has changed. For example, the victim may have been at the surface of the water, but may have submerged before a lifeguard approached.
3. **Safely enter the water.** If the victim is near a pool wall or pier, minimize water movement by using a slide-in entry rather than a compact jump or stride jump. If a running entry is used, slow down before reaching the victim.
4. **Perform an appropriate rescue.** Swim to the victim to make contact and use an in-line stabilization technique to minimize movement of the victim's head, neck and back. Use an appropriate in-line stabilization technique based on the victim's location and whether the victim is face-up or face-down.
5. **Move the victim to shallow water whenever possible.** It is much easier to care for the victim in shallow water. If the victim cannot be moved to shallow water—for example, the victim is in a deep-water pool—both the victim and lifeguard can be supported with a rescue tube. Whenever possible, seek the help of other rescuers for head, neck and back injuries in deep water.
6. **Check for consciousness and signs of life.** A victim who can talk is conscious and breathing. If the victim is unconscious, look for movement and check for normal breathing for no more than 10 seconds. If there are no signs of life, immediately remove the victim

The Spine

The spine is a flexible column that supports the head and trunk and protects the spinal cord. The *spinal column* extends from the base of the skull to the tip of the tailbone. It is made of small bones called vertebrae. The *vertebrae* are separated by cushions of cartilage, called disks. This cartilage acts as a shock absorber when you walk, run or jump. The *spinal cord*, a bundle of nerves extending from the skull to the lower back, runs through openings inside the vertebrae. Nerves reach the body through openings on the sides of the vertebrae.

The spine is divided into five regions: cervical (neck), thoracic (mid-back), lumbar (lower back), sacrum and coccyx (small triangular bone at the bottom of the spine). Although injuries can occur anywhere along the spine, most aquatic injuries damage the cervical region. A serious injury is likely to cause temporary or permanent paralysis, even death. The extent of paralysis depends on which area of the spinal cord is damaged.

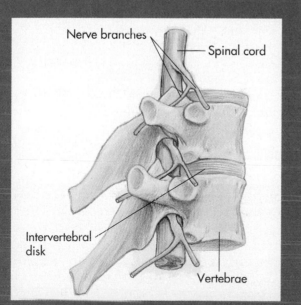

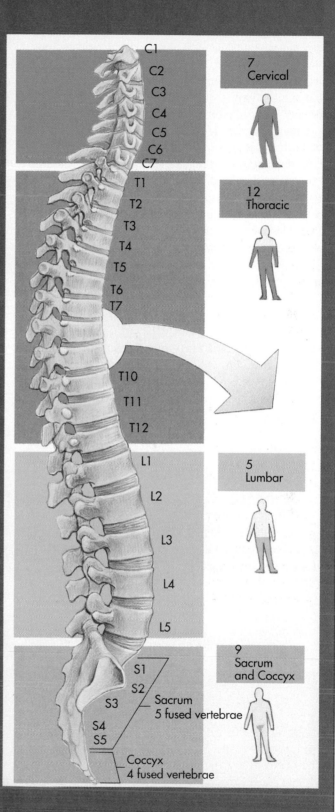

from the water using a backboard (see page 169, Caring for Head, Neck and Back Injuries—An Unconscious Victim).

7. **Remove the victim from the water.** Place and secure the victim on a backboard and remove the victim from the water.

8. **Provide emergency care as needed.** Once the victim is out of the water—

   - Use personal protective equipment, such as disposable gloves and breathing barriers.
   - Perform an initial assessment and perform rescue breathing, cardiopulmonary resuscitation (CPR) or first aid, if needed.
   - Continue to monitor the victim.
   - Minimize shock by keeping the victim from getting chilled or overheated.
   - Administer emergency oxygen, if available and trained to do so.
   - If the victim vomits, tilt the backboard on its side to help clear the vomit from the victim's mouth.

Manual In-Line Stabilization Techniques

Two different techniques are used in the water to minimize movement of the victim's head and neck: the head splint technique and the head and chin support. Both techniques can be used in shallow or deep water and with a face-up or face-down victim at, near or below the surface.

Head Splint

To perform the head splint technique on a face-down victim in shallow or deep water who is at or near the surface, the lifeguard should—

1. Approach the victim from the side. In deep water, use the rescue tube for support (**Fig. 10-1**).
2. Grasp the victim's arms midway between the shoulder and elbow. Grasp the victim's right arm with the right hand and the victim's left arm with the left hand. Gently move the victim's arms up alongside the head.
3. Squeeze the victim's arms against his or her head to help hold the head in line with the body (**Fig. 10-2**).
4. Glide the victim slowly forward. If in shallow water, the lifeguard should lower him or herself to shoulder depth before gliding the victim forward. Continue moving slowly and turn the victim until he or she is face-up. To do this, push the victim's arm that is closest to the lifeguard under the water while pulling the victim's other arm across the surface toward the lifeguard (**Fig. 10-3**).
5. Position the victim's head close to the crook of the lifeguard's arm, with the head in line with the body (**Fig. 10-4**).
6. Hold the victim in this position until help arrives. If the victim is in deep water, move the victim to shallow water, if possible.

Fig. 10-1

Fig. 10-2

Fig. 10-3

Fig. 10-4

7. Check for consciousness and signs of life. If there are no signs of life, immediately remove the victim from the water.

To perform the head splint technique on a face-up victim in shallow or deep water at or near the surface, the lifeguard should—

1. Approach the victim's head from behind, or stand behind the victim's head. In shallow water, the lifeguard should lower his or her body so that the water level is at his or her neck. In deep water, the lifeguard should use the rescue tube for support.

2. Grasp the victim's arms midway between the shoulder and elbow with the thumbs to the inside of each of the victim's arms **(Fig. 10-5, A-B)**. Grasp the victim's right arm with the right hand and the victim's left arm with the left hand. Gently move the victim's arms up alongside the head while the lifeguard repositions him or herself to the victim's side while trapping the victim's head with his or her arms.

3. Slowly and carefully squeeze the victim's arms against his or her head to help hold the head in line with the body. Do not move the victim any more than necessary **(Fig. 10-5, C-D)**.

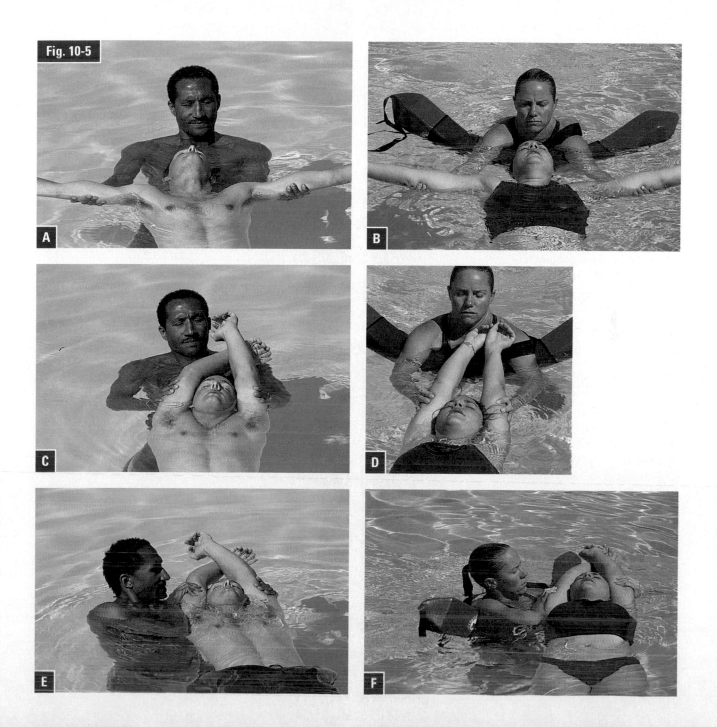

Fig. 10-5

4. Position the victim's head close to the crook of the lifeguard's arm, with the head in line with the body (**Fig. 10-5, E-F**).
5. Hold the victim in this position until help arrives. If the victim is in deep water, move the victim to shallow water if possible.
6. Check for consciousness and signs of life. If there are no signs of life, immediately remove the victim from the water.

Head and Chin Support

The head and chin support is used for face-down or face-up victims who are at or near the surface in shallow water at least 3 feet deep. In deep water, the head and chin support can be used for a face-up victim. Use a rescue tube for support. The head and chin support is not appropriate in all situations:

- Do not use the head and chin support for a face-down victim in water less than 3 feet deep. This technique requires the lifeguard to submerge and roll under the victim while maintaining in-line stabilization. It is difficult to do this in water less than 3 feet deep without risking injury to the lifeguard or the victim.

- Do not use the rescue tube for support when performing the head and chin support on a face-down victim in deep water. This impedes the lifeguard's ability to turn the victim over. However, once the victim is turned face-up, another lifeguard can place a rescue tube under the rescuer's armpits to help keep the victim and rescuer afloat (**Fig. 10-6**).

To perform the head and chin support for a face-up or face-down victim at or near the surface, the lifeguard should—

1. Approach the victim from the side (**Fig. 10-7, A**).
2. With the lifeguard's body at about shoulder depth in the water, place one forearm along the length of the victim's breastbone and the other forearm along the victim's spine.
3. Use the hands to gently hold the victim's head and neck in line with the body. Place one hand on the victim's lower jaw and the other hand on the back of the

Fig. 10-6

Fig. 10-7

lower head. Be careful not to place pressure or touch the front and back of the neck (**Fig. 10-7, B-C**).
4. Squeeze the forearms together, clamping the victim's chest and back. Continue to support the victim's head and neck.
   - If the victim is face-down, the lifeguard must turn him or her face-up. Using the head and chin support to stabilize the spine, slowly move the victim forward to help lift the victim's legs. The lifeguard should turn the victim toward him or herself while submerging (**Fig. 10-7, D**).
   - Roll under the victim while turning the victim over (**Fig. 10-7, E**). Avoid twisting the victim's body. The

Fig. 10-7

Fig. 10-8

D

A

E

B

F

C

victim should be face-up when surfacing on the other side (**Fig. 10-7, F**).

5. Hold the victim face-up in the water until help arrives. If the victim is in deep water, move the victim to shallow water if possible.

6. Check for consciousness and signs of life. If there are no signs of life, immediately remove the victim from the water.

Submerged Victims

The head and chin support or head splint technique can be used for a submerged victim found face-up, face-down or on one side (**Fig. 10-8, A-B**). Lifeguards

should follow the general steps for the head and chin support or the head splint while bringing the victim to the surface at an angle. Turn the victim face-up, if needed, just before reaching the surface or at the surface (**Fig. 10-8, C**).

Using a Backboard in Shallow Water

At least two lifeguards are needed to place and secure a victim on a backboard, but additional lifeguards or bystanders should also help, if available. After stabilizing the victim's head and neck with either the head splint or the head and chin support, the lifeguards should place and secure the victim on a backboard. Lifeguards should

The Backboard

A backboard is a standard piece of rescue equipment at all aquatic facilities. Lifeguards place and secure a victim suspected of head, neck or back injury on a backboard to restrict motion of the head, neck and back when removing the victim from water. Backboards come in different shapes, sizes and buoyancy. They vary in materials, such as plastic or marine plywood, and should have a non-absorptive surface that can be cleaned easily. Desirable qualities for a backboard at an aquatic facility include—

- Ample handholds positioned on all sides of the backboard.
- Multiple anchoring points for the straps to permit adjustments for victims of various sizes.
- Slats or "runners" under the bottom of the backboard to allow for easier lifting.
- Large size and width to place and secure victims of various sizes.
- Features that allow for the attachment of head immobilizers.

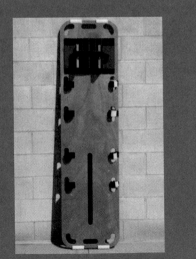

Lifeguards should be familiar with the backboard(s) used at their facility and should practice backboarding techniques regularly during in-service training to maintain their skills.

follow these steps to backboard a victim in shallow water:

1. **Rescuer 1** continues to provide manual in-line stabilization until another rescuer(s) arrives **(Fig. 10-9, A)**. **Rescuer 2** enters the water, submerges the backboard and positions it under the victim so that it extends slightly beyond the victim's head **(Fig. 10-9, B)**.
2. While **Rescuer 2** raises the backboard into place, depending on the manual in-line stabilization technique used, both rescuers should follow the steps below.

Head Splint

- **Rescuer 1** moves the elbow that is under the victim toward the top of the backboard while continuing to apply pressure on both arms. **Rescuer 2** uses the head and chin support to stabilize the victim (one hand and arm on the chin and chest, the other hand and arm under the backboard) **(Fig. 10-10, A)**.
- Once the backboard is in place, **Rescuer 1** lowers the victim's arms, moves to the victim's head and places the rescue tube under the head of the backboard **(Fig. 10-10, B)**. **Rescuer 1** supports the backboard with his or her forearms. Lastly, **Rescuer 1** stabilizes the victim's head by placing his or her hands along each side of the victim's head **Fig. 10-10, C)**.

Head and Chin Support

- **Rescuer 1** carefully removes his or her arm from beneath the victim. **Rescuer 1** then keeps the hand on the chin and arm on the chest and places the other hand and arm under the backboard **(Fig. 10-11, A)**.
- Once the backboard is in place, **Rescuer 2** moves to the victim's head and places a rescue tube under the head of the backboard **(Fig. 10-11, B)**. **Rescuer 2** then supports the backboard with his or her forearms. Lastly, **Rescuer 2** stabilizes the victim's head by placing his or her hands along each side of the victim's head **(Fig. 10-11, C)**.

3. The rescuer who is not positioned at the victim's head secures the victim on the backboard **(Fig. 10-12, A)**. The victim should be secured with a minimum of three straps: across the victim's chest, hips and thighs. Secure the straps in the following order:

   - Strap high across the chest and under the victim's armpits. This helps prevent the victim from sliding on the backboard during the removal.

Fig. 10-9

A

B

Fig. 10-10

A

Fig. 10-11

A

B

B

C

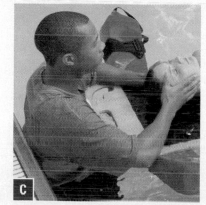

C

- Strap across the hips with the victim's arms and hands secured.
- Strap across the thighs.
- Recheck straps to be sure that they are secure **(Fig. 10-12, B)**.

4. After all the straps have been checked and properly secured, the lifeguard secures the victim's head to the backboard, using a head immobilizer and a strap across the victim's forehead **(Fig. 10-13, A-B)**.

5. If not done so already, the rescuers should bring the victim to the side of the pool.

If additional lifeguards are available to assist in the backboarding of a victim in shallow water, they can assist the rescuers by—

- Assuming a position at the victim's head to provide stabilization.
- Assisting in submerging and positioning the backboard under the victim.
- Supporting the backboard while the straps and head immobilizer are secured.
- Retrieving the head immobilizer.

Removal from the Water

Once the victim is secured on the backboard, the rescuers should remove the victim from the water. To remove the victim from a pool—

1. Position the backboard with the head end by the side of the pool and the foot end straight out into the pool.

2. With one rescuer at each side, lift the head of the backboard slightly and place it on the edge of the gutter or on the edge of the pool deck, if possible **(Fig. 10-14)**. Use one or two rescue tubes if needed to support the foot end of the board **(Fig. 10-15)**.

3. One rescuer gets out of the pool while the other rescuer maintains control of the backboard. Once out of the pool, the rescuer on deck then grasps the head of the backboard while the other rescuer gets out of the pool **(Fig. 10-16)**.

4. Together, the rescuers stand and step backward, pulling the backboard and sliding it up over the edge of the deck and out of and away from the water **(Fig. 10-17)**. Use proper lifting techniques to prevent injury:
   - Keep the back straight.
   - Bend at the knees.
   - Move in a controlled way without jerking or tugging.

If additional lifeguards are available to assist, they can help guide and remove the backboard and victim onto the deck.

Fig. 10-12

A

B

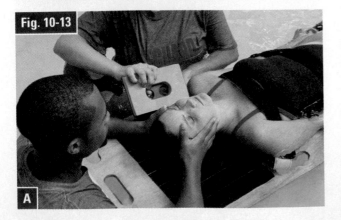

Fig. 10-13

A

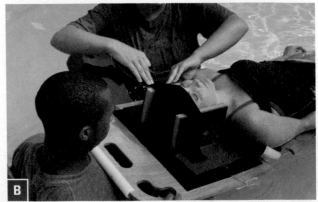

B

Fig. 10-14

Fig. 10-15

Fig. 10-16

Fig. 10-17

Removal from the Water—Extreme Shallow Water (Zero-Depth)

Many facilities have extreme shallow water areas, such as zero-depth pools, wave pools and sloping beaches at waterfront facilities. Some pools may also have zero-depth entries, such as a wheel chair ramp. To remove a victim from a zero-depth, have sufficient rescuers on each side of the backboard to support the victim's weight. After the victim is secured to the backboard, the rescuers—

- Carefully lift the backboard and victim up using proper lifting techniques to prevent injury.
- Remove the backboard and victim from the water by slowly walking out. Keep the board as level as possible during the removal (**Fig. 10-18**).
- Gently lower the backboard and the victim to the ground once out of the water using proper lifting techniques to prevent injury.

Caring for Head, Neck and Back Injuries— An Unconscious Victim

Even though it is difficult to determine in the water if an unconscious victim is breathing, a lifeguard should attempt to check for signs of life by looking for movement

and looking, listening and feeling for normal breathing for no more than 10 seconds while maintaining in-line stabilization (**Fig. 10-19**). If a second lifeguard is available to assist, he or she can check for signs of life while the first lifeguard maintains in-line stabilization (**Fig. 10-20**). If the victim is not breathing or shows no signs of life, immediately remove the victim from the water.

- Remove the victim from the water using the two-person removal (see Chapter 5) or, if the facility has a zero-depth entry, by placing the victim on the back-

Fig. 10-18

Fig. 10-19

Fig. 10-20

board and removing the backboard and victim by lifting the backboard and walking out of the water. Make every effort to minimize movement of the victim's head and neck.

- Do not waste time strapping the victim to the backboard because this would delay urgently needed care.

Once the victim is removed from the water—
- Use personal protective equipment, such as disposable gloves and breathing barriers.
- Perform an initial assessment. Use the two-handed jaw-thrust technique to open the airway to minimize movement of the head, neck and back. If the jaw-thrust maneuver does not open the airway, use the head-tilt/chin-lift technique to open the airway.
- Perform rescue breathing, CPR or first aid, if needed.
- Minimize shock by keeping the victim from getting chilled or overheated.
- Administer emergency oxygen if available and trained to do so.

Caring for Head, Neck and Back Injuries in Deep Water

Fortunately, head, neck or back injuries rarely occur in deep water. If one does occur, the victim often can be moved to shallow water. A lane line or safety line may

need to be removed to reach shallow water. If the victim cannot be moved to shallow water, such as in a separate diving well, a lifeguard should use the rescue tube to help support him or herself and the victim until help arrives.

To stabilize the victim's spine and secure the victim on the backboard in deep water, the lifeguards should slightly modify the procedures used in shallow water and follow these steps:

1. **Rescuer 1** minimizes movement of the victim's head, neck and back by using either the head splint technique or the head and chin support for a face-up victim **(Fig. 10-21, A-B)**. If the victim is submerged, **Rescuer 1** leaves the rescue tube on the surface and does a feet-first surface dive to the victim. He or she brings the victim to the surface using the head and chin support or the head splint. **Rescuer 2** retrieves **Rescuer 1's** rescue tube and inserts it under **Rescuer 1's** armpits.

2. To place and secure the victim on a backboard, **Rescuer 1** moves the victim to the side of the pool or, if possible, toward the corner of the pool. **Rescuer 2** places a rescue tube under the victim's knees to raise the legs **(Fig. 10-22)**. This makes it easier to place the backboard under the victim. **Rescuer 2** then places the backboard under the victim while **Rescuer 1** continues to maintain manual in-line stabilization **(Fig. 10-23)**. Both rescuers should follow the steps below when perform-

Fig. 10-21

A

B

Fig. 10-22

Fig. 10-23

ing either the head splint technique or a head and chin support:

Head Splint

- As the backboard is raised into place, **Rescuer 1** moves the elbow that is under the victim toward the top of the backboard while continuing to apply pressure on both arms. **Rescuer 2** uses the head and chin support to stabilize the victim (one hand and arm on the chin and chest, the other hand and arm under the backboard) **(Fig. 10-24)**.
- Once the backboard is in place, **Rescuer 1** removes the rescue tube under the victim's knees by sliding the rescue tube towards him or herself. **Rescuer 1** then lowers the victim's arms, moves to the victim's head and places a rescue tube under the head of the backboard **(Fig. 10-25)**. **Rescuer 1** supports the backboard with his or her forearms. **Rescuer 1** then stabilizes the victim's head by placing his or her hands along each side of the victim's head **(Fig. 10-26)**.

Head and Chin Support (Face-Up)

- As the backboard is raised into place, **Rescuer 1** carefully removes his or her arm from beneath the victim. **Rescuer 1** then keeps the hand on the chin and the arm on the chest and places the other hand and arm under the backboard.
- Once the backboard is in place, **Rescuer 2** removes the rescue tube under the victim's knees by sliding the rescue tube towards him or herself **(Fig. 10-27)**. **Rescuer 2** then moves to the victim's head and places a rescue tube under the head of the backboard. **Rescuer 2** supports the backboard with his or her forearms and stabilizes the victim's head by placing his or her hands along each side of the victim's head **(Fig. 10-28)**.

Fig. 10-24

Fig. 10-25

Fig. 10-26

Fig. 10-27

Fig. 10-28

Fig. 10-29

Fig. 10-30

Fig. 10-31

Fig. 10-32

3. The rescuer who is not positioned at the victim's head secures the victim on the backboard by placing straps at least across the victim's chest, hips and thighs (Fig. 10-29). After all the straps have been checked and properly secured, the rescuer secures the victim's head to the board, using a head immobilizer and a strap across the victim's forehead (Fig. 10-30).

4. Position the backboard with the head end by the side of the pool and the foot end straight out into the pool.

5. With one rescuer at each side, lift the head of the backboard slightly and place it on the edge of the gutter or the edge of the pool deck, if possible. Use one or two rescue tubes if needed to support the foot end of the board (Fig. 10-31).

6. One rescuer gets out of the pool while the other rescuer maintains control of the backboard. Once out of the pool, the rescuer on deck then grasps the head of the backboard while the other rescuer gets out of the pool (Fig. 10-32).

Fig. 10-33

Fig. 10-34

Fig. 10-35

Fig. 10-36

Fig. 10-37

7. Together the rescuers stand and step backward, pulling the backboard and sliding it up over the edge of the deck and out of and away from the water. Use proper lifting techniques to prevent injury:

■ Keep the back straight.

■ Bend at the knees.

■ Move in a controlled way without jerking or tugging.

If additional lifeguards are available to assist in the backboarding of a victim in deep water, they can assist the rescuers by—

● Supporting the rescuer at the head of the backboard (**Fig. 10-33**).

● Placing and securing the straps along the chest, hips and thighs (**Fig. 10-34**).

● Placing the head immobilizer and securing the strap across the forehead (**Fig. 10-35**).

● Guiding the backboard as it is being removed from the water (**Fig. 10-36**).

● Removing the backboard from the water (**Fig. 10-37**).

Caring for Head, Neck and Back Injuries— Special Situations

In-line stabilization and backboarding can be more diffi-cult to perform in some waterpark attractions and water-front facilities that have waves, currents and extreme shallow water. Moving water and confined spaces can cause problems. Facility management should provide in-formation and skills practice for in-line stabilization and backboarding procedures used at the facility for specific attractions and environments during orientation and in-service trainings, which include emergency shut-off pro-cedures for water flow and movement.

Caring for Head, Neck and Back Injuries in Extreme Shallow Water

Caring for a victim of a head, neck or back injury who is face-down in extreme shallow water takes practice. If the water level is such that the victim's upper body is partially out of the water (including the mouth and nose), the care for the victim is the same as care for a head, neck or back injury on land.

If a victim is found face-down in extreme shallow water, modify the head splint technique as follows:

1. The lifeguard should approach the victim from the side and move his or her arms slowly and carefully into po-

Fig. 10-38

Fig. 10-39

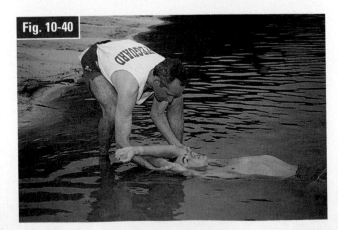

Fig. 10-40

sition. The lifeguard grasps the victim's right arm with his or her right hand and the left arm with his or her left hand and traps the victim's head between the arms (**Fig. 10-38**).

2. After the head is trapped between the arms, the lifeguard begins to roll the victim toward him or herself.

3. While rolling the victim, the lifeguard steps from the victim's side toward the victim's head and begins to turn the victim face-up (**Fig. 10-39**).

4. The lifeguard then lowers his or her arm on the victim's side that is closest to the lifeguard so that the victim's arms go over the top of the lifeguard's arm as he or she steps toward the victim's head. It is important to maintain arm pressure against the victim's head, since the lifeguard's hand position will change during this maneuver. The lifeguard will now be positioned above and behind the victim's head (**Fig. 10-40**).

5. The lifeguard should hold the victim in this position.

6. The lifeguard can comfort the victim while another rescuer monitors the victim's ABCs until EMS personnel arrive and take over.

Moving Water

Lifeguards may need to modify the care provided to a person with a head, neck or back injury if waves or currents are moving the water. In water with waves, a lifeguard should move the victim to calmer water, if possible. At a waterfront, a pier or raft may reduce the waves. If there is no barrier from the waves, have other rescuers form a "wall" with their bodies to block the waves. At a wave pool, stop the waves by pushing the emergency stop button. Remember, even though the button has been pushed, residual wave action will continue for a short time.

Lifeguard orientation and in-service trainings will cover the specific conditions at the facility and teach lifeguards how to adapt the head, neck and back injury management procedures learned previously in this chapter.

Rivers, Streams and Winding River Attractions. A special problem in rivers, streams and winding rivers at waterparks is that the current can pull or move the victim. At waterparks, a facility's EAP may include signaling another lifeguard to stop the flow of water in a winding river by pushing the emergency stop button. In all cases, lifeguards should—

- Ask other lifeguards or patrons for help in keeping objects and people from floating into the rescuer while he or she is supporting the victim.

- Not let the current press sideways on the victim or force the victim into a wall. This would twist the victim's body. Keep the victim's head pointed upstream into the current (**Fig. 10-41**).

- This position also reduces the splashing of water on the victim's face. Once a manual in-line stabilization

Fig. 10-41

Fig. 10-42

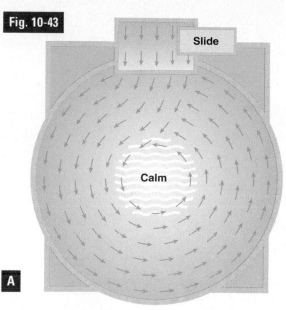

Fig. 10-43

A

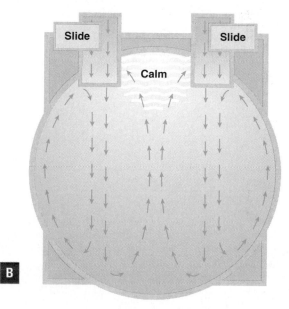

B

technique is performed and the victim is turned face-up, slowly turn the victim so that the current pulls his or her legs around to point downstream (**Fig. 10-42**).

- Place the victim on a backboard following the facility's backboarding procedures.

Catch Pools. The water in a catch pool moves with more force than in a winding river and can make it difficult to hold a victim still.

- If a person is suspected of having a head, neck or back injury in a catch pool, the lifeguard should immediately signal other lifeguards to stop sending riders.
- If possible, someone should stop the flow of water by pushing the emergency stop button.
- Once a manual in-line stabilization technique is performed and the victim is turned face-up, the lifeguard should move the victim to the calmest water in the catch pool if water is still flowing. If there is only one slide, the calmest water is usually at the center of the catch pool (**Fig. 10-43, A**). If several slides empty into the same catch pool, calmer water is usually between two slides (**Fig. 10-43, B**).
- The lifeguard should place the victim on a backboard following the facility's backboarding procedures.

Speed Slides. The narrow space of a speed slide causes an extra problem for a head, neck or back injury. A head, neck or back injury may happen if the victim's body twists or turns the wrong way, someone strikes his or her head on the side of the slide or a patron sits up and tumbles down the slide. Backboarding can be a challenge because the water in the slide is only 2 or 3 inches deep and does not help support the victim.

This backboarding procedure requires several lifeguards:

1. The first rescuer performs manual in-line stabilization by placing his or her hands on both sides of the

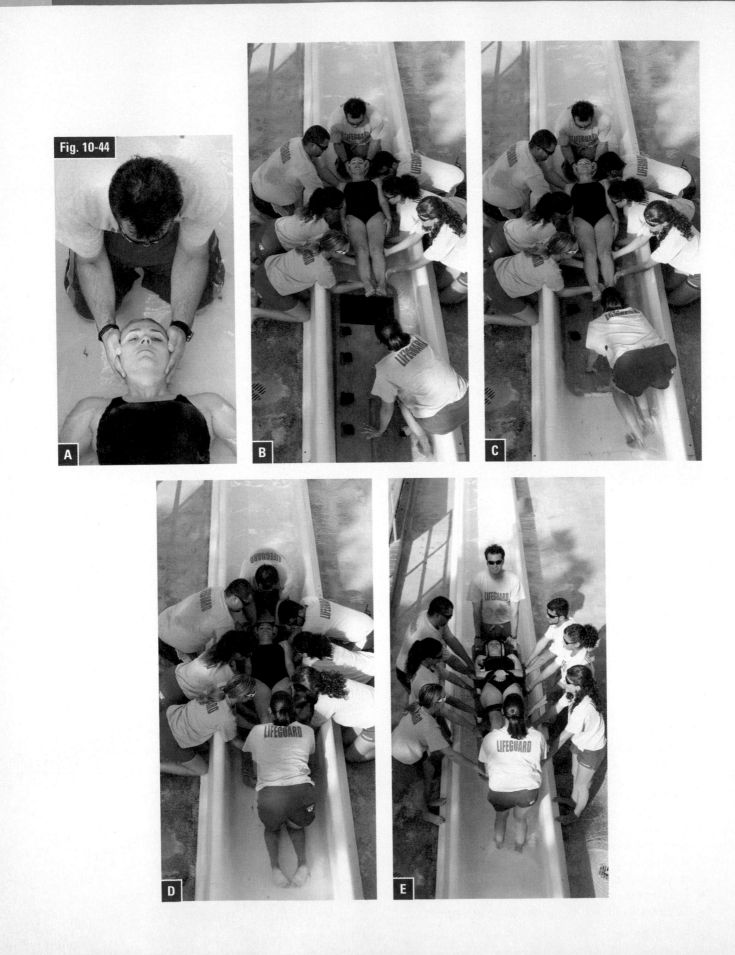

Fig. 10-44

victim's head while the victim is on the slide
(Fig. 10-44, A).
2. Other rescuers should carefully lift the victim so
that the backboard may be slid in place
(Fig. 10-44, B).
3. The backboard should be slid beneath the victim from
the feet to the head **(Fig. 10-44, C)**.
4. The victim should then be lowered onto the backboard
(Fig. 10-44, D).
5. After the victim is secured to the backboard and the
head is immobilized, the rescuers should lift the backboard and victim out of the slide **(Fig. 10-44, E)**.

HEAD, NECK AND BACK INJURIES ON LAND

If a head, neck or back injury is suspected, activate the
facility's EAP and follow the general procedures for injury
or sudden illness on land:
- Size up the scene.
- Perform an initial assessment.
- Summon EMS personnel.
- Perform a secondary assessment.

Use appropriate personal protective equipment, such
as disposable gloves and breathing barriers.

Caring for Head, Neck and Back Injuries on Land

If a victim is suspected of having a head, neck or back injury, the lifeguard should tell him or her not to nod or
shake his or her head but to say yes or no. The goal is to
minimize movement of the head, neck and back. To care
for injuries to the head, neck or back for a victim who is
sitting or lying down, the lifeguard should—
- Minimize movement of the victim's head, neck and
back by putting the lifeguard's hands on both sides of
the victim's head. Have the victim remain in the position in which he or she was found until EMS personnel
arrive and take over.
    - For a victim in a sitting position, the lifeguard faces
the victim and places his or her hands on both
sides of the victim's head **(Fig. 10-45, A)**.
    - For a victim lying down, the lifeguard positions him or
herself behind the victim's head and places his or her
hands on both sides of the victim's head **(Fig. 10-45, B)**.
- Continue to monitor the victim—watch for changes in
consciousness and breathing.

Caring for a Standing Victim

If encountering a patron who is standing with a suspected head, neck or back injury, a lifeguard should not

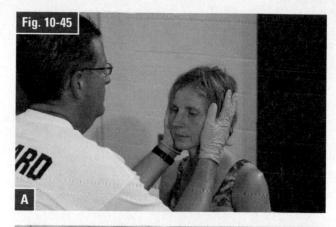
Fig. 10-45

have the person sit or lie down. Minimize movement of
the victim's head by placing his or her hands on both
sides of the victim's head **(Fig. 10-46)**.

If the victim's condition becomes unstable (e.g.,
the victim complains of dizziness, has a potential life-
threatening condition or begins to lose consciousness),
slowly lower the victim to the ground with the assistance
of other lifeguards. Try to maintain in-line stabilization
while the victim is being lowered.

If the victim's condition is stable and the facility's procedures require the victim to be secured to a backboard

Fig. 10-46

Fig. 10-47

Fig. 10-48

and lowered to the ground, the following procedure can be used with a minimum of three lifeguards:

1. **Rescuer 1** approaches the victim from the front and performs in-line stabilization of the victim's head and neck by placing one hand on each side of the head **(Fig. 10-47).**

2. **Rescuer 2** retrieves a backboard and places it against the victim's back, being careful not to disturb **Rescuer 1's** in-line stabilization of the victim's head. **Rescuer 3** assists **Rescuer 2** in positioning the backboard so that the board is centered behind the victim **(Fig. 10-48).**

Fig. 10-49

A

B

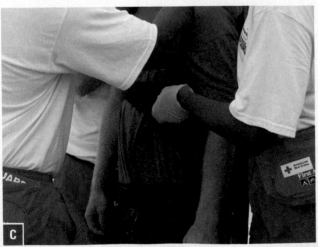
C

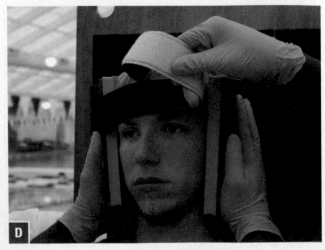
D

3. While **Rescuer 3** holds the backboard, **Rescuer 2** secures the victim to the backboard by placing and securing straps across the victim's chest and under the victim's armpits, hips and thighs (**Fig. 10-49, A-B**). This helps prevent the victim from sliding on the backboard when it is lowered. **Rescuer 2** rechecks the straps to be sure that they are secure (**Fig. 10-49, C**). **Rescuer 2** then secures the victim's head to the backboard using a head immobilizer and strap across the victim's forehead (**Fig. 10-49, D**).

4. **Rescuer 2** and **Rescuer 3** place their inside hands underneath the victim's armpit, in between the victim's arm and torso, and grasp the backboard. These rescuers should grasp a handhold that is at the victim's armpit level or higher (**Fig. 10-49, E**).

5. When the victim is secured to the board, **Rescuer 1** moves to the back of the board and grasps the top of the backboard (**Fig. 10-49, F**). **Rescuer 1** informs the victim that they will now begin to lower him or her to the floor. **Rescuer 1** then gives the signal to the other two rescuers to begin lowering the victim to the ground. While lowering the victim to the ground, **Rescuer 2** and **Rescuer 3** should walk forward and bend at the knees to avoid back injury (**Fig. 10-49, G**).

Fig. 10-49

E

F

G

Concussions

Any significant force to the head can cause an injury ranging from bleeding to a concussion. A *concussion* is a temporary impairment of brain function. It usually does not cause permanent physical damage to the brain. In most cases, the victim may lose consciousness for only an instant and may say that he or she "blacked out" or "saw stars." A concussion sometimes results in a loss of consciousness for longer periods of time. Other times, a victim may be confused or have memory loss. Be aware that a person in the water who receives a severe blow to the head could lose consciousness temporarily and submerge. Anyone suspected of having any head injury in or out of the water should be examined by a health-care provider immediately.

PUTTING IT ALL TOGETHER

Lifeguards need to recognize and be able to care for victims with head, neck or back injuries. To decide whether an injury could be serious, consider both its cause and the signs and symptoms. If a victim in the water is suspected of having a head, neck or back injury, make sure EMS personnel are summoned immediately. Minimize movement by using manual in-line stabilization. Secure the victim to a backboard to restrict motion of the head, neck and back. Avoid injury by always removing a victim from the water using proper lifting techniques. When the victim is out of the water, provide care as needed until EMS personnel arrive and take over.

Chapter 11

The Benefits of Lifeguarding

As this manual has shown, lifeguarding is a challenging and important job. Being an effective lifeguard requires commitment and a lot of work, but the personal and professional benefits are well worth the effort.

PERSONAL BENEFITS

One of the most important personal benefits of being a successful lifeguard is the satisfaction of knowing that a lifeguard's actions can save a life. A related benefit is the self-confidence built by meeting the many physical and mental challenges of the job. Other benefits of lifeguarding include—

- **Improved self-discipline.** Professional lifeguards must be mature and reliable. For example, they must arrive at work on time, accept assignments willingly and respond to incidents quickly and effectively. Lifeguards also must stay healthy and fit in order to react to emergencies with a burst of energy. This requires exercising regularly, eating properly, using sun protection and avoiding the use of alcohol and other drugs.
- **Better decision-making skills.** Decision making is important in lifeguarding, as it is in other areas in life. Lifeguards often make important decisions, many under the intense stress of an emergency. These include—
  - How to prevent a swimmer in trouble from becoming a drowning victim.
  - How to ensure patron safety.
  - When and how to make a rescue.
  - When and how to perform first aid and provide other emergency care.
- **Increased leadership opportunities.** Professional lifeguards are leaders at their facilities and, as such, they are expected to act responsibly, obey all of the facility rules and lead others by their example.
- **Development of public relations, customer service and conflict-resolution skills.** Lifeguards represent their facilities to the public in a professional way. Any time they interact with the public, their actions should promote an atmosphere of trust and goodwill. Lifeguards learn to interact successfully with patrons and deal with both emergency and non-emergency problems.
- **Understanding how to properly enforce the rules.** Among a lifeguard's many responsibilities is enforcing the facility's rules and regulations. However, no matter how fairly a lifeguard enforces the rules, he or she may encounter an uncooperative patron. An effective lifeguard must learn how to resolve these conflicts— as well as conflicts between patrons—in a respectful, positive manner.
- **Teamwork skills development.** Whenever more than one lifeguard is on duty at the same time, those lifeguards are part of a team **(Fig. 11-1)**. Learning to work as a member of a team is a very valuable skill because—
  - A team can do its work and accomplish its goals more efficiently than a group of individuals working separately.

Fig. 11-1

- Individuals are better motivated to do a good job when they feel part of a team.
- Everyone has more fun cooperating and working together.

PROFESSIONAL BENEFITS

The skills learned and developed as a lifeguard hold great value, not only for careers in aquatics or recreation, but for any career or life situation that involves working with others. Employers value employees with decision-making, leadership, public relations, customer service, conflict-resolution and teamwork skills. Self-confidence and self-discipline are also highly valued in the workplace.

Using these skills and experiences, many lifeguards have gone on to become successful in a variety of professions including business, law and politics. At least one president of the United States, Ronald Reagan, began his professional career as a lifeguard.

Careers in Aquatics

If aquatics is one's chosen career, consider enrolling in an American Red Cross Lifeguard Management course, which prepares qualified candidates to become lifeguard supervisors **(Fig. 11-2)**. Lifeguard supervisors gain experience in minimizing risks—a skill that is crucial for moving into higher positions in both aquatics and recreation. Lifeguard supervisors also take on a higher level of leadership responsibilities, including assisting with staff hiring and recruitment, conducting trainings and developing work schedules.

Employment as a lifeguard supervisor is the next step on a career path at many aquatics facilities, including the following:
- Pool or aquatic facility manager
- Aquatics director
- Aquatics and sports and leisure clubs director

Fig. 11-2

- Aquatics programmer, supervisor or coordinator
- Instructional specialist
- Swim, dive, water polo or synchronized swimming coach

Other Careers

While working as a lifeguard, one may develop an interest in working as an emergency medical technician (EMT). First aid, CPR and AED training will help one prepare and adapt to a career in the emergency medical field.

PUTTING IT ALL TOGETHER

To be a successful professional lifeguard, candidates must work hard and be dedicated. However, if a candidate chooses to make the commitment, the personal and professional rewards gained will last a lifetime.

Lifeguarding for Life

It would be hard to find a better example of a successful lifeguard than Luiz Morizot-Leite.

Morizot-Leite supervises 40 guards at Haulover Beach, Florida, and trains American Red Cross lifeguards in his spare time.

Morizot-Leite is one of the most sought-after instructors, according to officials at the American Red Cross of Greater Miami and the Keys. The 36-year-old teaches lifeguarding, water safety and other Red Cross courses. People keep asking for him," said Elba Taveras, a Red Cross coordinator. "Wherever he goes, he keeps the class interesting."

Teaching is only the beginning of Morizot-Leite's efforts to smash stereotypes about lifeguarding and revitalize its appeal. "The public has this image that you're only a lifeguard when you are a kid, but lifeguarding is a professional career," he said. Several career lifeguards work for him. One, a former university teacher with a master's degree, worked at Morizot-Leite's facility for 18 years until a hip fracture forced him to retire at the age of 69. Morizot-Leite wants to be like him. "I'll be doing this 25 years from now," he said.

Brazilian born, Morizot-Leite was 4 years old when he began dreaming of being a lifeguard like his father, who guarded for several years before entering medical school. After arriving in the United States, Morizot-Leite decided to become an EMT to improve his lifeguard qualifications. In 2003, he completed his master's degree in sports management, which brings up another stereotype. "I hate that people think we become lifeguards because we don't like to study," he said. In fact, he said, his facility may soon require a college degree.

Whatever their education, lifeguards need training, Morizot-Leite believes. "The Red Cross gives lifeguards the foundation they need."

GLOSSARY

Abandonment – Ending care of an ill or injured person without that person's consent or without ensuring that someone with equal or greater training will continue that care.

Abdomen – The middle part of the trunk (torso) containing the stomach, liver and other organs.

Abrasion – A wound in which skin is rubbed or scraped away.

Active drowning victim – A person exhibiting universal behavior that includes struggling at the water's surface for 20 to 60 seconds before submerging.

Anaphylactic shock – A severe allergic reaction in which air passages may swell and restrict breathing; a form of shock. See also anaphylaxis.

Anaphylaxis – A severe allergic reaction; a form of shock. See also anaphylactic shock.

Anatomic splint – A part of the body used to immobilize an injured body part.

Anatomical obstruction – Complete or partial blockage of the airway by the tongue or swollen tissues of the mouth or throat.

Angina pectoris – Chest pain that comes and goes at different times; commonly associated with cardiovascular disease.

Antihistamine – Drugs used to treat the signals of allergic reactions.

Aquatic environment – An environment in which recreational water activities are played or performed.

Aquatic safety team – A network of people in the facility and emergency medical services system who can plan for, respond to and assist in an emergency at an aquatic facility.

Area of responsibility – The zone or area in which a lifeguard conducts surveillance.

Ashen – A grayish color; darker skin often looks ashen instead of pale.

Assess – To examine and evaluate a situation carefully.

Asthma – A condition that narrows the air passages and makes breathing difficult.

Asystole – A condition in which the heart has stopped generating electrical activity.

Atherosclerosis – A form of cardiovascular disease marked by a narrowing of the arteries in the heart and other parts of the body.

Atria – The upper chambers of the heart.

Atrioventricular node (AV) – The point along the heart's electrical pathway midway between the atria and ventricles that sends electrical impulses to the ventricles.

Automated external defibrillator (AED) – An automatic device used to recognize a heart rhythm that requires an electric shock and either delivers the shock or prompts the rescuer to deliver it.

Avulsion – A wound in which soft tissue is partially or completely torn away.

Backboard – A standard piece of rescue equipment at all aquatic facilities used to maintain in-line stabilization while securing and transporting a victim with a suspected head, neck or back injury.

Bag-valve-mask resuscitator (BVM) – A handheld breathing device used on a victim in respiratory distress or respiratory arrest. It consists of a self-inflating bag, a one-way valve, and a face mask and can be used with or without supplemental oxygen.

Bandage – Material used to wrap or cover an injured body part; often used to hold a dressing in place.

Blind spots – Areas within a lifeguard's area of responsibility that cannot be seen or are difficult to see.

Bloodborne pathogens – Bacteria and viruses present in blood and body fluids, which can cause disease in humans.

Bloodborne pathogens standard – A federal regulation designed to protect employees from exposure to bodily fluids that might contain a disease-causing agent.

Body substance isolation (BSI) precautions – An approach to infection control that considers all body fluids and substances to be infectious.

Bone – A dense, hard tissue that forms the skeleton.

Buddy board – A board with identification tags used to keep track of swimmers and reinforce the importance of the buddy system.

Bulkhead – A moveable wall placed in a swimming pool to separate activities or water of different depths.

Buoy – A float in the water anchored to the bottom.

Buoyancy – The tendency of a body to float or to rise when submerged in a fluid.

Buoyant – Tending to float, capable of keeping an object afloat.

Bystanders – People at the scene of an emergency who do not have a duty to provide care.

Carbon dioxide – A colorless, odorless gas; a waste product of respiration.

Carbon monoxide (CO) – A clear, odorless, poisonous gas produced when carbon or other fuel is burned, as in gasoline engines.

Cardiac arrest – A condition in which the heart has stopped or beats too ineffectively to generate a pulse.

Cardiopulmonary resuscitation (CPR) – A technique that combines chest compressions and rescue breaths for a victim whose heart and breathing have stopped.

Cartilage – An elastic tissue in the body; in the joints, it acts as a shock absorber when a person is walking, running or jumping.

Catch pool – A small pool at the bottom of a slide where patrons enter water deep enough to cushion their landing.

Chain of command – The structure of employee and management positions in a facility or organization.

Chemical hazard – A harmful or potentially harmful substance in or around a facility.

Chest – The upper part of the trunk (torso), containing the heart, major blood vessels and lungs.

Chronic – Persistent over a long period of time.

Closed wound – An injury that does not break the skin and in which soft tissue damage occurs beneath the skin.

Concussion – A temporary impairment of brain function.

Conduction system – Specialized cells of the heart that initiate and carry on electrical activity.

Confidentiality – Protecting a victim's privacy by not revealing any personal information learned about a victim except to law enforcement personnel or emergency medical services personnel caring for the victim.

Consent – Permission to provide care given by an ill or injured person to a rescuer.

Convulsions – Sudden, uncontrolled muscular contractions.

Critical incident – Any situation that causes a person to experience unusually strong emotional reactions that interfere with his or her ability to function during and after a highly stressful incident.

Critical incident stress – The stress a person experiences during or after a highly stressful emergency.

Cross bearing – A technique for determining the place where a submerged victim was last seen, performed by two persons some distance apart, each pointing to the place such that the position is where the lines of their pointing cross.

Cryptosporidium – A parasitic disease found in the feces of infected humans or animals. It can be spread by swallowing water that has been in contact with the contaminated feces and is difficult to kill with chlorine.

Current – Fast-moving water.

Cyanosis – A blue discoloration of the skin around the mouth and fingertips resulting from a lack of oxygen in the blood.

Daily log – A written journal kept by lifeguards, the head lifeguard and management containing a daily account of safety precautions taken and significant events.

Deep-water line search – An effective pattern for searching in water that is greater than chest deep.

Defibrillation – An electrical shock that disrupts the electrical activity of the heart long enough to allow the heart to spontaneously develop an effective rhythm on its own.

Diabetes – A condition in which the body does not produce enough insulin or does not use insulin effectively enough to regulate the amount of sugar (glucose) in the bloodstream.

Diabetic – A person with the condition called diabetes mellitus, which causes a body to produce insufficient amounts of the hormone insulin.

Diabetic emergency – A situation in which a person becomes ill because of an imbalance of sugar (glucose) and insulin in the bloodstream.

Direct contact transmission – Occurs when infected blood or body fluids from one person enter another person's body at a correct entry site.

Disability – The loss, absence or impairment of sensory, motor or mental function.

Dislocation – The movement of a bone away from its normal position at a joint.

Disoriented – Being in a state of confusion; not knowing place, identity or what happened.

Dispatch – The method for informing patrons when it is safe to proceed on a ride.

Distressed swimmer – A person capable of staying afloat, but likely to need assistance to get to safety. If not rescued, the person becomes an active drowning victim.

Dressing – A pad placed on a wound to control bleeding and prevent infection.

Drop-off slide – A slide that ends with a drop of several feet into a catch pool.

Droplet transmission – Transmission of disease through the inhalation of droplets from an infected person's cough or sneeze.

Drowning – Death by suffocation when submerged in water.

Drug – Any substance other than food intended to affect the functions of the body.

Duty to act – A legal responsibility of certain people to provide a reasonable standard of emergency care; may be required by case law, statute or job description.

Elapid snake – Family of venomous snakes that includes coral snakes, cobras, mambas and others, such as the Australian brown snake or death adder.

Electrocardiogram (ECG) – A graphic record produced by a device that records the electrical activity of the heart from the chest.

Embedded object – An object that remains embedded in an open wound.

Emergency – A sudden, unexpected incident demanding immediate action.

Emergency action plan (EAP) – A written plan detailing how facility staff are to respond in a specific type of emergency.

Emergency medical services (EMS) personnel – Trained and equipped community-based personnel dispatched through an emergency number, usually 9-1-1, to provide medical care for ill or injured people.

Emergency medical technician (EMT) – A person who has successfully completed a state-approved emergency medical technician training program; paramedics are the highest level of EMTs.

Emergency stop button – A button or switch used to immediately turn off the waves or water flow in a wave pool, water slide or other water attraction in the event of an emergency.

Emphysema – A disease in which the lungs lose their ability to exchange carbon dioxide and oxygen effectively.

Engineering controls – Safeguards intended to isolate or remove a hazard from the workplace.

Epilepsy – A chronic condition characterized by seizures that vary in type and duration; can usually be controlled by medication.

Exhaustion – The state of being extremely tired or weak.

Facility surveillance – Checking the facility to help prevent injuries caused by avoidable hazards in the facility's environment.

Fainting – A temporary loss of consciousness.

Fibrillation – A quivering of the heart's ventricles.

Forearm – The upper extremity from the elbow to the wrist.

Fracture – A chip, crack or complete break in bone tissue.

Free-fall slide – A type of speed slide with a nearly vertical drop, giving riders the sensation of falling.

Frostbite – The freezing of body parts exposed to the cold.

Heat cramps – Painful spasms of skeletal muscles after exercise or work in warm or moderate temperatures; usually involve the calf and abdominal muscles.

Heat exhaustion – The early stage and most common form of heat-related illness; often results from strenuous work or exercise in a hot environment.

Heat stroke – A life-threatening condition that develops when the body's cooling mechanisms are overwhelmed and body systems begin to fail.

Heat-related illnesses – Illnesses, including heat exhaustion, heat cramps and heat stroke, caused by overexposure to heat.

Hepatitis B – A liver infection caused by the hepatitis B virus; may be severe or even fatal and can be in the body up to 6 months before symptoms appear.

Hepatitis C – A liver disease caused by the hepatitis C virus; it is the most common chronic bloodborne infection in the United States.

Hull – The main body of a boat.

Human immunodeficiency virus (HIV) – A virus that destroys the body's ability to fight infection. A result of HIV infection is referred to as acquired immunodeficiency syndrome (AIDS).

Hydraulic – Strong force created by water flowing downward over an obstruction and then reversing its flow.

Hypothermia – A life-threatening condition in which the body is unable to maintain warmth and the entire body cools below normal temperature.

Hypoxia – A condition in which insufficient oxygen reaches the cells, resulting in cyanosis and changes in consciousness and in breathing and heart rates.

Immobilize – To use a splint or other method to keep an injured body part from moving.

Implied consent – Legal concept that assumes a person would consent to receive emergency care if he or she were physically able to do so.

Incident – An occurrence or event that interrupts normal procedure or brings about a crisis.

Incident report – A report filed by a lifeguard or other facility staff who responded to an emergency or other incident.

Indirect contact transmission – Occurs when a person touches objects that have the blood or body fluid of an infected person, and that infected blood or body fluid enters the body through a correct entry site.

Inflatables – Plastic toys or equipment that are filled with air to function as recommended.

Inhaled poison – A poison that a person breathes into the lungs.

Injury – The physical harm from an external force on the body.

In-service training – Regularly scheduled staff meetings and practice sessions that cover lifeguarding information and skills.

Instinctive drowning response – A universal set of behaviors exhibited by an active drowning victim that include struggling to keep the face above water, extending arms to the side and pressing down for support, not making any forward progress in the water and staying at the surface for only 20 to 60 seconds.

Joint – A structure where two or more bones are joined.

Laceration – A cut.

Laryngospasm – A spasm of the vocal cords that closes the airway.

Life jacket – A type of personal flotation device (PFD) approved by the United States Coast Guard for use during activities in, on or around water.

Lifeguard – A person trained in lifeguarding, CPR and first aid skills who ensures the safety of people at an aquatic facility by preventing and responding to emergencies.

Lifeguard competitions – Events and contests designed to evaluate the skills and knowledge of individual lifeguards and lifeguard teams.

Lifeguard team – A group of two or more lifeguards on duty at a facility at the same time.

Ligaments – A tough, fibrous connective tissue that holds bones together at a joint.

Material Safety Data Sheet (MSDS) – A form that provides information about a hazardous substance.

Mechanical obstruction – Complete or partial blockage of the airway by a foreign object, such as a piece of food or a small toy, or by fluids, such as vomit or blood.

Muscle – Tissue in the body that lengthens and shortens to create movement.

Myocardial infarction – A heart attack.

Nasal cannula – A device used to deliver oxygen to a breathing person; used mostly for victims with minor breathing problems.

Negligence – The failure to follow the standard of care or to act, thereby causing injury or further harm to another.

Nonfatal submersion – To survive, at least temporarily, following submersion in water (drowning). Also known as near drowning.

Non-rebreather mask – A mask used to deliver high concentrations of oxygen to breathing victims.

Occupational Safety and Health Administration (OSHA) – A government agency that helps protect the health and safety of employees in the workplace.

Open wound – An injury to soft tissue resulting in a break in the skin, such as a cut.

Opportunistic infections – Infections that strike people whose immune systems are weakened by HIV or other infections.

Oxygen – A tasteless, colorless, odorless gas necessary to sustain life.

Paralysis – A loss of muscle control; a permanent loss of feeling and movement.

Partial thickness burn – A burn that involves both layers of skin. Also called a second-degree burn.

Passive drowning victim – An unconscious victim face-down, submerged or near the surface.

Pathogen – A disease-causing agent. Also called a microorganism or germ.

Patron surveillance – Maintaining a close watch over the people using an aquatic facility.

Peripheral vision – What one sees at the edges of one's field of vision.

Personal flotation device (PFD) – Coast Guard-approved life jacket, buoyancy vest, wearable flotation aid, throwable device or other special use flotation device.

Personal water craft – A motorized vehicle designed for one or two riders that skims over the surface of the water.

Pier – A wooden walkway or platform built over the water supported by pillars that is used for boats to dock, fishing or other water activities.

Poison – Any substance that causes injury, illness or death when introduced into the body.

Poison Control Center (PCC) – A specialized kind of health center that provides information in cases of poisoning or suspected poisoning emergencies.

Policies and procedures manual – A manual that provides detailed information about the daily and emergency operations of a facility.

Preventive lifeguarding – The methods that lifeguards use to prevent drowning and other injuries by identifying dangerous conditions or behaviors and then taking steps to minimize or eliminate them.

Professional rescuers – Paid or volunteer personnel, including lifeguards, who have a legal duty to act in an emergency.

Public address system – An electronic amplification system, used at an aquatic facility so that announcements can be easily heard by patrons.

Puncture – An open wound created when the skin is pierced by a pointed object.

Purkinje fibers – A vast network of microscopic fibers, which spread electrical impulses across the heart.

Rapids ride – A rough-water attraction that simulates white-water rafting.

Reaching assist – A method of helping someone out of the water by reaching to that person with your hand, leg or an object.

Reaching pole – An aluminum or fiberglass pole, usually 10- to 15-feet long, used for rescues.

Refusal of care – The declining of care by a victim; the victim has the right to refuse the care of anyone who responds to an emergency.

Rescue board – A plastic or fiberglass board shaped like a surf board that is used by lifeguards to paddle out and make a rescue.

Rescue tube – A 45- to 54-inch vinyl, foam-filled tube with an attached tow line and shoulder strap that lifeguards use to make rescues.

Respiratory arrest – A condition in which breathing has stopped.

Respiratory distress – A condition in which breathing is difficult.

Resuscitation mask – A pliable, dome-shaped device that fits over a person's mouth and nose; used to assist with rescue breathing.

RID factor – Three elements—recognition, intrusion and distraction—related to drownings at guarded facilities.

Ring buoy – A buoyant ring, usually 20 to 30 inches in diameter; with an attached line, allows a rescuer to pull a victim to safety without entering the water.

Risk management – Identifying and eliminating or minimizing dangerous conditions that can cause injuries and financial loss.

Rules – Guidelines for conduct or action that help keep patrons safe at pools and other swimming areas.

Runout – The area at the end of a slide where water slows the speed of the riders.

Safety check – An inspection of the facility to find and eliminate or minimize hazards.

Scanning – A visual technique used by lifeguards to properly observe and monitor patrons participating in water activities.

Seizure – A disorder in the brain's electrical activity, marked by loss of consciousness and often by convulsions.

Shepherd's crook – A reaching pole with a large hook on the end. See also reaching pole.

Shock – A life-threatening condition in which the circulatory system fails to deliver blood to all parts of the body, causing body organs to fail.

Sighting – A technique for noting where a submerged victim was last seen, performed by imagining a line to the opposite shore and estimating the victim's position along that line. See also cross bearing.

Sink – To fall, drop or descend gradually to a lower level.

Sinoatrial (SA) node – The origin of the heart's electrical impulse.

Soft tissue – Body structures that include the layers of skin, fat and muscles.

Spa – A small pool or tub in which people sit in rapidly circulating hot water.

Spasm – An involuntary and abnormal muscle contraction.

Speed slide – A steep water slide on which patrons may reach speeds in excess of 35 mph.

Spinal column – Small bones that extend from the base of the skull to the tip of the tailbone that protect the spinal cord.

Spinal cord – A bundle of nerves extending from the base of the skull to the lower back and protected by the spinal column.

Splint – A device used to immobilize body parts; applying such a device.

Spokesperson – The person at the facility designated to speak on behalf of others.

Sprain – The stretching and tearing of ligaments and other tissue structures at a joint.

Standard of care – The minimal standard and quality of care expected of an emergency care provider.

Standard precautions – Safety measures, such as body substance isolation, taken to prevent occupational-risk exposure to blood or other potentially infectious materials, such as body fluids containing visible blood.

Starting blocks – Platforms from which competitive swimmers dive to start a race.

Sterile – Free from germs.

Stern – The back of a boat.

Stoma – An opening in the front of the neck through which a person whose larynx has been removed breathes.

Strain – The stretching and tearing of muscles or tendons.

Stress – A physiological or psychological response to real or imagined influences that alter an existing state of physical, mental or emotional balance.

Stroke – A disruption of blood flow to a part of the brain, causing permanent damage.

Submerged – Underwater, covered with water.

Sun protection factor (SPF) – The ability of a substance to prevent the sun's harmful rays from being absorbed into the skin; a concentration of sunscreen.

Sunscreen – A cream, lotion or spray used to protect the skin from harmful rays of the sun.

Superficial burn – A burn involving only the outer layer of skin, the epidermis, characterized by dry, red or tender skin. Also referred to as a first-degree burn.

Surveillance – A close watch kept over someone or something, such as patrons or a facility.

Thermocline – A layer of water between the warmer, surface zone and the colder, deep-water zone in a body of water in which the temperature decreases rapidly with depth.

Throwable device – Any object that can be thrown to a drowning victim to aid him or her in floating.

Throwing assist – A method of helping someone out of the water by throwing a floating object with a line attached.

Tornado warning – A warning issued by the National Weather Service notifying that a tornado has been sighted.

Tornado watch – A warning issued by the National Weather Service notifying that tornadoes are possible.

Universal precautions – Practices required by the federal Occupational Safety and Health Administration (OSHA) to control and protect employees from exposure to blood and other potentially infectious materials.

Vector-borne transmission – Transmission of a disease by an animal or insect bite through exposure to blood or other body fluids.

Ventricles – The two lower chambers of the heart.

Ventricular fibrillation (V-fib) – An abnormal heart rhythm characterized by disorganized electrical activity, which results in the quivering of the ventricles.

Ventricular tachycardia (V-tach) – An abnormal heart rhythm characterized by rapid contractions of the ventricles.

Vertebrae – Small bones that make up the spinal column. See also spinal column.

Waterfront – Open water areas, such as lakes, rivers, ponds and oceans.

Waterpark – An aquatic theme park with attractions such as wave pools, speed slides or winding rivers.

Work practice controls – Employee and employer behaviors that reduce the likelihood of exposure to a hazard at the job site.

Wound – An injury to the soft tissues.

REFERENCES

2005 International Consensus on CPR and ECC Science with Treatment Recommendations Guidelines 2005 for First Aid, *Circulation.* Volume 112, Issue 22 Supplement; November 29, 2005.

American Alliance for Health, Physical Education, Recreation and Dance. *Safety Aquatics.* Sports Safety Series, Monograph #5. American Alliance for Health, Physical Education, Recreation and Dance, 1977.

American Heart Association and the American National Red Cross, 2005 Guidelines for First Aid, Supplement to *Circulation*, www.circulationaha.org

The American National Red Cross. *Adapted Aquatics: Swimming for Persons With Physical or Mental Impairments.* Washington, D.C.: The American National Red Cross, 1977.

_____. *Basic Water Rescue.* Boston: StayWell, 1998.

_____. *CPR/AED for the Professional Rescuer.* Yardley, Pennsylvania: StayWell, 2006.

_____. *Emergency Response.* Yardley, Pennsylvania: StayWell, 2001.

_____. *First Aid/CPR/AED for the Workplace Participant's Workbook.* Yardley, Pennsylvania: StayWell, 2006.

_____. *First Aid—Responding to Emergencies.* Yardley, Pennsylvania: StayWell, 2006.

_____. *Lifeguarding.* Washington, D.C.: The American National Red Cross, 1990.

_____. *Lifeguarding Today.* Boston: StayWell, 1994.

_____. *Lifeguard Training.* Yardley, Pennsylvania: StayWell, 2001

_____. *Safety Training for Swim Coaches.* Boston: StayWell, 1998.

_____. *Swimming and Water Safety.* Yardley, Pennsylvania: StayWell, 2004.

American Red Cross Advisory Council on First Aid and Safety (ACFAS). *Advisory Statement on Aspirin Administration,* 2001.

_____. *Advisory Statement on Epinephrine Administration,* 2001.

_____. *Advisory Statement on Asthma Assistance,* 2003.

_____. *Advisory Statement on the Use of the Heimlich Maneuver in Near-Drowning Victims,* 2000.

_____. *Advisory Statement on Cervical Collar Application in Water Rescue,* 2000.

Armbruster, D.A.; Allen, R.H.; and Billingsley, H.S. *Swimming and Diving.* 6th ed. St. Louis: The C.V. Mosby Company, 1973.

Association for the Advancement of Health Education. "Counting the Victims." HE-XTRA 18 (1993):8.

Baker, S.P.; O'Neill, B.; and Ginsburg, M.J. *The Injury Fact Book.* 2nd ed. Lexington, Massachusetts: Lexington Books, D.C. Heath and Co., 1991.

Beringer, G.B., et al. "Submersion Accidents and Epilepsy." *American Journal of Diseases of Children* 137 (1983):604–605.

Bierens, Joost J.L.M.; *Handbook on Drowning.* Berlin/Heidelberg: Springer-Verlag, 2006.

Brewster, C.B. *Open Water Lifesaving: The United States Lifesaving Association Manual.* 2nd ed. Boston: Pearson Custom Publishing, 2003.

Brown, V.R. "Spa Associated Hazards—An Update and Summary." Washington, D.C.: U.S. Consumer Product Safety Commission, 1981.

Bruess, C.E.; Richardson, G.E.; and Laing, S.J. *Decisions for Health.* 4th ed. Dubuque, Iowa: William C. Brown Publishers, 1995.

Centers for Disease Control and Prevention. "Drownings at U.S. Army Corps of Engineers Recreation Facilities, 1986–1990." *Morbidity and Mortality Weekly Report* 41 (1992):331–333.

_____. "Drownings in a Private Lake—North Carolina, 1981–1990." *Morbidity and Mortality Weekly Report* 41 (1992):329–331.

_____. "Suction-Drain Injury in a Public Wading Pool—North Carolina, 1991." *Morbidity and Mortality Weekly Report* 41 (1992):333–335.

_____. *Suggested Health and Safety Guidelines for Recreational Water Slide Flumes.* Atlanta, Georgia: U.S. Department of Health and Human Services, 1981.

_____. *Swimming Pools—Safety and Disease Control Through Proper Design and Operation.* Atlanta, Georgia: United States Department of Health, Education, and Welfare, 1976.

Chow, J.M. "Make a Splash: Children's Pools Attract All Ages." *Aquatics International* (1993):27–32.

Clayton, R.D., and Thomas, D.G. *Professional Aquatic Management.* 2nd ed. Champaign, Illinois: Human Kinetics, 1989.

Committee on Trauma Research; Commission on Life Sciences; National Research Council; and the Institute of Medicine. *Injury in America.* Washington, D.C.: National Academy Press, 1985.

Consumer Guide with Chasnoff, I.J.; Ellis, J.W.; and Fainman, Z.S. *The New Illustrated Family Medical & Health Guide.* Lincolnwood, Illinois: Publications International, Ltd., 1994.

Council for National Cooperation in Aquatics. *Lifeguard Training: Principles and Administration.* New York: Association Press, 1973.

Craig, A.B., Jr. "Underwater Swimming and Loss of Consciousness." *The Journal of the American Medical Association* 176 (1961):255–258.

DeMers, G.E., and Johnson, R.L. *YMCA Pool Operations Manual.* 3rd ed. Champaign, Illinois: Human Kinetics, 2006.

Ellis, et al. *National Pool and Waterpark Lifeguard Training Manual.* Alexandria, Virginia: National Recreation and Park Association, 1993 and 1991.

Fife, D.; Scipio, S.; and Crane, G. "Fatal and Nonfatal Immersion Injuries Among New Jersey Residents." *American Journal of Preventive Medicine* 7 (1991):189–193.

Forrest, C., and Fraleigh, M.M. "Planning Aquatic Playgrounds With Children In Mind: Design A Spray Park Kids Love." *California Parks & Recreation* (Summer 2004): 12.

Gabriel, J.L., editor. *U.S. Diving Safety Manual.* Indianapolis: U.S. Diving Publications, 1990.

Gabrielsen, M.A. "Diving Injuries: Research Findings and Recommendations for Reducing Catastrophic Sport Related Injuries." Presented to the Council for National Cooperation in Aquatics. Indianapolis, 2000.

_____. *Swimming Pools: A Guide to Their Planning, Design, and Operation.* 4th ed. Champaign, Illinois: Human Kinetics, 1987.

Getchell, B.; Pippin, R.; and Varnes, J. *Health.* Boston: Houghton Mifflin Co., 1989.

Hedberg, K., et al. "Drownings in Minnesota, 1980–85: A Population-Based Study." *American Journal of Public Health* 80 (1990):1071–1074.

Huint, R. *Lifeguarding in the Waterparks.* Montreal: AquaLude, Inc., 1990.

Ideas For Spray Park Take Shape. Available at: www.billingsgazette.com. Accessed on December 28, 2005.

Kowalsky, L., editor. *Pool-Spa Operators Handbook.* San Antonio, Texas: National Swimming Pool Foundation, 1990.

Lierman, T.L., editor. *Building a Healthy America: Conquering Disease and Disability.* New York: Mary Ann Liebert, Inc., Publishers, 1987.

Lifesaving Society. *Alert: Lifeguarding in Action.* 2nd ed. Ottawa, Ontario: Lifesaving Society, 2004.

Litovitz, T.L.; Schmitz, B.S.; and Holm, K.C. "1988 Annual Report of the American Association of Poison Control Centers National Data Collection System." *American Journal of Emergency Medicine* 7 (1989):496.

Livingston, S.; Pauli, L.L.; and Pruce, I. "Epilepsy and Drowning in Childhood." *British Medical Journal* 2 (1977):515–516.

Marion Laboratories. *Osteoporosis: Is It in Your Future?* Kansas City: Marion Laboratories, 1984.

MayoClinic.com. Dehydration Overview. Available at www.mayoclinic.com/health/dehydration/ds00561. Accessed on July 3, 2006.

Mitchell, J.T. "Stress: The History, Status and Future of Critical Incident Stress Debriefings." *JEMS: Journal of Emergency Medical Services* 13 (1988):47–52.

_____. "Stress and the Emergency Responder." JEMS: *Journal of Emergency Medical Services* 15 (1987):55–57.

Modell, J.H. "Drowning." *New England Journal of Medicine* 328 (1993):253–256.

National Committee for Injury Prevention and Control. *Injury Prevention: Meeting the Challenge.* New York: Oxford University Press as a supplement to the *American Journal of Preventive Medicine,* Volume 5, Number 3, 1989.

National Safety Council. *Injury Facts, 1999 Edition.* Itasca, Illinois: National Safety Council, 1999.

National Spa and Pool Institute. *American National Standard for Public Swimming Pools.* Alexandria, Virginia: National Spa and Pool Institute, 1991.

New York State Department of Public Health. *Drownings at Regulated Bathing Facilities in New York State, 1987–1990.* Albany, New York: New York State Department of Health, 1990.

O'Connor, J. "A U.S. Accidental Drowning Study, 1980–1984." Thesis, University of Oregon, 1986.

O'Donohoe, N.V. "What Should the Child With Epilepsy Be Allowed to Do?" *Archives of Disease in Childhood* 58 (1983):934–937.

Orlowski, J.P.; Rothner, A.D.; and Lueders, H. "Submersion Accidents in Children With Epilepsy." *American Journal of Diseases of Children* 136 (1982):777–780.

Payne, W.A., and Hahn, D.B. *Understanding Your Health.* 7th ed. St. Louis: McGraw Hill Companies, 2002.

Pearn, J. "Epilepsy and Drowning in Childhood." *British Medical Journal* 1 (1977):1510–1511.

Pearn, J.; Bart, R.; and Yamaoka, R. "Drowning Risks to Epileptic Children: A Study From Hawaii." *British Medical Journal* 2 (1978):1284–1285.

Pia, F. "Observations on the Drowning of Nonswimmers." *Journal of Physical Education* (July 1974):164–167.

_____. *On Drowning,* Water Safety Films, Inc. (1970).

_____. "Reducing Swimming Related Drowning Fatalities." *Pennsylvania Recreation and Parks* (Spring 1991):13–16.

_____. "The RID Factor as a Cause of Drowning." *Parks and Recreation* (June 1984):52–67.

Quan, L., and Gomez, A. "Swimming Pool Safety—An Effective Submersion Prevention Program." *Journal of Environmental Health* 52 (1990):344–346.

Rice, D.P.; MacKenzie, E.J.; et al. *Cost of Injury in the United States: a Report to Congress 1989.* San Francisco, California: Institute for Health and Aging, University of California, and Injury Prevention Center, The Johns Hopkins University, 1989.

Robertson, L.S. *Injury Epidemiology.* 2nd ed. New York: Oxford University Press, 1998.

The Royal Life Saving Society Australia; *Lifeguarding.* 3rd ed. Marrickville, NSW: Elsevier Australia, 2001.

The Royal Life Saving Society UK. *The Lifeguard.* 2nd ed. RLSS Warwickshire, UK, 2003.

Spinal Cord Injury Information Network. Facts and Figures at a Glance—June, 2006. Available at: www.spinalcord.uab.edu. Accessed on September 8, 2006.

Spray Parks, Splash Pads, Kids-Cool! Available at: www.azcentral.com. Accessed on December 28, 2005.

Strauss, R.H., editor. *Sports Medicine.* Philadelphia: W.B. Saunders Co., 1984.

Torney, J.A., and Clayton, R.D. *Aquatic Instruction, Coaching and Management.* Minneapolis: Burgess Publishing Co., 1970.

_____. *Aquatic Organization and Management.* Minneapolis: Burgess Publishing Co., 1981.

Williams, K.G.. *The Aquatic Facility Operator Manual.* 3rd ed. The National Recreation and Park Association, National Aquatic Section, 1999.

Wintemute, G.J., et al. "The Epidemiology of Drowning in Adulthood: Implications for Prevention." *American Journal of Preventive Medicine* 4 (1988):343–348.

World Waterpark Association. *Considerations for Operating Safety.* Lenexa, Kansas: World Waterpark Association, 1991.

YMCA of the USA. *On the Guard II.* 4th ed. Champaign, Illinois: Human Kinetics, 2001.

Index

MISSION OF THE AMERICAN RED CROSS

The American Red Cross, a humanitarian organization led by volunteers and guided by its Congressional Charter and the Fundamental Principles of the International Red Cross Movement, will provide relief to victims of disaster and help people prevent, prepare for, and respond to emergencies.

ABOUT THE AMERICAN RED CROSS

The American Red Cross has helped people mobilize to help their neighbors for 125 years. Last year, victims of a record 72,883 disasters, most of them fires, turned to the nearly 1 million volunteers and 35,000 employees of the Red Cross for help and hope. Through more than 800 locally supported chapters, more than 15 million people each year gain the skills they need to prepare for and respond to emergencies in their homes, communities and world. Almost 4 million people give blood—the gift of life—through the Red Cross, making it the largest supplier of blood and blood products in the United States. The Red Cross helps thousands of U.S. service members separated from their families by military duty stay connected. As part of the International Red Cross and Red Crescent Movement, a global network of more than 180 national societies, the Red Cross helps restore hope and dignity to the world's most vulnerable people. An average of 91 cents of every dollar the Red Cross spends is invested in humanitarian services and programs. The Red Cross is not a government agency; it relies on donations of time, money, and blood to do its work.

FUNDAMENTAL PRINCIPLES OF THE INTERNATIONAL RED CROSS AND RED CRESCENT MOVEMENT

HUMANITY
IMPARTIALITY
NEUTRALITY
INDEPENDENCE
VOLUNTARY SERVICE
UNITY
UNIVERSALITY